# EXPLORING
## WITH WISCONSIN
## FAST PLANTS

## PAUL WILLIAMS
*University of Wisconsin-Madison*

 KENDALL/HUNT PUBLISHING COMPANY
4050 Westmark Drive   Dubuque, Iowa 52002

| | |
|---|---|
| *Program Director* | Paul Williams |
| *Program Manager* | Coe Williams |
| *Writers* | Paul Williams<br>Richard Green |
| *Writer/Editor* | Coe Williams |
| *Design/Editors* | Lori Graham<br>Christie Roden |
| *Illustrators* | Paul Williams<br>Kirk Anderson<br>Jane Scharer |

The Wisconsin Fast Plants Program would like to extend thanks to Nan Alexander, Gail Coray, Irving Granderson, Arie Korporaal, Phoebe Roeder and Shirley Splittstoesser for their editing suggestions and additions to the 1995 edition of *Exploring with Wisconsin Fast Plants*.

Wisconsin Fast Plants is funded by a grant from the National Science Foundation administered by the University of Wisconsin-Madison.

**Teachers may copy selected pages for student use.**

On the cover: Students involved in the AstroPlants pilot project, Roger Evans' classroom, Leland High School, San Jose, CA. Photo by Linda Baham.

ISBN 0-7872-1578-3

Printed in the United States of America
10 9 8 7 6 5 4 3 2 1

# Table of Contents

# Introduction

# Friendly and Accessible Science with Fast Plants

Wisconsin Fast Plants offers you an exciting new teaching tool with which to explore all aspects of plant growth and development while introducing students to the process of scientific investigation. "The science that can be explored with Fast Plants allows kids to ask good questions" (Arie Korporaal, Science Consultant, Los Angeles Unified School District). Fast Plants lend themselves easily to investigating those "what if " questions.

Wisconsin Fast Plants are rapid-cycling brassicas, members of the cabbage and mustard family. They have been developed through fifteen years of selective breeding to be used by plant researchers and by teachers in the classroom. They have a life cycle of 35-40 days (seed to seed) and can be grown in the classroom under continuous fluorescent light.

This manual is intended to give you all the information necessary to successfully grow a life cycle of Fast Plants with students, plus ideas for more Fast Plants explorations:

- **Section 1** explains how Fast Plants were created and their relationship to other plants.
- **Section 2** is called "Let's Grow Fast Plants." It contains basic information for the teacher who is using Fast Plants for the first time, including necessary materials and set-up, illustrated growing instructions for students, tips, troubleshooting, and ideas for investigations.
- **Section 3** contains explorations pertaining to specific points in the life cycle—germination, plant growth, flowering, pollination, double fertilization and seed pod development and seed maturation and dispersal.
- **Section 4** has additional explorations in plant physiology and ecology.
- **Section 5** addresses variation and inheritance via activities that can be investigated at a beginning level or carried into more advanced concepts and questions.

- **Section 6** deals with energy and nutrient recycling, e.g., composting and fermentation.
- **Section 7** contains stories, modeling ideas and games.
- **Section 8** explains optimal growing conditions and lighting requirements for Fast Plants, and includes inexpensive ways to construct your own growing systems, e.g., using film cans and 2-liter soda bottles.
- **Section 9** includes supplementary materials for the teacher — background information, interdisciplinary ideas, some learning objectives and a glossary.

The manual is entitled *"Exploring With Wisconsin Fast Plants."* Fast Plants offer you the opportunity to help students learn more about plants and their processes while developing and practicing important science process skills — observing, questioning, hypothesizing, planning, measuring, recording, interpreting, critical reflecting and communicating. Content and process go hand in hand in both learning and doing science. The design of the Fast Plants classroom explorations in Sections 3 and 4 is consistent with the steps of the "Science Exploration Flowchart" found with each exploration. See page viii for a combined flowchart of these steps in language for teachers and in questions for students as found in the Science Exploration Flowchart in each chapter of Sections 3 and 4.

*A complete classroom observational experiment is written out at the beginning of each chapter of Sections 3 and 4.* It includes teaching concepts, background information for you, the teacher, and step by step illustrated instructions to be used with your students. The remainder of these chapters contains the additional steps needed to complete a full science investigation. You and the students can plan and carry out investigations to answer questions generated in the previous "observation." Each chapter presents one or more sample questions and carries them through these subsequent steps. A worksheet, "Setting Up an Experiment," is included to help the student design an experiment (pages 41-43).

The first time you use Fast Plants in your classroom, listen to the questions students ask. From these "what if" questions will come many science investigations which give the students the chance to construct their own learning experiences. The results of these will vary. Keep in mind that the *results of science investigations are never wrong* — they provide a vehicle for critical thinking in figuring out what happened.

Above all, have fun! Feel comfortable in the knowledge that even scientists do not know all the answers to questions surrounding some of the plant processes. Relax and be an "explorer" along with the students.

---

### Look for Concept Statements!

The first pages of Sections 3-6 contain general concept statements that address the Fast Plants activities in that section. The concept statements should assist you, the teacher, in aligning Fast Plants with the AAAS Benchmarks and to the National Research Council's National Standards for Science.

---

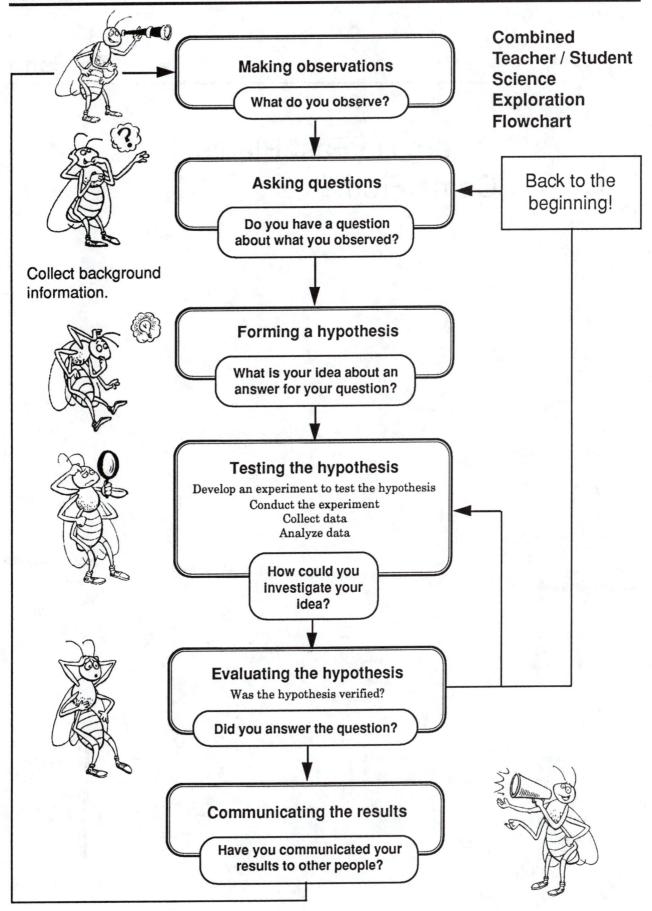

**Making observations**

What do you observe?

**Asking questions**

Do you have a question about what you observed?

Collect background information.

**Forming a hypothesis**

What is your idea about an answer for your question?

**Testing the hypothesis**

Develop an experiment to test the hypothesis
Conduct the experiment
Collect data
Analyze data

How could you investigate your idea?

**Evaluating the hypothesis**

Was the hypothesis verified?

Did you answer the question?

**Communicating the results**

Have you communicated your results to other people?

**Combined Teacher / Student Science Exploration Flowchart**

Back to the beginning!

# Where Do Fast Plants Come From?

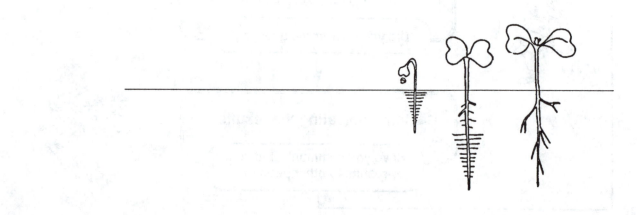

# The Making of Wisconsin Fast Plants

The life cycle of a plant begins and ends with a seed. For a yellow-flowered plant, whose scientific name is *Brassica rapa*, this happens in just five weeks. This plant is a variant of wild mustard and completes its life cycle in one fifth the time of its ancestors. It has been selectively bred by Dr. Paul H. Williams, University of Wisconsin-Madison Professor of Plant Pathology.

turnip

Dr. Williams had been working to improve the disease resistance of plants in the family Cruciferae, a large diverse group that includes mustards, radishes, cabbages and other cole crops. In order to speed up the genetic research in the crucifers, he spent almost 20 years breeding *Brassica rapa* and six related species from the subgroup or tribe Brassicaceae. The end result was a genetic line of small, prolific, rapid-cycling brassicas. These plants, now known as Wisconsin Fast Plants, are a valuable tool that helps to shorten traditional breeding programs and aid in cellular and molecular research. Additionally, the Fast Plants have become extremely useful as a teaching tool in the classroom since all aspects of plant growth and development can be easily demonstrated.

Chinese cabbage

pak choi

Dr. Williams refined the rapid-cycling brassicas to have characteristics most suitable for laboratory and classroom use. He kept selecting seed from stock that met the following criteria:

- shortest time from seeding to flowering
- ability to produce seed at high plant density
- petite plant type
- rapid seed maturation
- absence of seed dormancy
- ability to grow under continuous fluorescent lighting
- ability to grow well in a potting mix

rapini

Rbr

After about 15 years of planting, growing and selecting, his breeding process had reduced a six month life cycle to five weeks. Further breeding produced relative uniformity in flowering time, size and growing conditions and yet the Fast Plants retained much variety. Over 150 genetically controlled traits have been recorded and can be useful in experiments.

The educational potential for students, kindergarten through college level, to learn more about plant biology through "hands-on" explorations with Fast Plants in the classroom led to the development of the Wisconsin Fast Plant kits.

With support from the Educational Materials Development Program of the National Science Foundation, seed stocks and growing systems were especially designed for a wide range of learning activities. This manual enables teachers of varying backgrounds to easily use Fast Plants with their students and addresses these broad educational goals: 1) teaching basic concepts of biology; 2) stimulating inquiry and problem solving and 3) bringing new excitement into the classroom.

Third graders in Martha Ann Bull's class at Claymont Elementary School, in Ballwin, MO.

Photo courtesy of photographer Doug Miner, and the West County Suburban Journal.

## References

### Books

Lerner, C. 1989. *Plant Families*. New York: Morrow Junior Books. Concise, informative text explains how to recognize characteristics shared by the twelve largest plant families, accompanied by detailed color illustrations.

Williams, P. H. 1989. Rapid-Cycling Brassicas. Carolina Tips 52:2. The world of brassicas and the science of Fast Plants. Ordering information from the Carolina Biological Supply Co., Burlington, NC, 1-800-334-5551.

Williams, P. H. and C. B. Hill. 1986. Rapid-Cycling Populations of Brassicas. Science 232:1385-1389. The genetics research and science behind the Fast Plants story.

# The Relationship of Fast Plants in the Plant Kingdom

The Wisconsin Fast Plants, rapid-cycling brassicas, are members of a large family of plants called crucifers (Latin, Cruciferae).  Crucifers are named, and easily distinguished, because of the characteristic shape of their flowers – always four petals in the shape of a cross or crucifix.  One of the sections, or genera, of the crucifer family is the genus *Brassica*.

Some common brassica crops are mustard, Brussels sprouts, kohlrabi, cabbage, cauliflower, broccoli, turnip, Chinese cabbage, collard, kale, and rapeseed.  Tumbleweed, shepherds purse and pepper cress are weeds belonging to the same family.  Wall flower, silver dollar, candy tuff, alysum and sweet stocks are crucifers.  Watercress and horseradish also are crucifers.

**turnip**

From a world perspective the brassicas have great economic and commercial value, and play a major part in feeding the world's population.  These important crops range from nutritious vegetables, mustards and oil-producing crops to animal fodders and noxious weeds.  Interestingly enough, they have traditionally been less important in the U.S. than they are in most other parts of the world.

Historically, there have been very practical reasons for brassica vegetables being a main food supply in so many countries around the world.  Good refrigeration has been a fairly recent phenomenon; although it is taken for granted in most affluent and developed nations, it is still a luxury, or even nonexistent, in many parts of the world.  Vegetables that grow in a mild winter situation, such as Brussels sprouts, or those that store well, such as kohlrabi or heading cabbages, are relied upon in northern European countries.  The outer wrapper leaves of the cabbage and cauliflower, for instance, wilt down and form a protective layer for the inside of the head.  In India, a country with over 500 million people, cauliflower is the main vegetable and several different kinds are available on the market.

**cauliflower**

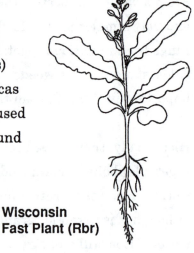

**Giant
Jersey
Kale**

Kale is used extensively for feeding sheep in many parts of the world, from New Zealand to Scotland. Other forms of kale are consumed by humans or seen in flower gardens of Japan. The brassica oilseed rape is a major source of cooking oils and margarine in India, China, Japan, Europe and Canada.

Millions of people all over the world get essential vitamins from the brassica known as Chinese cabbage. There are more than 200 different varieties of Chinese cabbage growing all over China. In terms of mathematics this totals 250 million pounds of brassicas eaten in China every day. In Korea, Chinese cabbage is fermented to make kimchee, the mainstay of the Korean diet.

**Chinese
cabbage**

Another group of brassicas are the mustards. Some are eaten in the form of mustard greens and many people use mustard as a spice or condiment. The strong mustard flavor is helpful to the plants. It repels certain insect pests and attracts others. In mammals, the mustard oils have been found to help detoxify cancer-causing chemicals in the liver.

From this tremendous resource of brassicas collected all over the world (both wild plants and domesticated forms) selective breeding has produced the rapid-cycling brassicas known as Wisconsin Fast Plants. These are now being used effectively in the classroom and in research projects around the world.

**Wisconsin
Fast Plant (Rbr)**

## References

### Books

Fenton, C. L. and H. B. Kitchen. 1971. *Plants We Live On*. New York: John Day Co. Interesting views of vegetables and the families to which they belong, of their economic importance and of plant breeding. An entire geography lesson is incorporated throughout; excellent botanical illustrations.

Rupp, R. 1987. *Blue Corn and Square Tomatoes*. Pownal, VT: Storey Communications, Inc. Fascinating reading containing unusual facts about common garden vegetables — their origins, reputations, connections with human history, etc.

# Around the World with Brassicas

Wisconsin Fast Plants, rapid-cycling brassicas, are part of a large family of plants called **crucifers** (Latin = Cruciferae). Crucifers are easily distinguished by the characteristic shape of their flowers—four petals in the shape of a cross or crucifix. A section, or genus, of the crucifer family is the genus **Brassica**.

Brassicas have great economic and commercial value, and play a major role in feeding the world population. They range from nutritious vegetables, mustards and oil producing crops, to animal fodders and weeds.

Six of the most important *Brassica* species are closely interrelated. The relationship between these species can be represented as a triangle with the three diploid species forming the points of the triangle, and the amphidiploid species (crosses between the first three) on the sides (Figure 1).

*Brassica nigra* (2n = 16), popularly known as black mustard, is a common weed. It looks very much like the Wisconsin Fast Plants. Seeds of *B. nigra* will stay dormant in the soil for years. Once the ground is disturbed — for instance, by a tractor or bulldozer — black mustard is one of the first plants to appear.

*Brassica carinata* results from a cross between *B. nigra* and *B. oleracea*. It is a tall, leafy plant found almost exclusively in Ethiopia. The leaves are stripped off and eaten and the seed is pressed as a source of edible oil.

Reviewing *Brassica oleracea* is a bit like taking a trip through the produce section of your supermarket. Collards, cauliflower, broccoli, Brussels sprouts, kohlrabi and cabbage all belong in the species *Brassica oleracea*. Members of *B. oleracea* are used extensively in Northern Europe and Central Asia and are important vegetables in many countries.

Cauliflower is the main vegetable in India. One reason is that it can be stored without refrigeration. The outer leaves of the cauliflower wilt and form a protective layer around the head. In other parts of the world where refrigeration is still unavailable or considered a luxury, people also rely on other brassicas that store well (such as heading cabbage or kohlrabi) or those that continue to grow through a mild winter (collard, Brussels sprouts).

The forms of *B. oleracea* known as kale are used for a wide variety of purposes, including human food and animal fodder. Kale is used extensively in New Zealand and Scotland for feeding sheep. A particularly tall variety of kale, known as tree kale or Jersey kale, is grown in Portugal as a food crop and dates back to Roman times. On the Isle of Jersey the tree kale is grown as fodder for the Jersey cattle. Jersey kale is also a source of a cottage industry for island inhabitants who make walking sticks from the eight-foot kale stems. These walking sticks are popular in British hospitals, because they are very strong and lightweight. A different variety of kale,

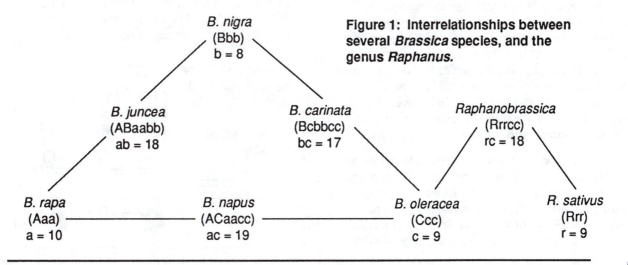

**Figure 1: Interrelationships between several *Brassica* species, and the genus *Raphanus*.**

developed in Japan for ornamental purposes, can be seen as a bedding plant. This ornamental kale spreads its curly leaves at ground level and looks like a big red, pink or white flower.

*Brassica napus* is a cross between *B. oleracea* and *B. rapa.* Rutabagas are a variety of *B. napus* as is oil seed rape. This crop is the third most important source of edible oil behind soybean and peanut oil. In the United States cooking oils and margarines are produced mainly from corn or soybeans. In other parts of the world the main source of edible oil is pressed from the seed of oil seed rape. Oil seed rape flourishes in Canada and Europe where the climate is too cool to produce a corn crop. In the summer the Canadian prairies are literally 'fields of sunshine' due to the yellow flowers of oil seed rape, also known as canola.

The last of the diploid *Brassica* species is *Brassica rapa* (2n = 20). Both turnips and Chinese cabbage fit into this species. Chinese cabbage is consumed by millions of people all over the world. Over 200 different varieties of Chinese cabbage can be found in China. The per capita consumption of brassicas in China is 1/4 pound each day. Multiplied by China's population, this approximates 250 million pounds of brassicas eaten in China every day. In northern China, where winters are long and cold, heading forms of Chinese cabbage are harvested in the fall. Stored anywhere and everywhere there is room (including under the beds), Chinese cabbage provides a major source of vitamins through the winter. One can easily imagine that by spring no one in China ever wants to see Chinese cabbage again!

In Korea Chinese cabbage is again a mainstay in the diet, but is processed in a different way. As the Germans ferment cabbage to make sauerkraut, the Koreans ferment cabbage to make kimchee, the national dish. Kimchee is made in large earthenware jars by layering Chinese cabbage, radish, garlic, hot peppers and salt. Every family has its special recipe — some even add fish to the kimchee. Whatever the recipe, kimchee is eaten three times a day, for breakfast, lunch and supper.

The final of the six *Brassica* species is *Brassica juncea* (2n = 36), the cross between *B. rapa* and *B. nigra.* *Brassica juncea* includes the group known as mustard. In the southern United States the foliage of *B. juncea* is often eaten as mustard greens. The distinctive flavor of mus-

tard, present to some extent in all the brassicas, is strongest in the various types of *B. juncea.* Most people use mustard as a condiment or spice. Mustard contains oils called glucosinolates which are activated by saliva and release the strong 'mustard' flavor. These glucosinolates are a help to both plants and humans. Certain pests are repelled and others attracted by glucosinolates. The strong flavor also helps to discourage deer and rabbits from eating brassica crops. In mammals certain glucosinolates have been found to help detoxify cancer-causing nitrosamine chemicals in the liver.

Other intergeneric crosses are possible between various brassicas and other crucifers. An example is *Raphanobrassica,* the cross between *B. oleracea* and *Raphanus sativus* (2n = 18), the common radish. *Raphanobrassica* was first produced in the 1920's by a Russian plant breeder named Karpechenko. He had hoped to breed a 'supervegetable' with both the large head of a cabbage and the large root of a radish. The cross resulted in a big, leafy plant. Disappointed, he didn't pursue the plant cross any further. Recently *Raphanobrassica* has been revived by the Scottish Plant Breeding Station in Dundee, Scotland. Its high dry matter content makes it an excellent fodder for sheep and cattle.

Selective breeding has produced Wisconsin Fast Plants from this tremendous resource of brassicas collected from all over the world (both wild and domesticated forms). Bred for their small size and rapid life cycle (35 days, seed-to-seed), Wisconsin Fast Plants are being used for research and classroom teaching.

Preview color slides of the brassicas on the Fast Plants World Wide Web server, at http://fastplants.cals.wisc.edu.

Individual slides or complete sets are available from the Fast Plants office, at $2.00 per slide.

Table 1: Names of the subspecies of agriculturally important brassicas and radish

| Species  (genome) | Subspecies or variety | Cultivar group or common name |
|---|---|---|
| *Brassica nigra*  (bb = 16) | --- | Black mustard |
| *Brassica oleracea*   (cc = 18) | *acephala*<br>*alboglabra*<br>*botrytis*<br>*capitata*<br>*costata*<br>*gemmifera*<br>*gongylodes*<br>*italica*<br>*medullosa*<br>*palmifolia*<br>*ramosa*<br>*sabauda*<br>*sabellica*<br>*selensia* | Kales<br>Chinese kale, Kailan<br>Cauliflower, heading broccoli<br>Cabbage<br>Portuguese cabbage, Tronchuda<br>Brussels sprouts<br>Kohlrabi<br>Broccoli, Calabrese<br>Marrow stem kale<br>Tree cabbage, Jersey kale<br>Thousand-head kale<br>Savoy cabbage<br>Collards<br>Borecole |
| *Brassica rapa*  (aa = 20) | *chinensis*<br>*narinosa*<br>*nipposinica*<br>*oleifera*<br>*parachinensis*<br>*pekinensis*<br>*perviridis*<br>*rapifera*<br>*trilocularis*<br>*utilis* | Pak choi<br>Tsatsai<br>Mizuna, Mibuna<br>Turnip rape, Toria<br>Saichin, Choy sum<br>Chinese cabbage<br>Tendergreen, Komatsuna<br>Turnip<br>Yellow sarson<br>Broccoletto, Broccoli raab |
| *Brassica carinata*  (bbcc = 34) | --- | Ethiopian mustard |
| *Brassica juncea*  (aabb = 36) | *capitata*<br>*crispifolia*<br>*faciliflora*<br>*lapitata*<br>*multiceps*<br>*oleifera*<br>*rapifera*<br>*rugosa*<br>*spicea*<br>*tsa-tsai* | Head mustard<br>Cut leaf mustard<br>Broccoli mustard<br>Large petiole mustard<br>Multishoot mustard<br>Indian mustard, Raya<br>Root mustard<br>Leaf mustard<br>Mustard<br>Big stem mustard |
| *Brassica napus*  (aacc = 38) | ---<br>*oleifera*<br>*rapifera* | Fodder rape<br>Oil rape<br>Swede, Rutabaga |
| *Raphanus sativus*  (rr = 18) | *radicola*<br>*oleifera*<br>*caudatus* | Radish, dikon<br>Oil radish<br>Rat tail radish |

The haploid complement of chromosomes is a = 10, b = 8 and c and r = 9.

## Morphotypes of the subspecies of *Brassica rapa*

choy sum
*Brassica rapa parachinensis*

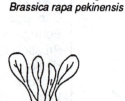
Chinese cabbage
*Brassica rapa pekinensis*

broccoli raab
*Brassica rapa utilis*

mibuna
*Brassica rapa nipposinica*

turnip
*Brassica rapa rapifera*

turnip rape or sarson
*Brassica rapa oleifera or
B. r. trilocularis*

pak choi
*Brassica rapa chinensis*

Wisconsin Fast Plants
Rapid-cycling *Brassica rapa*

tsa-tsai
*Brassica rapa narinosa*

tendergreen
*Brassica rapa perviridis*

## The Phylogeny of Fast Plants

**Kingdom: Planta**
- plants have cell walls and chlorophyll
- other kingdoms are: Monera (bacteria), Protista (protozoans), Fungi and Animalia

**Division: Tracheophyta**
- vascular plants

**Subdivision: Spermatophyta**
- seed plants

**Class: Angiospermae**
- flowering plants

**Subclass: Dicotyledonae (dicots)**
- two cotyledons, branching veins in leaves

**Order: Papaverales**
- special anatomy of fruit and embryo
- contains several families

**Family: Cruciferae or Brassicaceae**
- (e.g., mustards and cabbages)
- 4 petals, 4 sepals, 6 stamens, ovary consists of two fused carpels
- contains 375 genera

**Genus: *Brassica***
- pod a silique, embryos conduplicate
- contains over 3200 species

**Species: *rapa***
- chromosome number 2n = 20
- contains 11 subspecies

**Subspecies: e.g.:**

    *chinensis* (pak choi), *pekinensis* (Chinese cabbage), *rapifera* (turnip)

**Cultivar: <u>culti</u>vated <u>vari</u>ety name**
- domesticated through selection and breeding

# Let's Grow Fast Plants

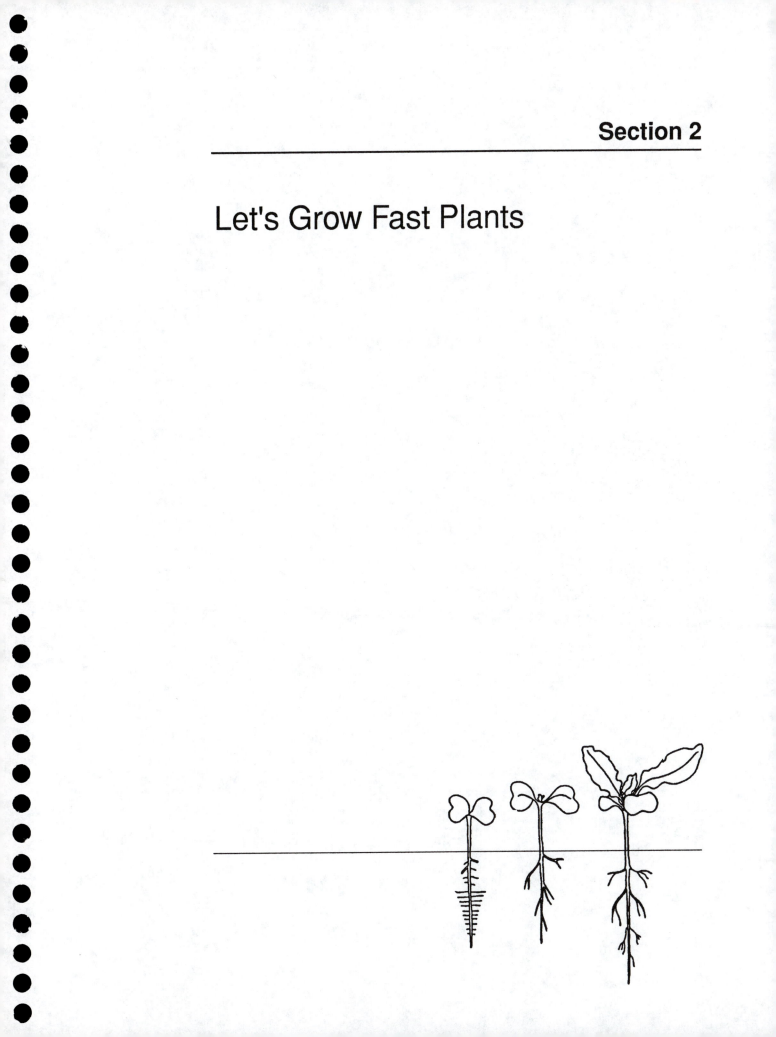

# Before you begin ...

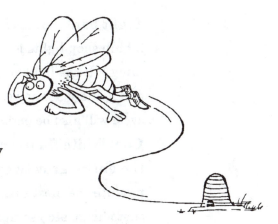

To optimize the Fast Plants experience and to prevent any disappointment for your students, **read this entire section thoroughly prior to conducting any experiment.**

### Time requirements

How long will it take? The entire life cycle takes 35-40 days, from planting to harvesting the seed you have produced. The seed will be ready to replant the day it is harvested, if you wish. The amount of time required each day varies, depending on the task. On the days when students are just observing the plants, checking the water level in the reservoirs, or making notes in their logs, only a few minutes are required. And once the students have pollinated, the plants require little care (except for watering) until the day of harvesting the seed.

### What you will need

- A Fast Plants kit (seed is included)
- A bank of **Cool White** fluorescent lights– a minimum of six bulbs is necessary for optimal plant growth, eight bulbs are ideal. See "Seeing the Light" (pages 245-248)
- A light rack to hold the bank of lights (see page 249 for construction plans)
- An extension cord

### The Light Bank

Why do you need fluorescent lights? Fast Plants grow best near an intense source of light. Fast Plants will not be successful with the light available on a windowsill or in a greenhouse. To grow strong, healthy plants and complete the growth cycle in 40 days, you must consider the following:

- **Use 4-foot, Cool White fluorescent bulbs, either the old 40 watt bulbs or the new 32 watt energy savers.** Many other types of bulbs **will not** produce satisfactory results; this includes specialized "plant" light bulbs. New federal requirements specify 32 watt, high efficiency bulbs instead of the old 40 watt bulbs. These will require different fixtures than the 40 watt bulbs.

- **Light banks must have at least *six* 4-foot Cool White bulbs.** Use three 2-bulb shop lights joined together. (Choose a lightweight set for easier handling.) If the light source is less, i.e. two or four bulbs, plants will grow tall and spindly as they stretch toward the light. The time to complete the life cycle will also be extended.

- **Cool White fluorescent lighting is necessary *24 hours a day* during the entire growth cycle.** Keeping the Fast Plants under constant light will produce the most satisfactory results. Be sure to make arrangements (with custodians, etc.) so light banks are not turned off at any time.

- **There should be 40 cm of clearance available under the light bulbs.** Suspend the light bank from a wooden rack so that the height of the light bank can be adjusted as the plants grow. (Instructions for assembling a suitable light rack are on page 249.) Forty centimeters are necessary to allow enough height for the mature plants under the light bulbs. The growing tips of the plants should be maintained 5-10 cm from the lights, but never touching the lights.

- **Illustrated directions for building your own light bank are found on page 250.**

## The Kit

**How can I get a Fast Plants kit?** Carolina Biological Supply Company is the market distributor of Fast Plants kits and manuals. Particular questions should be directed to Dr. Lisa Darmo, 1-800-227-1150. The complete address is: **Carolina Biological Supply Company**, 2700 York Road, Burlington, NC 27215, tel: 1-800-334-5551, fax: 1-800-222-7112.

---

## What does the kit contain? The kit components consist of:

**a) Fast Plants seed,** rapid-cycling *Brassica rapa* (Rbr). Seeds are small and have to be handled with care.

**b) quads** — 4-celled planting units in which you will grow one plant to maturity in each cell.

**f) fertilizer pellets** — slow-release source of nitrogen (N), phosphorus (P) and potassium (K). Pellets are larger than the seeds.

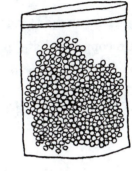

**c) potting mix** and **vermiculite**

**d) diamond wicks** — conduct water from water mat to soil in cell of quad.

**g) plant labels** — to record student name, planting date and experiment.

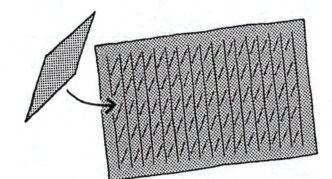

**h) pipet** — to water cells from above when necessary.

**e) water mat** — conducts water from reservoir to wicks.

**i) dried honeybees** — to make beesticks for pollinating.

 **2×**

**j) algae-squares (tinged blue)** — contain copper sulfate to prevent algae growth in reservoir.

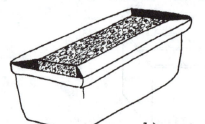

**k) water reservoir**

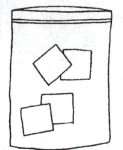

**l) wooden stakes and plastic support rings** — to support the plants if necessary.

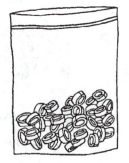

# Stages in the Life Cycle

Wisconsin Fast Plants are rapid-cycling brassicas, members of the cabbage and mustard family. Under proper growing conditions the life cycle of 35-40 days will be:

**Days 1-3:** The radicle (embryonic root) emerges. Seedlings emerge from the soil. Two cotyledons (seed leaves) appear and the hypocotyl (embryonic stem) extends upward. Green (chlorophyll) and purple (anthocyanin) pigments can be seen.

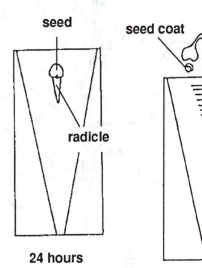
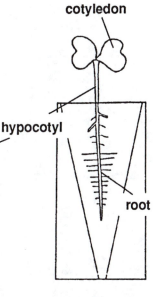

**Days 4-9:** Cotyledons enlarge. True leaves emerge and develop. Flower buds appear in the growing tip of the plant.

**Days 10-12:** Stem elongates between the nodes (points of leaf attachment). Flower buds rise above the leaves. Leaves and flower buds continue to enlarge.

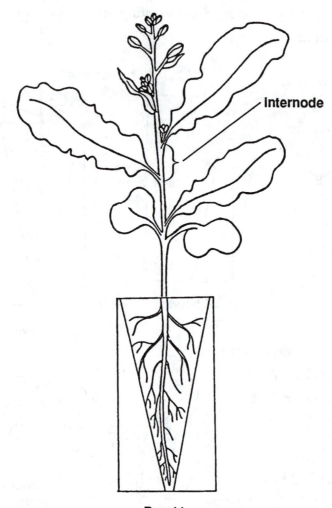

**Day 11**

**Days 13-17:** Flowers open. Floral parts can be identified. Flowers can be cross-pollinated (from one plant to another) for 3-4 days. Pollen is viable for 4-5 days and stigmas remain receptive to pollen for 2-3 days after a flower opens. After final pollination, prune off the remaining unopened flower buds and side shoots. Pruning directs the plant's energy into developing the seed.

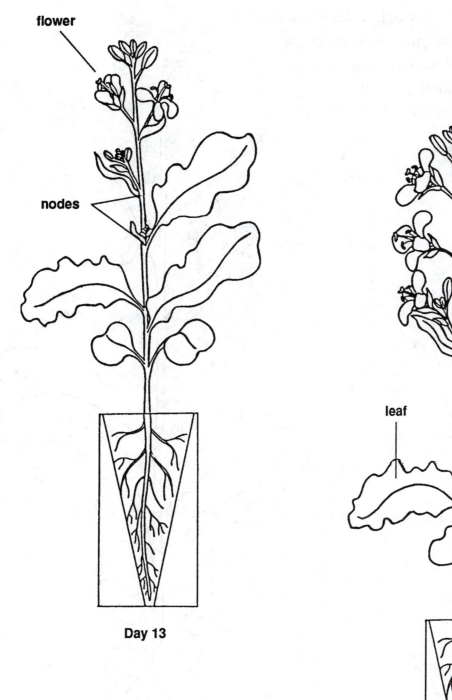

**flower**

**nodes**

**Day 13**

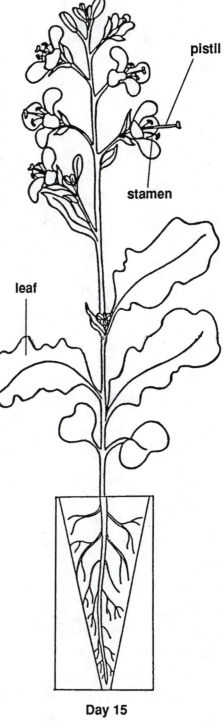

**pistil**

**stamen**

**leaf**

**Day 15**

**Days 18-22:** Petals drop from the pollinated flowers. Pods elongate and swell. Development of the seed and embryonic plant has begun and will continue until approximately Day 36.

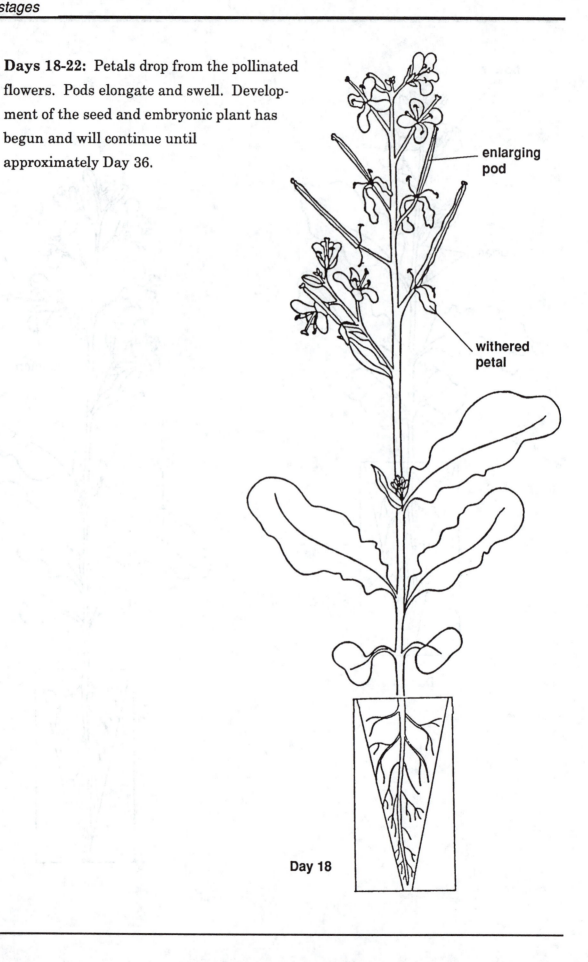

enlarging pod

withered petal

Day 18

**Days 23-36:** Seeds mature and ripen. Lower leaves yellow and dry. Twenty days after final pollination (about Day 36) plants should be removed from water.

**Days 36-40:** Plants dry down and pods turn yellow. On Day 40, pods can be removed from dried plants. Seed can be harvested. The cycle is complete.

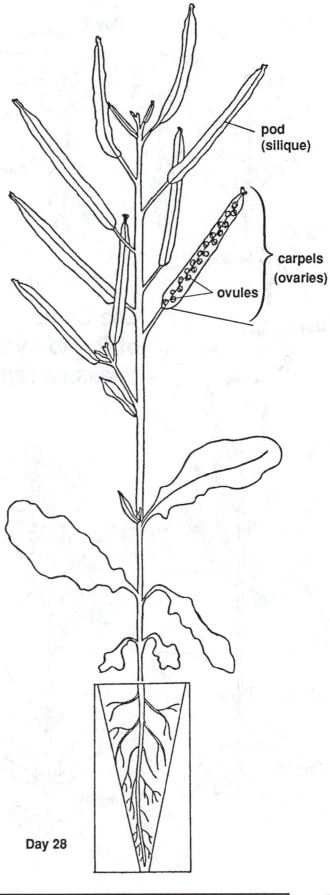

pod
(silique)

carpels
(ovaries)

ovules

**Day 28**

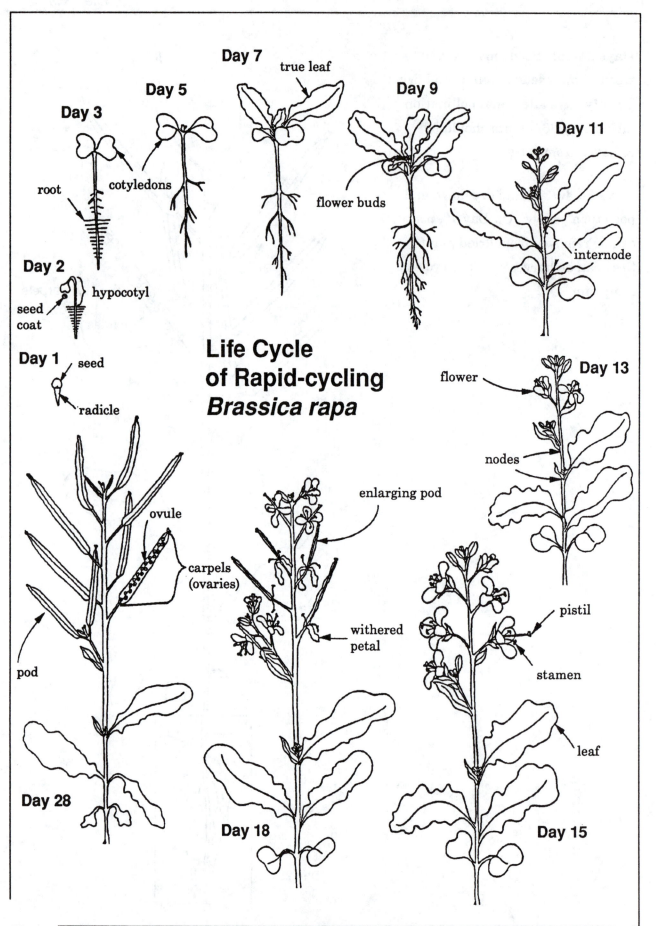

**Day 3**

root

cotyledons

**Day 5**

**Day 2**

seed
coat

hypocotyl

**Day 1**

seed

radicle

**Day 7**

true leaf

**Day 9**

flower buds

**Day 11**

internode

# Life Cycle
# of Rapid-cycling
# *Brassica rapa*

**Day 13**

flower

nodes

pistil

stamen

leaf

ovule

carpels
(ovaries)

enlarging pod

withered
petal

pod

**Day 28**

**Day 18**

**Day 15**

18

# The Cycle of Life:

## Exploring the Concept of a Life Cycle

Life on Earth comprises populations of individuals whose life span varies from a few hours (bacteria) to hundreds or even thousands of years (some trees). It is through the cycle of life of individuals, repeated from one generation to the next, that life of a group of organisms or species is continued on earth. Life, for many organisms, begins with fertilization, the time when specialized reproductive cells representing the contributions of a single egg (female) and a sperm (male) join to form the *zygote* (first cell of the new generation). In higher organisms the zygote divides repeatedly, progressing through stages of growth and development. It eventually becomes a mature adult, producing reproductive cells which contribute to yet another generation. The ways in which various organisms complete their life cycles is extremely varied and a fascinating part of biology.

The growing of rapid-cycling *Brassica rapa* (Rbr) through a life cycle, from seed to seed, can provide the basis for learning many aspects of biology that are relevant to the students' understanding of themselves as individual organisms among the many others inhabiting the planet Earth.

The table of Concepts in the Life Cycle of Fast Plants (page 20) will provide you with different ways of understanding of the cycle of life. By looking at the life cycle of Fast Plants from the perspective of the stages of growth and development from seed to seed, a framework can be developed for understanding the nature of the dependency between organisms and their environment.

**The explorations in this manual are all founded on an understanding of the life cycle of Fast Plants.**

### References

Burne, D. 1989. *Eyewitness Books, Plant*. New York: Alfred A. Knopf. A photoessay introducing the world of plants. Includes life cycles, plant defenses, uses of plants and plant collectors.

Stockley, C. 1986. *Dictionary of Biology (Usborne Illustrated)*. London: Usborne Publishing, Ltd. A densely illustrated, clear guide to key terms and subject areas of plants and animals.

# Concepts in the Life Cycle of Fast Plants

| Stage | State | Condition | Dependency |
|---|---|---|---|
| A. seed | • quiescence (dormant embryo) | • suspended growth of embryo | • independent of the parent and many components of the environment |
| B. germinating seed | • germination | • awakening of growth | • dependent on environment and health of the individual |
| C. vegetative growth | • growth and development | • roots, stems, leaves grow rapidly, plant is sexually immature | • dependent on environment |
| D. immature plant | • flower bud development | • gametogenesis — reproductive [male (pollen) and female (egg)] cell production | • dependent on healthy vegetative plant |
| E. mature plant | • flowering<br>• mating | • pollination — attracting or capturing pollen | • dependent on pollen carriers; bees and other insects |
| F. mature plant | • pollen growth | • gamete maturation<br>• germination and growth of pollen tube | • dependent on compatibility of pollen with stigma and style |
| G. mature plant | • double fertilization | • union of gametes<br>• union of sperm (n) and egg (n) to produce zygote (2n)<br>• union of sperm (n) and fusion nucleus (2n) to produce endosperm (3n) | • dependent on compatibility and healthy plant |
| H. mature parent plant *plus* embryo | • developing fruit<br>• developing endosperm<br>• developing embryo | • embryogenesis — growth and development of endosperm and embryo<br>• growth of supporting parental tissue of the fruit (pod) | • interdependency among developing embryo, endosperm, developing pod and supporting mature parental plant |
| I. aging parent plant *plus* maturing embryo | • senescence of parent<br>• maturation of fruit<br>• seed development | • withering of leaves of parent plant<br>• yellowing pods, drying embryo<br>• suspension of embryo growth, development of seed coat | • seed is becoming independent of the parent |
| J. dead parent plant *plus* seed | • death, desiccation<br>• seed quiescence | • drying of all plant parts, dry pods will disperse seeds | • seed (embryo) is independent of parent, but is dependent on the pod and the environment for dispersal |

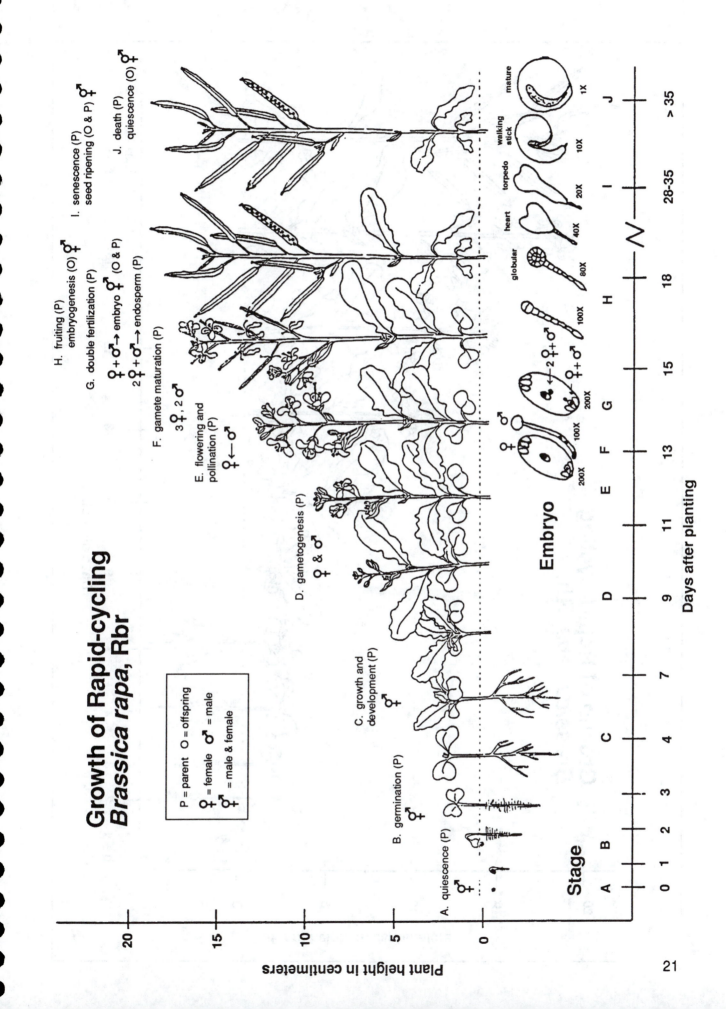

# Growth of Rapid-cycling
## *Brassica rapa*, Rbr

P = parent    O = offspring
♀ = female    ♂ = male
☿ = male & female

A. quiescence (P) ☿

B. germination (P) ☿

C. growth and development (P) ☿

D. gametogenesis (P) ♀ & ♂

E. flowering and pollination (P) ♀ ← ♂

F. gamete maturation (P) 3♀, 2♂

G. double fertilization (P)
♀ + ♂ → embryo ☿ (O & P)
2♀ + ♂ → endosperm (P)

H. fruiting (P) embryogenesis (O) ☿

I. senescence (P) seed ripening (O & P) ☿

J. death (P) quiescence (O) ☿

**Embryo**

| Stage | A | B | C | D | E | F | G | H | I | J |
|-------|---|---|---|---|---|---|---|---|---|---|
| Days after planting | 0 | 1 2 3 | 4 | 7 | 9 | 11 | 13 | 15 | 18 | 28-35 | > 35 |

Plant height in centimeters

20    15    10    5    0

21

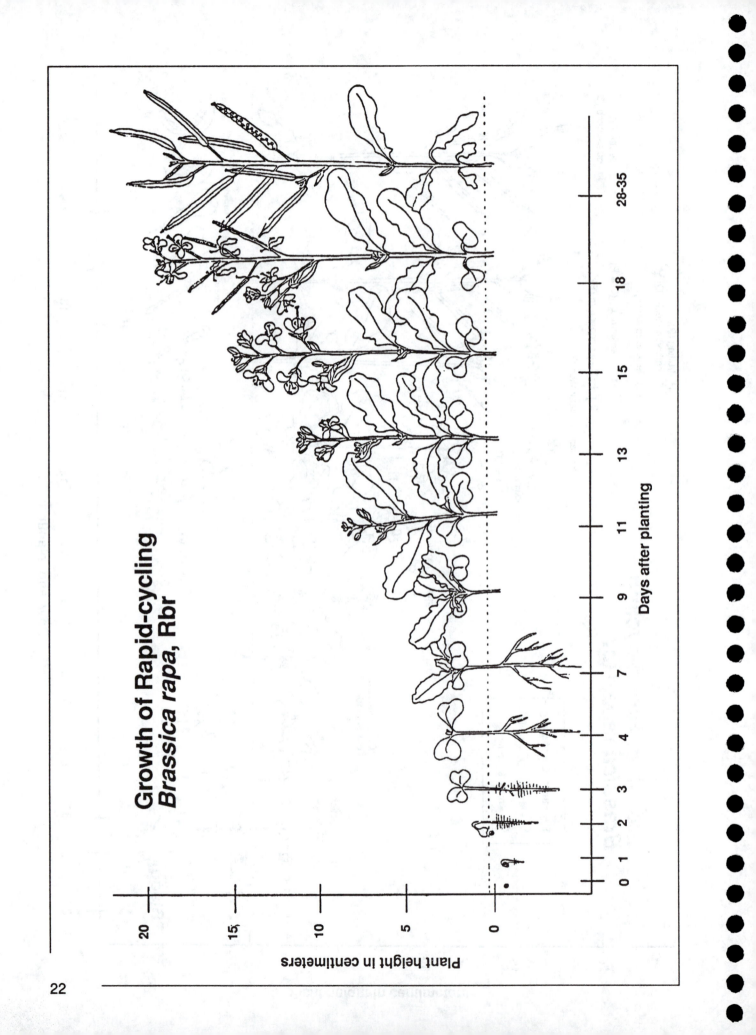

# Growth of Rapid-cycling
## *Brassica rapa*, Rbr

Plant height in centimeters

20

15

10

5

0

0   1   2   3   4   7   9   11   13   15   18   28-35

Days after planting

# Keeping Track of Things

**Observing.** Keen observation is the key to successful science explorations. Encourage observation throughout the life cycle, beginning with seeds, then plants and flowers, and finally seed pods. Unity and diversity among living things is obvious with Fast Plants. The plants will be green, form leaves, stems, flowers and require light, nutrients and a suitable temperature. Yet students will observe differences in height, leaf shape, leaf color, number of flowers and differences in seed size and color.

Paper, pencil, hand lenses and measuring materials are needed so that students can make specific observations. For example,

| Names _____ | | | | | |
| Date Seeds planted _____ | | | | | |

| Date | Age of Plants | Height in centimeters | | | |
|------|---------------|-----------|-----------|-----------|-----------|
|      |               | plant #1  | plant #2  | plant #3  | plant #4  |
|      |               |           |           |           |           |
|      |               |           |           |           |           |
|      |               |           |           |           |           |
|      |               |           |           |           |           |
|      |               |           |           |           |           |
|      |               |           |           |           |           |
|      |               |           |           |           |           |

what different leaf shapes occur? How tall is the plant at Day 8? How are the stamens arranged in the flower? Observing can be a class activity, especially with younger students.

**Asking questions.** As the Fast Plants cycle unfolds in your classroom and students observe their plants, questions will undoubtedly come up. Keep a class list of the questions students ask. This is your source of ideas for future Fast Plants explorations. See the "What If's " list (page 35).

**Questions might include:**
- What do the roots look like? (There is one main tap root.)
- What if you plant the seeds outdoors in the ground? (Fast Plants are not well adapted to outdoor growth.)
- What if the plants are grown without 24 hour/day fluorescent light? (Tall, spindly plants will result.)

- Why does one plant grow taller than another? (This is due to variation in nutrients, plant hormones, genetics.)
- What if you don't thin plants? (Overcrowding causes plants to take longer to complete the cycle.)
- What if you don't pollinate? (Little or no seed will be produced.)
- Why do the plants turn yellowish-brown near the end of the life cycle? (It's part of the preparation for release of seeds from the pods.)

**Prediction.** While students are observing and collecting information about a plant's life cycle, ask students to predict what will happen next.

### For example:

- Predict what the seeds need to sprout.
- Predict what the plant needs to grow.
- Predict where on the plant flowers will develop.
- Predict how tall the plants will become.
- Predict how long the plants will live.
- Predict the number of seeds the plant will produce.

Direct students to use their observations and collected information as they form their predictions. Write down the predictions in the form of a hypothesis or proposal. "Fast Plants require fertilizer to grow normally" is a hypothesis.

Names _____

Date Seeds planted _____   Date Harvested _____

| Number of seeds per plant | | | | |
|---|---|---|---|---|
| plant #1 | plant #2 | plant #3 | plant #4 | Average number |
|  |  |  |  |  |

**Labeling, measuring, recording data and graphing.** A science experiment requires precise labeling, careful observations, recording of data, and visualization of information in graphs, histograms, etc. Follow these guidelines in your Fast Plants experiment.

### Labeling:

- Use a waterproof marking pen.
- Number each plant in a quad.
- When seed is harvested, label the seed envelope with grower's name(s), date of harvest, and type of seed.

*Measuring*:

- Determine what you are going to measure — plant height, leaf length, number of flowers.
- Agree on how you are going to measure, from what point to what point. For example, from cotyledons (or edge of quad) to growing tip of plant.
- Decide what you will use to measure — plastic rulers, metric cubes, strips of paper, etc. Strips of paper can be cut off at the length measured and glued to a chart.

*Recording data:*

- Record keeping can be in the form of charts, logs, written journals, illustrated journals, or graphs. Encourage students to keep neat, accurate and complete written and illustrated records.
- Students will find variability as they measure Fast Plants. This is an ideal time to discuss human variation as well.
- Keep a record of class data. It's handy to look at the data from previous years before you begin again.

*Graphing:*

- Start simply by taking some common set of data like plant height and construct a histogram. This can be done as a class activity or in groups.
- Ask groups to evaluate the results graphed by other groups.
- Save graphs and histograms for comparison with next year's classes.

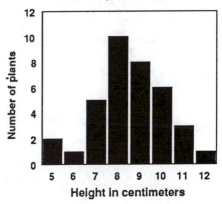

**Class Histogram of Plant Height at Day 12**

**Designing future investigations.** All real science investigations follow the steps that any scientist would use. After the students have made observations, kept good records and wondered "why" or "what if," they can design a subsequent investigation following the steps of the scientific method. These steps are found in the Science Exploration Flowchart (on page viii, page 40 and in all the chapters in Sections 3 and 4).

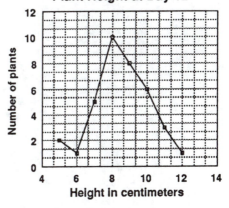

**Class Line Graph of Plant Height at Day 12**

**The investigation should include:**

- A statement of what the student will investigate.
- The procedure the student will follow.
- An analysis of the results obtained.
- A written explanation of what happened.

See the student worksheet "Setting Up An Experiment" (pages 41-43).

**Communicating the results.** The final step of written explanation is essential, though often overlooked. No science investigation is complete until it is communicated to others. A written conclusion can be done very simply, but should be understandable to anyone reading it, peers and/or teacher.

# Grower's Calendar

| Day of cycle (time required) | Activities |
| --- | --- |
| **Preparation** (1 1/2 hours)<br>*Date:* _____ | Assemble light bank and rack.<br>Set up reservoirs.<br>Saturate water mat according to growing instructions.<br>Arrange all planting materials. |
| **Day 1** (1 hour)<br>*Date:* _____ | **Plan to start life cycle on a Monday or Tuesday.**<br>Plant, water from above, label, set quads on water mat with top of quad 5-10 cm from the lights. |
| **Day 2-3**<br>*Date:* _____ | Water from top with pipet.<br>Cotyledons emerge. |
| **Day 4-5** (30 min.)<br>*Date:* _____ | Thin to 1 plant per cell.<br>Transplant if necessary to obtain 1 plant in every cell.<br>Check the water level in the reservoir! |
| **Day 6-11** (15 min/day)<br>*Date:* _____ | **Check plants and reservoir level daily throughout the rest of the life cycle.**<br>Observe growth and development. |
| **Day 12** (30 min.)<br>*Date:* _____ | Make beesticks.<br>Flower buds beginning to open. |
| **Day 13-18** (15 min./day)<br>*Date:* _____ | Pollinate for 2-3 consecutive days.<br>On the last day of pollination,<br>pinch off any remaining unopened buds. |
| **Day 17-35**<br>*Date:* _____ | Observe seed pod development.<br>Embryos mature in 20 days. |
| **Day 36**<br>*Date:* _____ | Twenty days after the last pollination, remove plants from water mat.<br>Allow plants to dry for 5 days. |
| **Day 40** (30 min.)<br>*Date:* _____ | Harvest seeds from dry pods.<br>Clean up all equipment.<br>Plant your own seeds or store them appropriately. |

# Suggested Activities with Fast Plants for Various Stages in the Life Cycle

| Day in the Life Cycle | Activity |
|---|---|
| Day 1 or earlier | • harvesting seed from pods ("Fast Plants and Families," pages 193-197) |
| Day 1-2 | • bioassays (pages 149-156) |
| Day 1-3 | • germination (pages 45-56)<br>• germination model (seed sponge model, page 228) |
| Day 1-4 | • tropisms (pages 157-170)<br>• effects of salt (pages 179-186) |
| Day 5-17 | • count developing leaves |
| Day 5-20 | • measure plant height |
| Day 7 | • modify the atmosphere (pages 171-178)<br>-- with volatiles<br>-- with particulates |
| Day 7-21 | • nutrition (pages 139-148)<br>-- needs to be set up at planting |
| Day 12 | • make beesticks (page 93) |
| Day 13-16 | • study flower parts (pages 73-90)<br>• flower models (page 230)<br>• pollinate (pages 91-112)<br>• plant breeding experiment (pages 205-208) |
| Day 13-20 | • count number of flowers |
| Day 17-35 | • seed pod development (pages 113-124)<br>-- open seed pods to observe ovules (Days 28-35)<br>-- measure pod length |
| Day 40 | • harvest pods<br>-- 20 days after last pollination or at Day 1 (see above)<br>-- count seeds per pod (pages 125-136)<br>-- after harvesting, compost (pages 211-216) |

# Tips and Suggestions

- Before you start, set up light banks as detailed on pages 249-250. Complete Steps 1, 2 and 3 of the Illustrated Growing Instructions (page 31).

- Lighting is critical for the success of your Fast Plants projects. Follow the equation below and see Section 8 (pages 243-260) for more information.

---

## Formula for growing successful Fast Plants:

| Six 40 W bulbs or new 32 W high efficiency bulbs should be used for growing Fast Plants | + | Rotate your plants. Irradiance (light intensity) grades off from the center of the light bank. | + | Keep tops of plants between 5 and 10 cm from the lights. | = | **Healthy Fast Plants** |

---

- Fertilizer pellets are larger than Fast Plants seeds.

- For easier seed handling, sprinkle a few seeds on a piece of scotch tape. Make a loop of the tape (sticky side out) and attach to a paper card. Each student can pick seeds off the seed tape when planting.

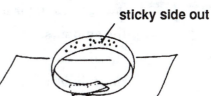

**sticky side out**

- The watering system is based on wicking (capillary) action. The water mat draws water from the reservoir onto the platform. Wicks in the bottom of each cell draw water into the potting mix.

- Careful watering with pipets will keep seed from washing out.

- Check placement of quads on water mat each day. Students may not have all of the wicks in contact with the water mat.

- Check plants and water level daily. Fill the reservoir to the brim before the weekend.

- Fast Plants must be thinned to one plant in each cell of the quad because space, potting mix and nutrient content is calculated for only one plant/cell.

- Staking plants as they get taller is optional.

- Discuss with students the information in "Bees and Brassicas" (pages 110-111), or "Speedy Bee and the Brassica Morning" (pages 225-227), before making beesticks and pollinating.

- Fast Plants are edible, flowers and all.

### In addition:

- Worksheets are found with each Life Cycle exploration in Section 3.

- Each exploration in Sections 3, 4 and 6 begins with helpful additional background information for the teacher and detailed, illustrated procedures for the students.

- "Modeling" in Section 7 details ways of demonstrating seed germination and the process of fertilization through the use of simple, but effective models. It also includes suggestions for making model flowers and bees.

# Illustrated Growing Instructions

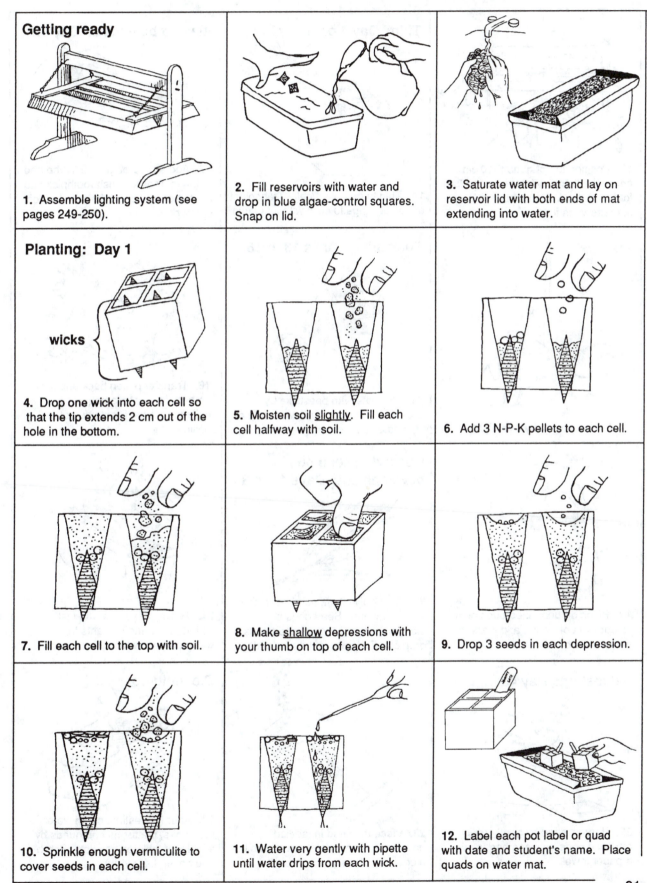

**Getting ready**

1. Assemble lighting system (see pages 249-250).

2. Fill reservoirs with water and drop in blue algae-control squares. Snap on lid.

3. Saturate water mat and lay on reservoir lid with both ends of mat extending into water.

**Planting: Day 1**

wicks

4. Drop one wick into each cell so that the tip extends 2 cm out of the hole in the bottom.

5. Moisten soil <u>slightly</u>. Fill each cell halfway with soil.

6. Add 3 N-P-K pellets to each cell.

7. Fill each cell to the top with soil.

8. Make <u>shallow</u> depressions with your thumb on top of each cell.

9. Drop 3 seeds in each depression.

10. Sprinkle enough vermiculite to cover seeds in each cell.

11. Water very gently with pipette until water drips from each wick.

12. Label each pot label or quad with date and student's name. Place quads on water mat.

# Illustrated Growing Instructions

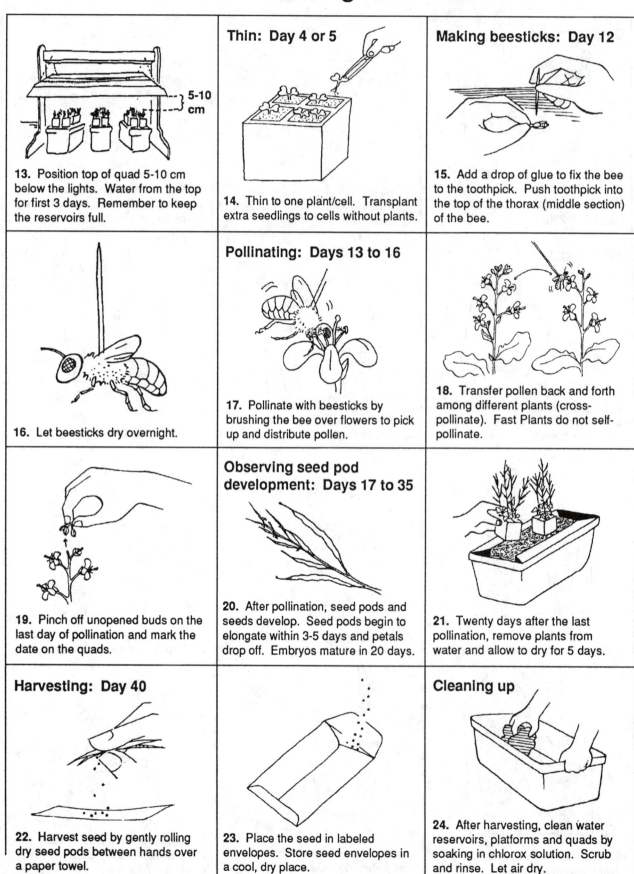

**13.** Position top of quad 5-10 cm below the lights. Water from the top for first 3 days. Remember to keep the reservoirs full.

5-10 cm

**Thin: Day 4 or 5**

**14.** Thin to one plant/cell. Transplant extra seedlings to cells without plants.

**Making beesticks: Day 12**

**15.** Add a drop of glue to fix the bee to the toothpick. Push toothpick into the top of the thorax (middle section) of the bee.

**16.** Let beesticks dry overnight.

**Pollinating: Days 13 to 16**

**17.** Pollinate with beesticks by brushing the bee over flowers to pick up and distribute pollen.

**18.** Transfer pollen back and forth among different plants (cross-pollinate). Fast Plants do not self-pollinate.

**19.** Pinch off unopened buds on the last day of pollination and mark the date on the quads.

**Observing seed pod development: Days 17 to 35**

**20.** After pollination, seed pods and seeds develop. Seed pods begin to elongate within 3-5 days and petals drop off. Embryos mature in 20 days.

**21.** Twenty days after the last pollination, remove plants from water and allow to dry for 5 days.

**Harvesting: Day 40**

**22.** Harvest seed by gently rolling dry seed pods between hands over a paper towel.

**23.** Place the seed in labeled envelopes. Store seed envelopes in a cool, dry place.

**Cleaning up**

**24.** After harvesting, clean water reservoirs, platforms and quads by soaking in chlorox solution. Scrub and rinse. Let air dry.

# Troubleshooting and Tips

| Condition of plants | Possible reasons and some solutions |
|---|---|
| **poor germination (no seedling emergence)** | • seeds planted too deep in quad<br>• potting mix compacted, or too wet when dropped into planting container<br>• quad not watered carefully from the top for the first three days<br>• seeds washed out of quad<br>• room temperature below 60°F (15.5°C)<br>• fertilizer pellets were planted instead of seeds<br>*If seedlings do not appear by Day 4, start over.* |
| **plants growing slowly** | • lower temperature in school than normal on weekends and holidays<br>• less than 6 cool-white fluorescent bulbs in light bank<br>• plants growing at lower temperature due to location near window in winter |
| **plants look spindly, unhealthy** | • check for aphids or other pests (see Problems, page 24)<br>• lights too far away from plants — should be 5-10 cm from growing tip<br>• fertilizer not added to each cell (insert fertilizer pellets at corners of cell and push below potting soil surface)<br>• too much fertilizer added to each cell |
| **plants die** | • wicks not placed correctly in bottom of quads<br>• water mat not in water, may be stuck to bottom of platform<br>• water mat not wet thoroughly and/or |

all air pockets not removed when watering system was set up
- water mat clogged and not wicking water (wash mat in 5% vinegar solution, rinse thoroughly)
- quad not completely on water mat (check quads at end of each day)
- water in tray ran out over weekend (always check water on Fridays!)
- plant damaged during thinning (handle gently)
- plant damaged during movement (as plants grow taller, stake and secure them with plastic rings)

| Problems | What to do |
| --- | --- |
| **insects** | • ladybug beetles can be used as a biological pest control. Call biological supply companies such as Carolina Biological or Nasco to order. |
| | • remove the insects from your plants by hand and pinch them |
| | • use an insecticidal soap. Consult a garden store. |
| **plants wilt** | • if the worst happens (i.e. you forgot to fill the reservoir on Friday) and the plants are wilting (but not yet crispy), you may be able to save your plants. Fill reservoirs with water and float the quads in the water while adding water from above with pipets. Allow the quads to float on the water until plants are turgid again. Re-soak the water mat and return the quads to the mat. |

## References

Bjork, L. and L. Anderson. 1978. *Linnea's Windowsill Garden.* New York: Farrar, Straus & Giroux. A tour of a young girl's indoor garden. Includes conversations about what keeps plants satisfied and what to do when plants are attacked by insect pests.

# "What-If's": What can we do now?

*What if . . .* Growing a life cycle of the Fast Plants should raise many questions and possibilities among the students. One good way to encourage them to articulate these questions is to phrase them as "What would happen if. . ." and to turn these questions into investigations. The ideas for follow-up investigations found below were generated by fifth graders in the classrooms of Debbie Bevan and Wesley Licht, Glendale Elementary, Madison, WI.

## What if we . . .

- don't cover seeds with soil?
- use a different soil, like sand or top soil, or pack the soil hard?
- change the seeds by soaking, boiling or freezing them?

- plant the seed in smaller containers?
- grow Fast Plants in the same pot as a larger plant (e.g., corn)?
- transplant our plants into bigger pots?
- don't transplant them or thin them?
- grow them in sunlight, not artificial light, or vary the amount of light?
- grow them in total darkness?
- snip off the first bloom, will it continue to grow?

- put different things in the water, i.e. food coloring, Coke, vinegar, soda?

- add different salt solutions, strong or weak?

## Explorations

See Germination exploration, pages 45-56.

See Plant Growth exploration, pages 57-72.

See Bioassay exploration, pages 149-156.

See Salt Effects on Plants exploration, pages 179-186.

- don't put any fertilizer in, or add a lot more, or put fertilizer on top of the soil?
- put fertilizer and seed at the bottom of the quad?
- use a different fertilizer like organic fertilizer or manure instead of the fertilizer pellets?

See Nutrition exploration, pages 139-148.

- don't pollinate?

See Pollination exploration, pages 91-112.

- grow the plants straight up, then lay them on their side for a few days?

See Tropisms exploration, pages 157-170.

- grow the plant in the same air, no new air getting to the plant?
- grow the plant in smoke filled air?

See Modifying the Atmosphere exploration, pages 171-178.

**Other What If's . . .**
- only plant one seed?
- grow plants in only water, no soil?
- give the plants no water?
- don't water plants from the top the first couple of days?
- don't use the water mat and wicks, just water from the top?
- take the cotyledons off when they first appear?

# Exploring the Life Cycle
# of Fast Plants

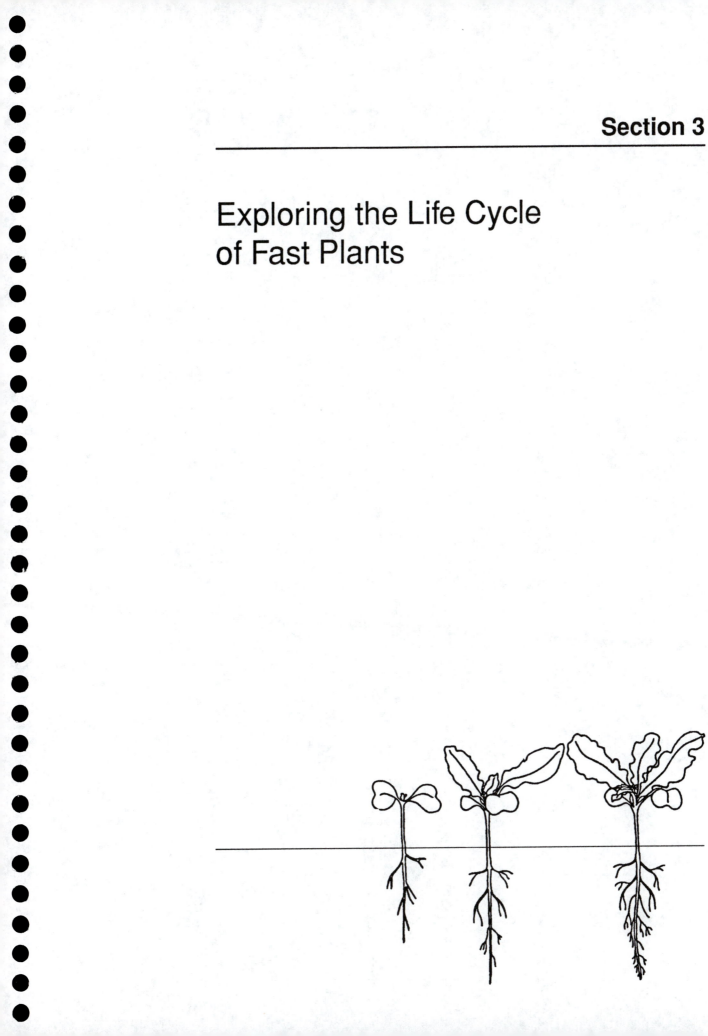

# Concepts: Exploring the Life Cycle of Fast Plants

## Germination

Germination is the awakening of a seed (embryo) from a resting state. It involves the harnessing of energy stored within the seed and is activated by components in the environment.

- *How does a seed awaken?*
- *What are the main components of the environment necessary for germination?*
- *How does the germinating seed go about harnessing its stored energy and use the environment?*
- *How does the seedling orient itself?*
- *What developmental events enable the emerging plant to shift its dependency from stored energy to the energy from light?*

## Plant Growth

Growth represents increase in size, number and complexity of plant cells and organs. Environment and genetics play fundamental roles in regulating growth. The energy for growth comes from photosynthesis and respiration.

- *What is the role of the environment in regulating plant growth?*
- *How do plants grow?*
- *How does a plant know when to produce leaves and when to produce flowers?*

## Flowering

Flowering is the initiation of sexual reproduction. The generation of male and female gametes (sperm and eggs) is one of the primary functions in flowering. The plant prepares for pollination by producing flowers. Each part of the flower has specific roles to play in sexual reproduction. The flower dictates the mating strategy of the species.

> Parts involved in the flower's primary and secondary functions:
> primary — pistil (carpels, ovules, style, stigma) and stamens (anther, pollen, sperm)
> secondary — sepals, petals, nectaries

- *Why does a plant have flowers?*
- *How do flower parts function to influence mating behavior?*

## Pollination

Pollination is the process of mating in plants. In flowers, pollen is delivered to the stigma through a wide range of mechanisms that insure an appropriate balance in the genetic makeup of the species. In brassicas, pollen is distributed by bees and other insects. The flower is the device by which the plant recruits the bee. Bees and brassicas have evolved an interdependent relationship.

- *How does the flower recruit the bee?*
- *How does pollination occur?*
- *How does the flower discriminate between self and non-self in the mix of pollens?*

## Double Fertilization and Seed Pod Development

Fertilization is the final event in sexual reproduction. In higher plants, two sperm from the pollen grain are involved in fertilization. One fertilizes the egg to produce the zygote and begin the new generation. The other sperm combines with the fusion nucleus to produce the special tissue (endosperm) that nourishes the developing embryo. In some plants endosperm nourishes the germinating seedling. Fertilization also stimulates the growth of the maternal tissue (seed pod or fruit) supporting the developing seed.

- *What is unique about fertilization in plants?*
- *What is endosperm and what is its relationship to the embryo?*
- *How does an embryo develop into a seed?*
- *How does the maternal parent contribute to the developing embryo?*

## Seed Maturation and Dispersal

Maturing embryos stimulate aging in the plant. Energy and nutrients from the leaves are directed to the developing seeds. As maturing embryos become seeds, they lose water and enter the resting state. Maternal tissues age and senesce (leaves wither, pods and stems yellow). Within the fruit (pods) the new generation (seeds) is ready for dispersal. Seeds are one way that plants withstand environmental adversity.

- *How has the plant solved the problem of packaging the new generation?*
- *How is Fast Plants seed dispersed?*

# How to use an exploration

The Fast Plants explorations in Sections 3 and 4 are designed to be used with the "Science Exploration Flowchart" on the next page. The Flowchart illustrates all the steps of a complete science exploration. By following the sequence in the flowchart, students will develop the skills of a scientist— 1) observing, measuring, collecting data; 2) asking questions; 3) developing the hypothesis*; 4) designing and conducting the experiment, analyzing data; 5) evaluating the hypothesis and 6) communicating new insights.

Each Exploration includes: a description of the exploration, background information for the teacher, teaching objectives, planning instructions and guidelines for carrying out scientific investigations to answer questions generated from the observational exercise. To aid the teacher, each exploration presents one or more sample questions and follows them through the remaining steps of the Flowchart. Different cartoons of "Speedy Bee" are used to clue each step of the text to the Flowchart.

> *The nature of truth is elusive. Many scientists believe that the closest we can come to an understanding of what is true is through a rigorous and exhaustive quest which seeks, yet fails, to disprove a hypothesis.*
>
> *Paul H. Williams*

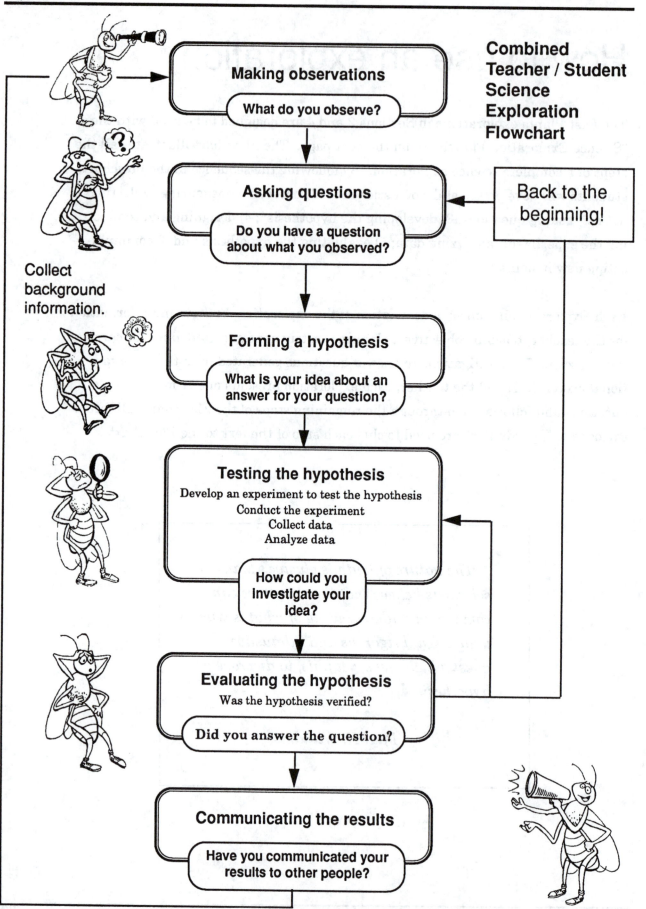

**Combined Teacher / Student Science Exploration Flowchart**

**Making observations**

What do you observe?

**Asking questions**

Do you have a question about what you observed?

Back to the beginning!

Collect background information.

**Forming a hypothesis**

What is your idea about an answer for your question?

**Testing the hypothesis**

Develop an experiment to test the hypothesis
Conduct the experiment
Collect data
Analyze data

How could you investigate your idea?

**Evaluating the hypothesis**

Was the hypothesis verified?

Did you answer the question?

**Communicating the results**

Have you communicated your results to other people?

# Setting Up An Experiment

1. Question you are exploring: _____

_____

2. Idea (hypothesis) you are testing: _____

_____

3. What variable will you change in your experiment? _____

_____

4. What variables will remain constant in your experiment?_____

_____

_____

5. Make a sketch of the set-up for your experiment.  Label all materials and state all conditions.  List the materials you need.

Materials needed:

_____

_____

_____

_____

_____

6. During the experiment:

   (a) What specific things will you observe? _____

   _____

   _____

   _____

   (b) What measurements will you make? _____

   _____

   _____

   (c) What plan do you have for recording your data? _____

   _____

   _____

7. Sketch a sample data table for your experiment:

| Time | Observations on conditions of seeds, number germinated, etc. | |
| | Dark | Light |
|------|------|-------|
| 24 hrs. | | |
| 48 hrs. | | |
| 72 hrs. | | |
| 96 hrs. | | |

8. Do the results of the experiment support your idea (hypothesis)? _____

Conclusions: _____

_____

_____

_____

_____

_____

_____

Credits: Debbie Bevan and Wesley Licht, Glendale Elementary, Madison, WI.

# Chapter 1: Germination

**The students will germinate Fast Plants seeds and will observe what affects germinating seeds.** This can be a stand-alone observational exercise. The steps of each chapter are consistent with the boxed steps of the Science Exploration Flowchart. You can develop a complete scientific investigation using the questions your students ask as a result of this observational exercise. Some examples for complete scientific investigations are provided and identified by following specific icons; ●, ▲, ■ and ◆. If you don't have time to complete a full investigation, you might plan to continue with it later in the year.

## Background Information for the Teacher

*Germination* is the beginning of growth of a plant from a previously dormant seed which contains the embryo. Germination begins when the seed takes up water (*imbibition*) and the seed coat cracks (Figure 1).

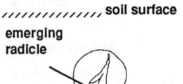

**soil surface**

**emerging radicle**

**Figure 1**

An embryonic root *(radicle)* emerges from the seed and grows root hairs that bring in water and nutrients (Figure 2). In Fast Plants, an embryonic stem *(hypocotyl)* elongates, pulling the seed leaves (or *cotyledons*) upwards through the soil (Figure 3). As they emerge from the soil the cotyledons expand. The cotyledons serve as a food source (energy) until true leaves form. These events happen on Days 1, 2 and 3 of the Fast Plants life cycle. For germination to take place, water and oxygen are needed and the temperature must be suitable.

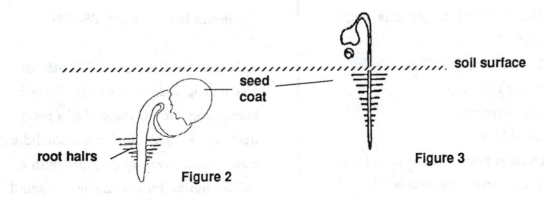

**seed coat**

**soil surface**

**root hairs**

**Figure 2**

**Figure 3**

## Teaching Objectives

**Beginning concepts:**

- Germination is the beginning of growth of a new plant from a seed.
- Major physical and chemical factors in the environment control and regulate growth — moisture, temperature and oxygen affect the germination of seeds.
- Other factors which affect germination are maturity of seed at harvest and seed dormancy.

**Advanced concepts:**

- A seed is a dry, dormant, embryonic plant complete with a reserve of stored energy to keep it alive and sustain germination.
- Fat, carbohydrate and protein stored in the seed serve as the energy source for germination.
- Emergence of the seedling and production of chlorophyll in the cotyledon prepares the plant for growth in the presence of sunlight.

## Preparation and Planning for Observational Exercise

**Time required:** 1 class hour on 3 to 4 consecutive days. Day 1: Set up germination dishes. Day 2-4: Observe and record.

**Tips and suggestions:**

- Set up the experiment early on Monday morning. This way students can observe the seed again just before leaving school. Also, the investigation can be completed by Friday.

- The germinated seedlings can be carefully transplanted into quads at Day 5 and grown to maturity.

- Optimum temperature, 65-80°F.

- **Alternative Procedural Method:** Use a deep peanut butter jar lid or something similar instead of a petri dish. After "planting," cover the lid with clear plastic wrap and secure with a rubber band. Punch one or two small holes at bottom of plastic to let in water.

---

**Materials needed per student/team:**

- 1 petri dish (or transparency film). See Tips and suggestions (page 183)
- 5 Wisconsin Fast Plants seeds
- paper toweling
- eye dropper
- hand lens
- shallow tray of water or bottom from a two-liter soda bottle

---

# Germination Observational Exercise

**1.** Cut two layers of paper towels to fit in the cover (larger half) of a petri dish.

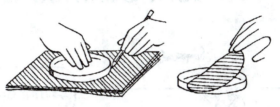

**2.** With a pencil, label the bottom of the paper towel with your name, the date and the time.

**6.** Set experiment in a warm location (optimum temperature: 65-80°F). Record the day and time of setting up the experiment.

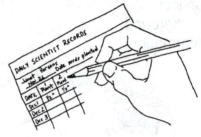

**3.** Moisten the towels in the petri dish with an eye dropper.

**7.** Over the next 3-4 days use a hand lens/magnifying glass to observe the stages of the germinating seeds and young plants. *Each day check the water level to be sure the paper toweling stays wet.*

**4.** Place five Fast Plants seeds on the top half of the towel and cover with the bottom (smaller half) of the petri dish.

**5.** Place petri dish at an angle in shallow water in the base of a two-liter soda bottle or in a tray so that the bottom 2 cm of the towel is below the water's surface.

water level

**8.** Record observations.

# Student Science Exploration Flowchart

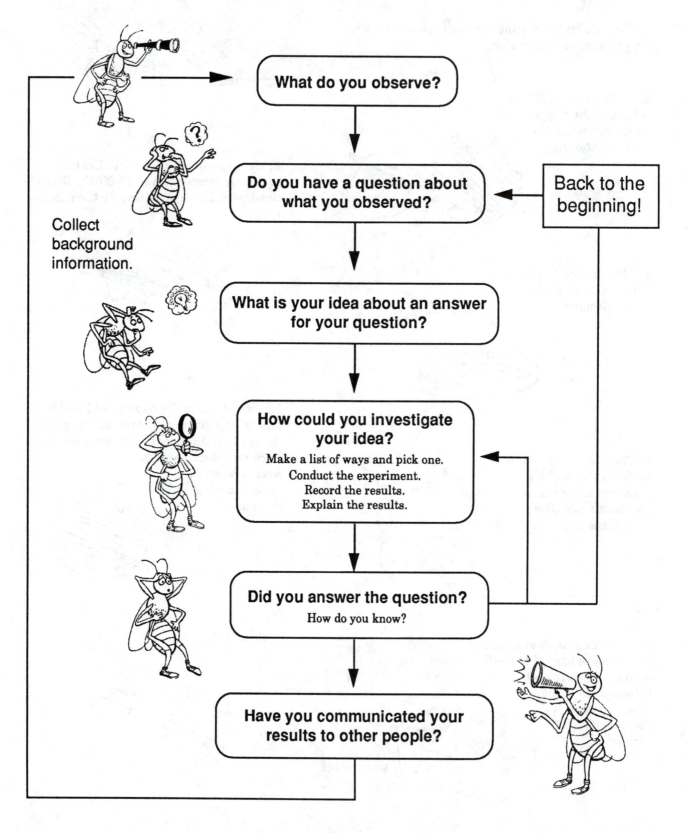

Collect
background
information.

**What do you observe?**

**Do you have a question about what you observed?**

Back to the beginning!

**What is your idea about an answer for your question?**

**How could you investigate your idea?**

Make a list of ways and pick one.
Conduct the experiment.
Record the results.
Explain the results.

**Did you answer the question?**

How do you know?

**Have you communicated your results to other people?**

## Exploring Germination

### Making observations

**Some preliminary questions:** Begin your exploration by asking your students some questions and discussing ideas they might have about seeds and germination.

**As you conduct the observational exercise illustrated on page 47,** your students will observe swelling of the seed, emergence of the root and root hairs, elongation of the hypocotyl, opening and spreading of the cotyledons and many other events associated with germination.

**Accompanying activities:**

- Germination model. Make a model seed sponge to demonstrate germination. See "Seed Sponge Model" (page 228).
- Before the students do the observational exercise, ask them to sketch what they think is inside a seed.

### Asking questions

**What questions have your students raised from observing?** The students should be curious about some of the things they have observed. A class discussion should generate questions. Have your students make a list of questions. Prompt them with the words "**What if.**"

**Example questions derived from the observation:**

- ● Do all seeds germinate as fast as Fast Plants? (Investigation #1)
- ▲ Would the seeds germinate if you changed the environment? For example, would the seeds germinate if you put them in the refrigerator? (Investigation #2)

**Other possible questions:** What is inside a seed? Where do seeds come from? Why did the seed swell? Does a seed germinating in the soil look the same?

### Forming a hypothesis

**What are your students' ideas about answers for their questions?**
Following the discussion of observations, students can turn their questions into statements and write them down as hypotheses.

**Example hypotheses derived from questions:**

● Fast Plants seeds germinate faster than other seeds. (Investigation #1)

▲ Fast Plants seeds germinate faster at warmer rather than at cooler temperatures. (Investigation #2)

**Tips and suggestions:** Ask students to check the Science Exploration Flowchart to see what the next steps need to be in their science investigation.

### Testing the hypothesis

**How could your students investigate their ideas?** Design an experiment. Devise ways to test the hypothesis, choose the best one and carry it out. Refer to worksheet "Setting Up An Experiment" (pages 41-43) for help in designing the experiment/s.

**Control Experiments:** A *control* serves as a standard of comparison for verifying the results of an investigation. By controlling the variable factors of the experiment, the effects of changing one variable at a time are easily observed.

**Examples of ways to test hypotheses:**

● Other seeds can be planted at the same time as Fast Plants seeds to compare germination rates. See worksheet "Comparing Germination Rates" (page 55). The control is the Fast Plants seed. (Investigation #1)
**Management Strategy:** The time to complete this investigation will vary from 5-10 days, depending on the other seeds used. Radish, broccoli and cabbage will germinate faster than lettuce, marigold, zinnia or nasturtium. Materials needed are: hand lenses, petri dishes, pipets or eyedroppers, paper toweling and a water reservoir as shown on page 47.

▲   Germinate half the seeds in petri dishes near a radiator, the other half in a cooler section of the room.  Or germinate half the seeds in the refrigerator and the other half near the radiator in a closed box.  This way the factor of light is missing from both locations, so the only difference is the temperature.  Keep a control set of seeds at normal room temperature.  (Investigation #2)

**Other suggestions for changing the germination environment:**

- Moistened paper toweling with light versus flooded paper toweling with light. Flooded seeds will be germinating in water.
- Dark and warm environment versus a dark and cool environment.
- Sand versus potting soil.
- Substances added to the water (vinegar, salt, sugar, soft drinks) versus clear water.
- Sound (different kinds of music) versus no sound.

**Collect data:**  See "Keeping Track of Things" (pages 23-26).

**Analyze the data:**  Have the students explain the results.  For example:

● Fast Plants seeds won the race, but there was a close second. (Investigation #1)

▲ The seeds placed in the refrigerator did not germinate at all.  The minimum temperature for germination is not reached in the refrigerator. (Investigation #2)

## Evaluating the hypothesis

**Was the hypothesis verified?**  How do your students know that they know?  For example: Was the test fair?  Did they answer the question?  Are they sure?

## Communicating the results

**Have your students communicated their results to others?**  *No science investigation is complete until it is communicated in writing.*  In addition, it can be communicated orally.  Students can write their conclusions very simply, but the report should be understandable to anyone reading it, peers and teacher.

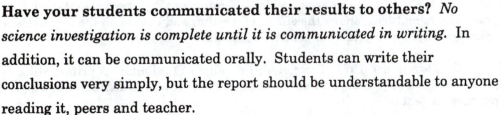

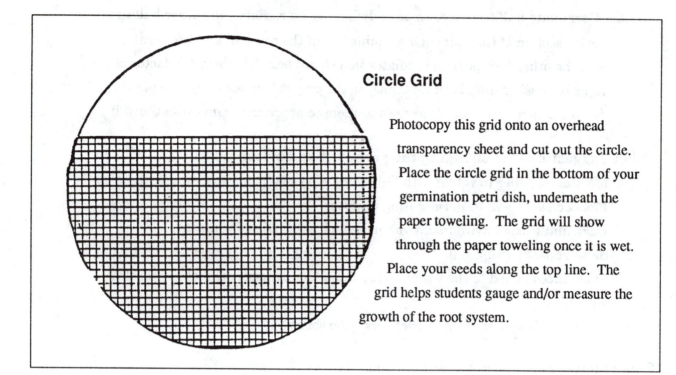

### Circle Grid

Photocopy this grid onto an overhead transparency sheet and cut out the circle. Place the circle grid in the bottom of your germination petri dish, underneath the paper toweling. The grid will show through the paper toweling once it is wet. Place your seeds along the top line. The grid helps students gauge and/or measure the growth of the root system.

## References

### Books

Lauber, P. 1981. *Seeds Pop, Stick, Glide*. New York: Crown Publishers, Inc. Engaging, clear text looks at the way plants disperse their seeds. Photography by Jerome Wexler.

Schuman, D. N. 1980. *Living with Plants, A Guide to Practical Botany*. Eureka, CA: Mad River Press, Inc. Excellent introductory chapter for background information entitled, "Introduction to a Plant," as well as other topics such as nutrients, soils and plant hormones.

Stockley, C. 1986. *Dictionary of Biology (Usborne Illustrated)*. London: Usborne Publishing, Ltd. A densely illustrated, clear guide to key terms and subject areas of plants and animals.

Suzuki, D. and B. Hehner. 1985. *Looking at Plants*. Toronto, Canada: Stoddart Publishing Co., Ltd. A tour through the plant world in clear and interesting language for students, plus short and long term projects.

Williams, P. H. 1993. *Bottle Biology*. Dubuque, IA: Kendall/Hunt Publishing Co. An idea book full of ways to use recyclable materials to teach about science and the environment.

### Films and videos

*Seeds and Seasons*. 1987. Churchill Farms. Video - 10 minutes. Primary presentation of a sunflower from seed to maturity, shows the effects of weather and insects on the plant. Uses time-lapse photography. Appropriate for primary students.

*What Do Seeds Need to Sprout?* 1973. Coronet Media. Film - 11 minutes. A primary film presenting three things for seeds to germinate: the right temperature, water and air. Appropriate for primary students.

germination

seed

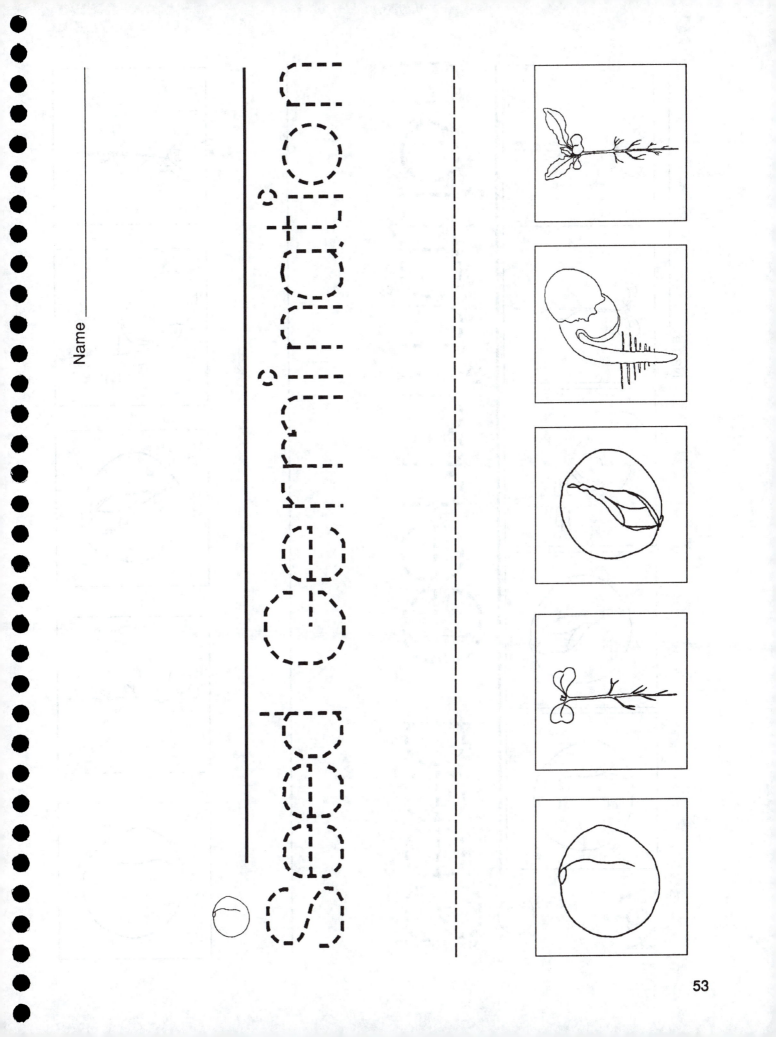

Name _____

## Key

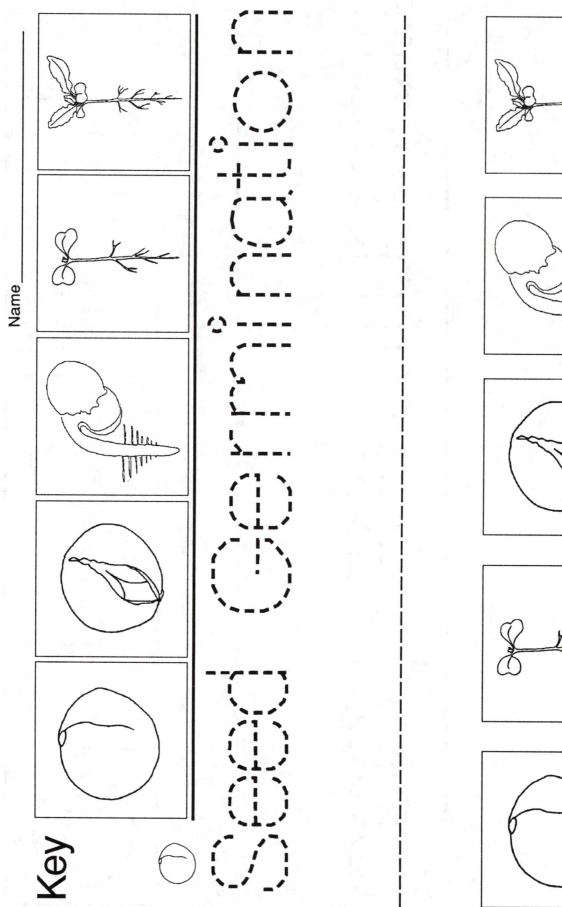

germination

seed

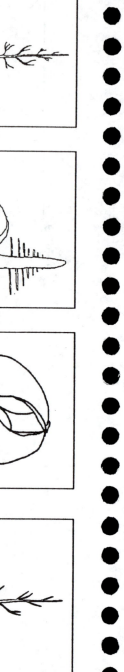

54

# Comparing Germination Rates

**Procedure**:

1. Cut two layers of paper toweling to fit in the cover (larger half) of a petri dish. With pencil, write a name of seed on paper towel at bottom.

2. Moisten the towels in the petri dish with an eye dropper.

3. Place five Fast Plants seeds on the towel and cover with the bottom (smaller half).

4. Place the petri dish at an angle in a tray of water so that water is just soaking one edge of the towel.

5. Repeat the set up for each of the other seed varieties.

**Materials needed**:

- petri dishes
- broccoli, radish, cabbage, bean and Fast Plants seeds
- paper toweling
- eye dropper
- hand lenses
- shallow trays of water

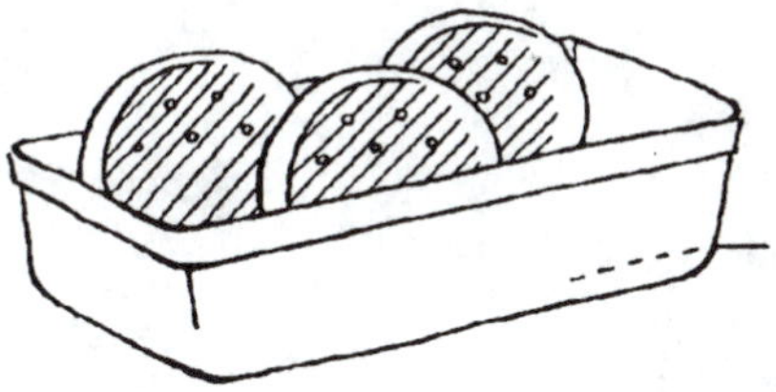

— water level

**Data**: Record dates and times on the chart below.

| Seed type | Day and time set up | Date seed swells | Date seed coat cracks | Date radicle emerges | Date cotyledons appear | Date true leaves appear |
|---|---|---|---|---|---|---|
| Fast Plants | | | | | | |
| Beans | | | | | | |
| Radish | | | | | | |
| Broccoli | | | | | | |
| Cabbage | | | | | | |

# Chapter 2: Plant Growth

Students will sow seed and grow Fast Plants through a life cycle, observing
and exploring the many changes in plant growth and development within a
life cycle. This can be a stand-alone observational exercise. The steps of
each chapter are consistent with the ⟨boxed⟩ steps of the Science Exploration Flowchart. You can develop a complete scientific investigation
using the questions your students ask as a result of this observational
exercise. Some examples for complete scientific investigations are
provided and identified by following specific icons; ●, ▲, ■ and ◆. If
you don't have time to complete a full investigation, you can continue with it later in the year.

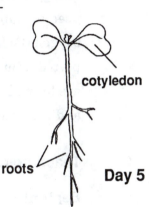

cotyledon

roots  **Day 5**

## Background Information for the Teacher

When conditions of the environment are favorable, growth occurs. The
environment includes physical (light, temperature, gravity), chemical
(water, air, minerals) and biological components (microbes and larger
organisms). All of these components interact to create the environment in which the plant grows. Following the emergence of the
germinating seedling from the soil, growth of the plant continues
through developmental stages in which new plant parts — leaves,
stem and flowers — are rapidly produced from the shoot growing
point known as the *shoot meristem*. Growth is observed as the
increase in size of the new leaves, stems and flowers.

In Fast Plants, growth is most dramatic in the 10-12 days between
seedling emergence and the opening of the first flowers. During this
period, students may explore important concepts that help them understand growth and development.

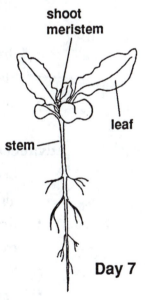

shoot
meristem

leaf

stem

**Day 7**

Each part of the plant performs important functions in the life cycle of the plant. The *roots* anchor the plant in the soil so that it doesn't wash or blow away. The roots also provide the means by which plants obtain water and minerals from the soil. The *stem* supports leaves and flowers and ensures that these parts are in the best position to perform their special tasks. The stem also transports water and minerals from the roots, and food manufactured in the leaves, to other plant parts.

The *leaves* are positioned to capture sunlight. In the process of photosynthesis, energy is trapped from sunlight by the green chlorophyll in leaves. This energy is used to manufacture food [carbohydrates (CHO)] by combining the carbon (C) and oxygen (O) from carbon dioxide ($CO_2$) in the air with hydrogen (H), which is transported from the roots as water ($H_2O$). Flowers contain many specialized parts that are formed to ensure that the seed of the next generation of plants will be produced and then dispersed to new locations for growth (see Chapters 3-6).

## Teaching Objectives

**Beginning concepts:**
- Plants grow and change.
- There are stages in the life cycle of a plant.
- Growth occurs through the appearance of new parts (for example, leaves, stems and flowers).
- Growth occurs through the increase in size of the new parts.
- Plants need adequate space to grow (thinning).
- Individuals within a population vary in their growth.

**Advanced concepts:**
- Each of the different parts of the plant (root, leaves, stems, flowers) perform specialized tasks supporting growth and the life-cycle of the plant.
- Growth is influenced by the ways in which the environment impacts on the growing plant.
- Normal growth requires a favorable environment.
- Variation in growth of individual plants in a population is related to variation in both the genetic constitution of the individuals and to variation in the growth environment of the individuals.

# Plant Growth Observational Exercise

**1.** Plant and grow following the steps in the illustrated growing instructions.

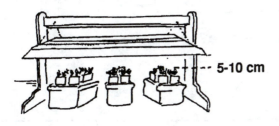

5-10 cm

**2.** As your plants grow, watch for the appearance of each new plant part. With your teacher, identify the part of the plant by name and discuss its function. Look for changes in the plants' appearance.

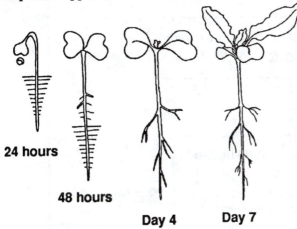

**24 hours**

**48 hours**

**Day 4**     **Day 7**

**3.** Each day, from Day 7 to Day 18, count and record the number of leaves and flowers on each of your plants.

**4.** Each day, measure and record the height of the plant.

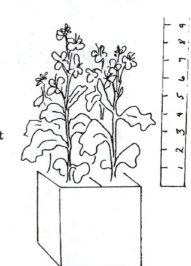

**5.** Notice the change in the distance between the leaves (internodes).

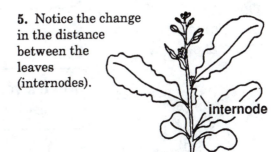

internode

**6.** Choose one plant and make a life-size sketch twice a week. Record the measurements for that day on the sketch.

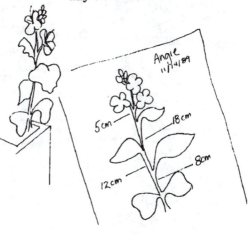

**7.** Do the plants continue to make new leaves? Do they continue to produce new flowers? Do the leaves continue to lengthen?

# Student Science Exploration Flowchart

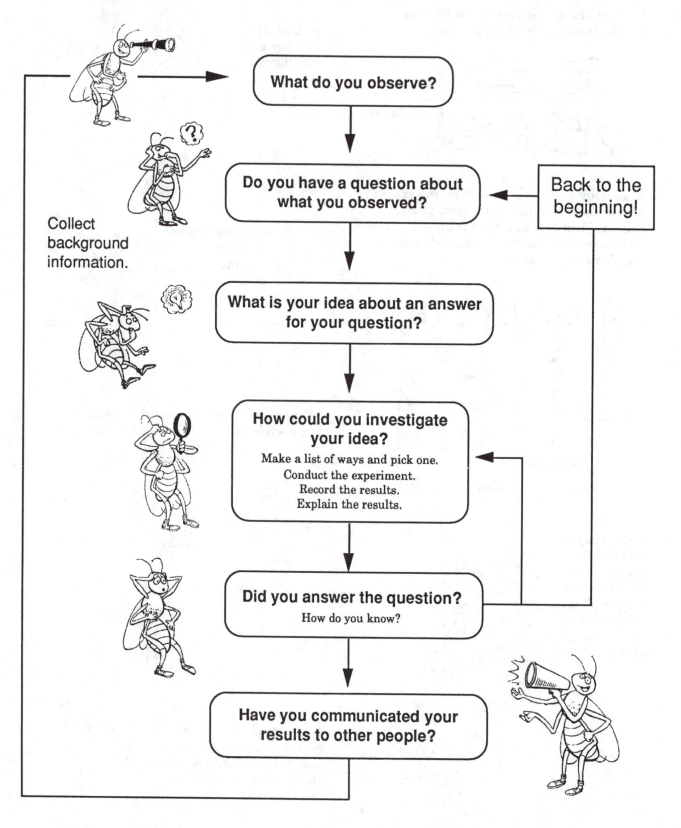

Collect background information.

**What do you observe?**

**Do you have a question about what you observed?**

Back to the beginning!

**What is your idea about an answer for your question?**

**How could you investigate your idea?**

Make a list of ways and pick one.
Conduct the experiment.
Record the results.
Explain the results.

**Did you answer the question?**

How do you know?

**Have you communicated your results to other people?**

## Preparation and Planning for Observational Exercise

**Time required:** 2 1/2 weeks total. One hour on the first day for planting, tending of plants; 1/2 hour each day (Days 7-18) for measuring and recording observations.

**Tips and suggestions:**

- Follow the Grower's Calendar (page 27) and all steps of the Illustrated Growing Instructions (pages 31-32) as you proceed with the exercise.
- The teacher should be thoroughly familiar with the concepts from "Concepts in the Life Cycle of Fast Plants" (page 20) as a basis for helping students make observations and ask questions.
- Be prepared to incorporate ideas from the record keeping section. See "Keeping Track of Things" (pages 23-26).

> **Materials needed per student/team:**
> - 1 quad of Fast Plants
> - sheets for record keeping

## Exploring Plant Growth

**Making observations**

**Some preliminary questions:** Begin your exploration by asking your students some questions and discussing ideas they might have about how plants grow and develop.

**As you conduct the observational exercise illustrated on page 59,** your students will watch the growth and development during the first two weeks of the life cycle of Fast Plants. They will look for daily changes in the plants as they grow and develop (seedlings emerging from the soil, cotyledons expanding and turning green, true leaves forming and enlarging, flower buds forming, stems elongating and flowers opening). They will keep accurate records on growth and development (the number of leaves and the number of flowers each plant produces, the height of the plant) as a way of focusing their attention on growth and development.

In the subsequent observational exercises (Chapters 3-6), students will observe flower parts, embryo and pod development, flowers withering and pods developing (if they pollinate their flowers), and, eventually, leaves withering, plants turning yellow and drying and seeds ripening.

**Accompanying activities:** Have students measure themselves — height, length of their arms, etc., and record the data.

## Asking questions

**What questions have your students raised from observing?** The students should be curious about some of the things they have observed. A class discussion should generate questions. Have your students make a list of questions. Prompt them with the words **"What if."**

**Example questions derived from the observations:**
- ● How would changing the light affect the growth of Fast Plants? (Investigation #1)
- ▲ What happens if you change the amount of soil and root space that a plant has? (Investigation #2)
- ■ What if you interrupt the growth of Fast Plants? (Investigation #3)

## Forming a hypothesis

**What are your students' ideas about answers for their questions?** Following the discussion of observations, students can turn their questions into statements and write them down as hypotheses.

**Example hypotheses derived from questions:**
- ● Fast Plants will look the same if they grow in daylight as under the light bank. (Investigation #1)
- ▲ Fast Plants will always grow to be the same size, regardless of how much soil they have. (Investigation #2)

■ If the flowering shoot (all buds and flowers) is removed (eaten by a rabbit or student) the plant will not complete its life cycle; it will not produce seed for the next generation. (Investigation #3)

**Tips and suggestions:** Have the students check the Science Exploration Flowchart to see what the next steps need to be in their science exploration.

---

### Testing the hypothesis

**How could your students investigate their ideas?** Design an experiment. Devise ways to test the hypothesis, choose the best one and carry it out. Refer to worksheet "Setting Up An Experiment" (pages 41-43) for help in designing the experiment/s.

**Control Experiments:** A *control* serves as a standard of comparison for verifying the results of an investigation. By controlling the variable factors of the experiment, the effects of changing one variable at a time are easily observed.

**Examples of ways to test hypotheses:**
- Grow half the plants in your class window and half under the lights (control). Hint: Each group of students should have some of their plants in each environment so they will not be disappointed in the growth (Investigation #1). Things that could be measured include: length of the internodes between the leaves, the time to the opening of the first flower, height of plant, general appearance of the plant.
  **Management Strategy:** The plants in the window will grow much more slowly. Several extra days will be needed to reach the flowering stage. The plants in the window will also grow to be much taller and more spindly than the lighted plants. Best results will be obtained with a south-facing window, and poor results with a north-facing window.
- ▲ Grow 1/3 of the plants in larger containers, 1/3 in quads (but do not thin any plants) and 1/3 as usual as the control (Investigation #2)
  **Management Strategy:** Try 2-, 3- and 4-inch pots, with 1 plant per pot. The larger the pot, the larger the Fast Plants will grow and the longer the life cycle.

■ Pinch off the growing tip of half of the plants (buds and flowers) at Day 12. Hint: Watch for the appearance of new shoots and buds. Record the date of the appearance of the first flowers compared to those on the unpruned control plants. Pollinate all plants, and grow to maturity (Investigation #3). **Management Strategy:** Lateral buds and flowers will appear 3-5 days after pinching off the first terminal buds and flowers.

**Collect data:** See "Keeping Track of Things" (pages 23-26).

**Analyze the data:** Have the students explain the results. For example:

● Fast Plants were developed to grow under continuous fluorescent light. Did they grow differently in your windows: Were they tall or spindly, or did they take a longer time to flower? How different is the environment of your window— consider the hours of light, quality of light, temperature, etc. (Investigation #1)

▲ Is there a difference in the height of the plants, in the size of the leaves, in the number of flowers, in the date at which the different groups flower? Does this lead to ideas for more experiments? (Investigation #2)

■ Why does a plant produce side shoots if the top is pinched off and growth is interrupted? Does this tell you anything about the main goal of a plant, namely, reproduction (see chapters 4 and 5)? Why would gardeners who want lots of flowers pinch off the growing tips of their plants? (Investigation #3)

### Evaluating the hypothesis

**Was the hypothesis verified?** How do your students know that they know? For example: Was the test fair? Did they answer the question? Are they sure?

### Communicating the results

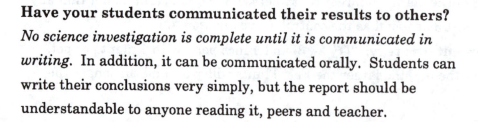

**Have your students communicated their results to others?** *No science investigation is complete until it is communicated in writing.* In addition, it can be communicated orally. Students can write their conclusions very simply, but the report should be understandable to anyone reading it, peers and teacher.

## References

### Books

Schuman, D. N. 1980. *Living with Plants, A Guide to Practical Botany.* Eureka, CA: Mad River Press, Inc. Excellent introductory chapter for background information entitled, "Introduction to a Plant," as well as other topics such as nutrients, soils and plant hormones.

Stockley, C. 1986. *Dictionary of Biology (Usborne Illustrated).* London: Usborne Publishing, Ltd. A densely illustrated, clear guide to key terms and subject areas of plants and animals.

# Life Cycle
# Concepts

Name _____

| |
|---|
| true leaves appear |
| flowers begin to grow |
| cotyledons emerge |
| pod development begins |
| pods are mature |
| flower buds appear |
| germination begins |
| stem elongates |

Copy this page and cut around all items.
Place them in order to show the sequence
of growth and glue on construction paper.

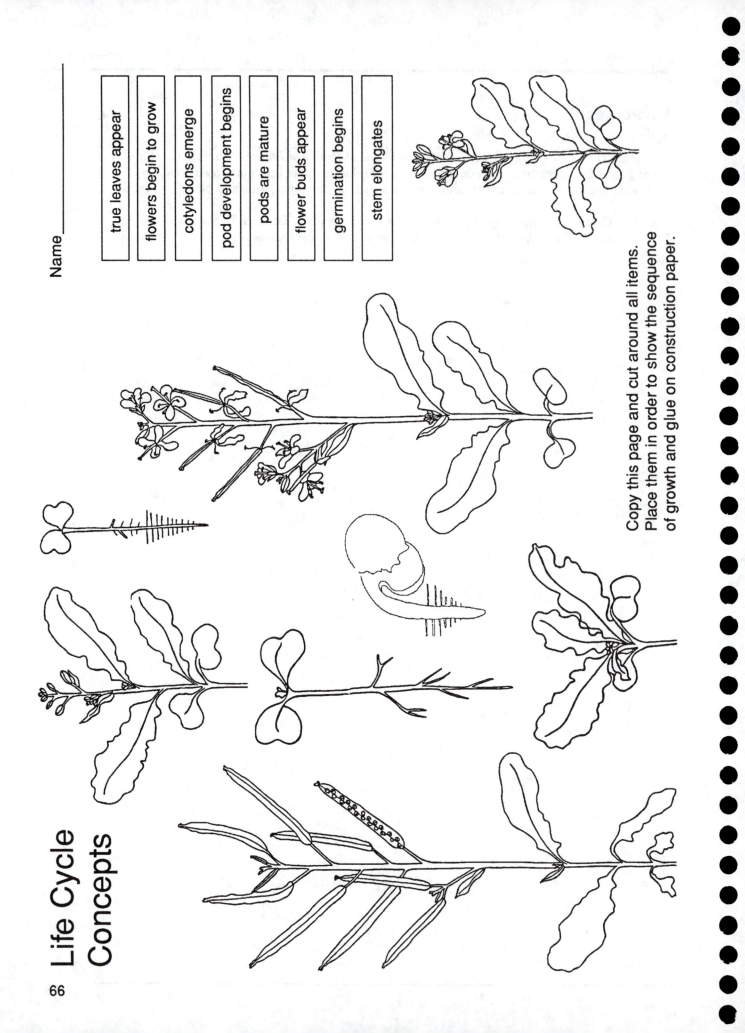

# Growth and development of rapid-cycling brassicas

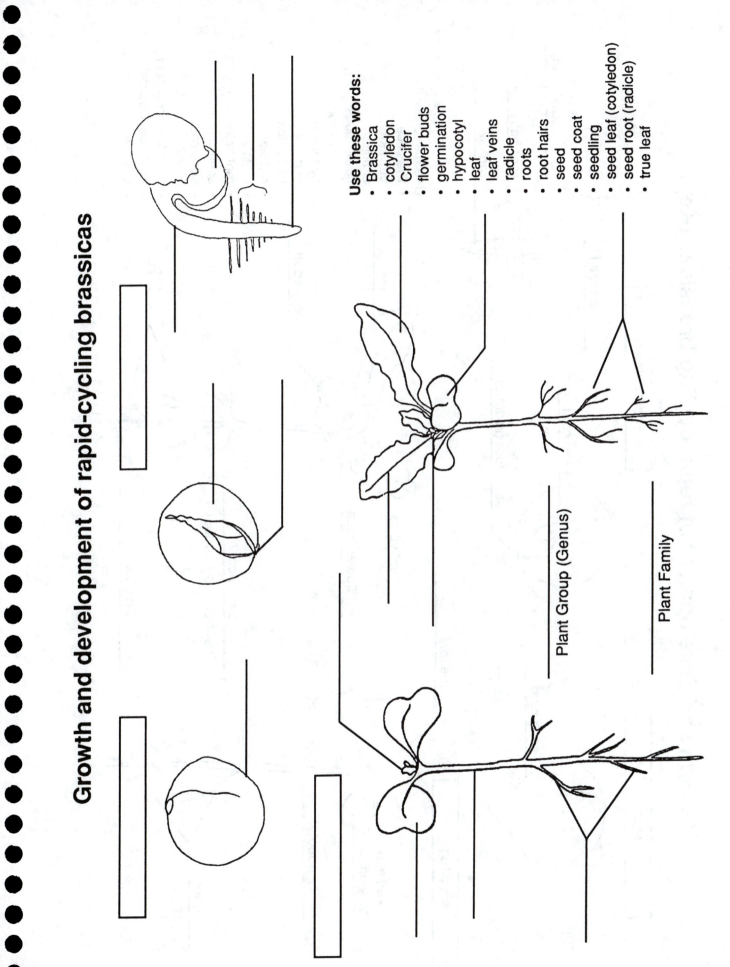

Use these words:
- Brassica
- cotyledon
- Crucifer
- flower buds
- germination
- hypocotyl
- leaf
- leaf veins
- radicle
- roots
- root hairs
- seed
- seed coat
- seedling
- seed leaf (cotyledon)
- seed root (radicle)
- true leaf

Plant Group (Genus)

Plant Family

# Growth and development of rapid-cycling brassicas (Key)

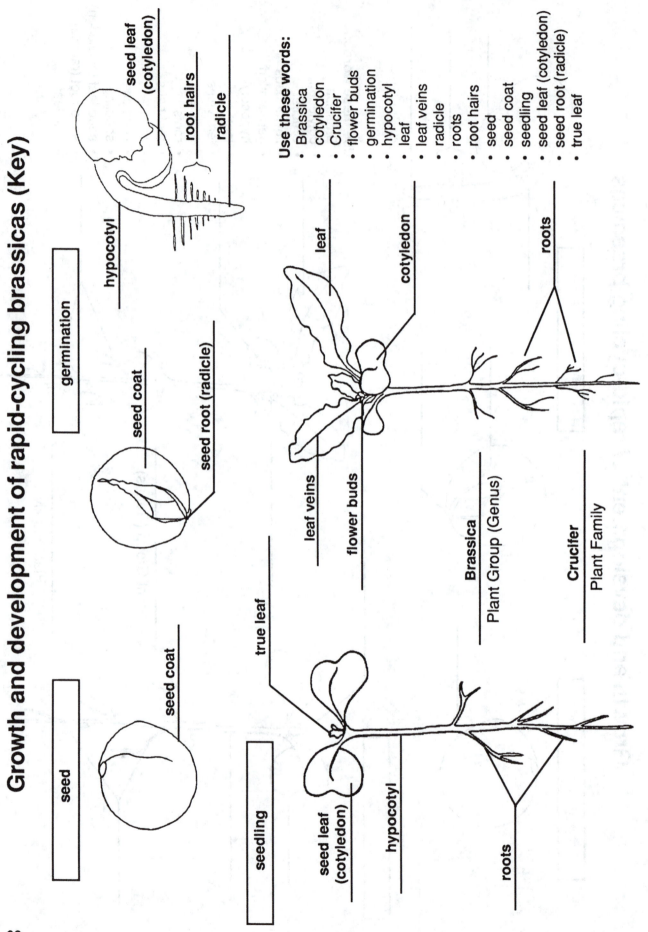

**Use these words:**
- Brassica
- cotyledon
- Crucifer
- flower buds
- germination
- hypocotyl
- leaf
- leaf veins
- radicle
- roots
- root hairs
- seed
- seed coat
- seedling
- seed leaf (cotyledon)
- seed root (radicle)
- true leaf

germination

seed leaf (cotyledon)

root hairs

radicle

hypocotyl

seed coat

seed root (radicle)

seed

seed coat

leaf

cotyledon

roots

leaf veins

flower buds

Brassica
Plant Group (Genus)

Crucifer
Plant Family

seedling

true leaf

seed leaf (cotyledon)

hypocotyl

roots

# Parts of a Fast Plant

Name

1. Fill in each flower part beside its correct definition.
2. Label the Fast Plant diagram.

**Use these words:**
- bud
- cotyledon
- flower
- internode
- leaf
- node
- root
- stem

_____ reproductive structure of a fruit-producing plant

_____ the part of a stem where one or more leaves are attached

_____ part of a plant that grows above the ground bearing the leaves and flowers

_____ the undeveloped flower protected by sepals

_____ the region of the stem between two nodes

_____ the part of a plant whose function is photosynthesis and transpiration

_____ the part of a plant that normally grows underground, anchors the plant, absorbs and conducts water and minerals

_____ seed leaf

Name _____

# Parts of a Fast Plant (Key)

1. Write each flower part beside its correct definition.
2. Label the Fast Plant diagram.

**Use these words:**
- bud
- cotyledon
- flower
- internode
- leaf
- node
- root
- stem

**flower** _____ reproductive structure of a fruit-producing plant

**node** _____ the part of a stem where one or more leaves are attached

**stem** _____ part of a plant that grows above the ground bearing the leaves and flowers

**bud** _____ the undeveloped flower protected by sepals

**internode** _____ the region of the stem between two nodes

**leaf** _____ the part of a plant whose function is photosynthesis and transpiration

**root** _____ the part of a plant that normally grows underground, anchors the plant, absorbs and conducts water and minerals

**cotyledon** _____ seed leaf

Diagram labels: **bud**, **flower**, **stem**, **node**, **internode**, **leaf**, **cotyledon**, **root**

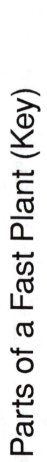

# Fast Plants Vocabulary

Fill in the word that goes with each definition.

_____ A.   The first root first growing from a seed.

_____ B.   Female part of a flower.

_____ C.   The pollen is transferred from stamen to the stigma.

_____ D.   The process of food-making by green plants.

_____ E.   Female egg cell that grows into a seed.

_____ F.   The outer layer of a seed which protects the inside.

_____ G.   Pollen grain sends tube down pistil and unites with ovule.

_____ H.   Produces a sweet liquid to attract insects.

_____ I.   Tiny growths on roots which bring in water and nutrients.

_____ J.   Male part of a flower.

_____ K.   Encloses a flower bud until blooming time.

_____ L.   The cotyledons (not true leaves) which pop out when seed sprouts.

_____ M.   The top part of a stamen that produces pollen.

_____ N.   Part of a flower that attracts insects with its color.

_____ O.   The seed coat bursts and a new plant begins growing.

**Use these words:**

- anther
- fertilization
- germination
- nectary
- ovule
- petal
- photosynthesis
- pistil
- pollination
- radicle
- root hairs
- seed coat
- seed leaves
- sepal
- stamen

# Fast Plants Vocabulary (Key)

Fill in the word that goes with each definition.

| | | |
|---|---|---|
| _____radicle_____ | A. | The first root first growing from a seed. |
| _____pistil_____ | B. | Female part of a flower. |
| _____pollination_____ | C. | The pollen is transferred from stamen to the stigma. |
| _____photosynthesis_____ | D. | The process of food-making by green plants. |
| _____ovule_____ | E. | Female egg cell that grows into a seed. |
| _____seed coat_____ | F. | The outer layer of a seed which protects the inside. |
| _____fertilization_____ | G. | Pollen grain sends tube down pistil and unites with ovule. |
| _____nectary_____ | H. | Produces a sweet liquid to attract insects. |
| _____root hairs_____ | I. | Tiny growths on roots which bring in water and nutrients. |
| _____stamen_____ | J. | Male part of a flower. |
| _____sepal_____ | K. | Encloses a flower bud until blooming time. |
| _____seed leaves_____ | L. | The cotyledons (not true leaves) which pop out when seed sprouts. |
| _____anther_____ | M. | The top part of a stamen that produces pollen. |
| _____petal_____ | N. | Part of a flower that attracts insects with its color. |
| _____germination_____ | O. | The seed coat bursts and a new plant begins growing. |

**Use these words:**
- anther
- fertilization
- germination
- nectary
- ovule
- petal
- photosynthesis
- pistil
- pollination
- radicle
- root hairs
- seed coat
- seed leaves
- sepal
- stamen

# Chapter 3: Flowering

The students will explore the parts of a Fast Plants flower. Further investigation compares other flowers to Fast Plants. This can be a stand-alone observational exercise. The steps of each chapter are consistent with the ⎡boxed⎤ steps of the Science Exploration Flowchart. You can develop a complete scientific investigation using the questions your students ask as a result of this observational exercise. Some examples for complete scientific investigations are provided and identified by following specific icons; ●, ▲, ■ and ◆. If you don't have time to complete a full investigation, you might plan to continue with it later in the year.

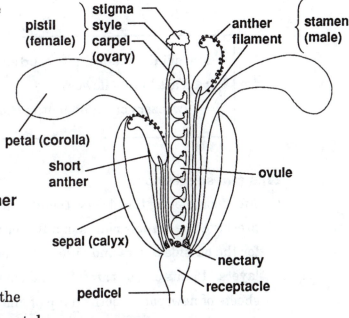

## Background Information for the Teacher

Most flowers have the same basic parts. Often they are arranged in different ways. The four main parts of a flower are: *petals, sepals, stamens* and *pistil*. The sepals are the green leaf-like structures at the base of the petals. The petals are the colored leaf-like structures within the sepals. The stamen has two parts, the *anther* and the *filament*. The anther contains the pollen grains. Pollen grains contain structures that will become the male gametes. The pistil usually has three parts, the *stigma* (which receives the pollen), the *style*, or neck below the stigma and the *carpel* (or *ovary*). Fast Plants have two fused carpels, separated by a thin membrane. Carpels house *ovules* (eggs) which contain the female gametes. When an egg is fertilized by a male gamete from a germinating pollen grain, an embryo grows to become a seed.

*Gametes* are the sex cells which each contain one set of chromosomes. One set of chromosomes equals n (n = haploid). Cells of most plants and other organisms contain two sets of chromosomes (2n = diploid). For more information on seed formation, see Double Fertilization and Seed Pod Development (pages 113-124).

## Teaching Objectives

**Beginning Objectives:**

- The flower is the reproductive center of most plants.
- Flowering plants have unique structures for insuring their survival.
- Although all flowers have common parts, variations occur in these parts.
- The colorful petals of flowers attract insects.

## Preparation and Planning for Observational Exercise

**Time required:** 1 to 2 class hours.

---

**Materials needed per student/team:**

- Fast Plants flowers
- tweezers or round toothpicks
- Brassica flower worksheet
- hand lenses

---

**Tips and suggestions:**

- After completing the observational exercise on page 75, students may wish to preserve one of their plants in a flower press. Use two 4" x 6" pieces of cardboard for the outside covers and either blotting paper or newspaper for the inside layers. Plants can be carefully laid out with one piece of blotting paper, or 5 sheets of newspaper, both on top of and below the plant in the press (Figure 1). Secure all layers with a rubber band at the top and bottom of the press (Figure 2). Eventually you can remove the flat, dry specimen and mount it with clear tape onto a 4" x 6" card.

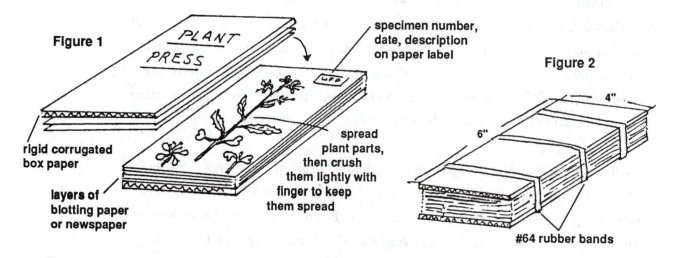

**Figure 1**

PLANT PRESS

rigid corrugated box paper

layers of blotting paper or newspaper

specimen number, date, description on paper label

spread plant parts, then crush them lightly with finger to keep them spread

**Figure 2**

4"

6"

#64 rubber bands

# Flowering Observational Exercise for younger students

**1.** Using a hand lens, carefully examine the brassica (Fast Plants) flower. Compare your flower to the worksheet of the brassica flower.

**2.** Identify the primary parts (sepals, stamens, petals, pistil) of your flower.

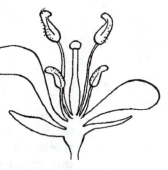

**3.** *Sepals* are usually green, looking like modified leaves. Sepals protect the flower before it opens.

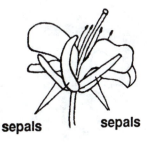

sepals          sepals

**4.** The *petals* attract insects with their bright colors.

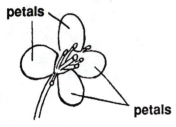

petals

petals

**5.** Inside the flower are the tall male flower parts, *stamens* — with knobs called *anthers* on top. Pollen is carried on the anthers. Count the number of stamens.

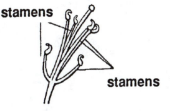

stamens

stamens

**6.** The *pistil* is the female part of the flower, and it collects pollen on its sticky top, the *stigma*. The *carpels* inside the pistil contain the eggs or ovules.

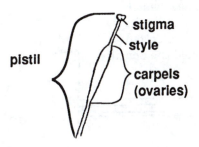

pistil

stigma

style

carpels (ovaries)

**7.** Make your own drawing of what you see. Label all the parts.

# Flowering Flower Model
## for younger students

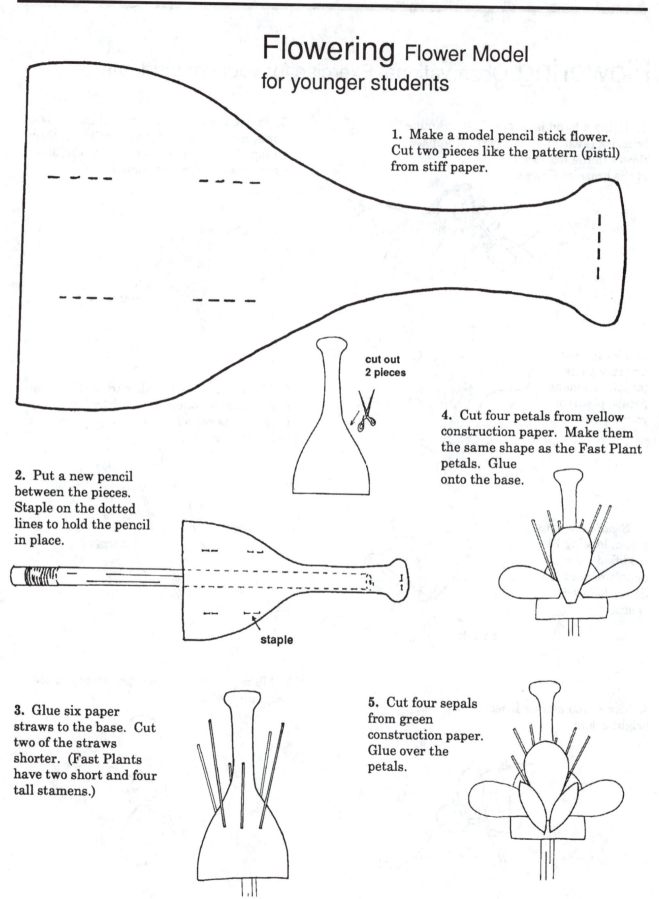

1. Make a model pencil stick flower. Cut two pieces like the pattern (pistil) from stiff paper.

cut out
2 pieces

2. Put a new pencil between the pieces. Staple on the dotted lines to hold the pencil in place.

staple

4. Cut four petals from yellow construction paper. Make them the same shape as the Fast Plant petals. Glue onto the base.

3. Glue six paper straws to the base. Cut two of the straws shorter. (Fast Plants have two short and four tall stamens.)

5. Cut four sepals from green construction paper. Glue over the petals.

# Flower Dissection Strip
## Observational Exercise for older students

**1.** Make a flower dissection strip as a permanent record of the flower. Tear off a 15 cm strip of clear tape and place it on your work surface sticky side up. Secure it at each end with a small strip of tape.

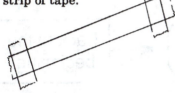

**2.** Pinch off a fresh flower from one of your plants. Optional: the flower can be secured in a slit cut across the top of a #3 black rubber stopper. Insert the flower stem by squeezing the stopper at both ends of the slit to create the opening.

**3.** Using a hand lens or dissection microscope, carefully examine the brassica (Fast Plants) flower. Compare your flower to the worksheet of the brassica flower.

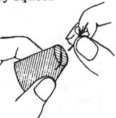

**4.** Identify the primary parts *(sepals, stamens, petals, and pistil)* of your flower.

**5.** A toothpick or tweezers will help to separate the flower parts.

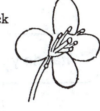

**6.** *Sepals* are usually green, looking like modified leaves. Sepals protect the flower in the bud stage.

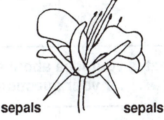

**sepals**          **sepals**

**7.** Notice the arrangement of the *petals*. The petals attract insects with their bright colors.

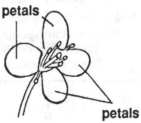

**petals**

**petals**

**8.** Inside the flower are the male flower parts, *stamens* — thread-like stalks *(filaments)* with pollen-carrying knobs called *anthers* on top. Count the number of stamens and notice how they are arranged around the pistil.

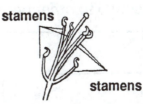

**stamens**

**stamens**

**9.** The *pistil* is the female part of the flower, and it collects pollen on its sticky top, the *stigma*. The *carpel* inside the base of the pistil contains the eggs *(ovules)*.

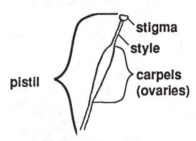

**stigma**

**style**

**pistil**          **carpels (ovaries)**

**10.** Working with a tweezers, remove the flower parts and lay them in order on the sticky tape. Remove the flower parts in order: the four sepals, the four petals, the six stamens (see illustration below).

**11.** Finally, you are left with just the pistil attached to the stem at the receptacle. With a hand lens, observe the *nectaries* around the bottom of the ovary. Touch a nectary with a toothpick and then touch the toothpick to your tongue. Can you taste the sugar? Then, stick the pistil at the end of your flower strip.

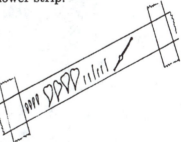

**12.** Take the complete flower strip off of your work surface and place it, sticky side down, onto a clean piece of paper. Now you have a "record" of your flower. Label the parts if you wish.

# Student Science Exploration Flowchart

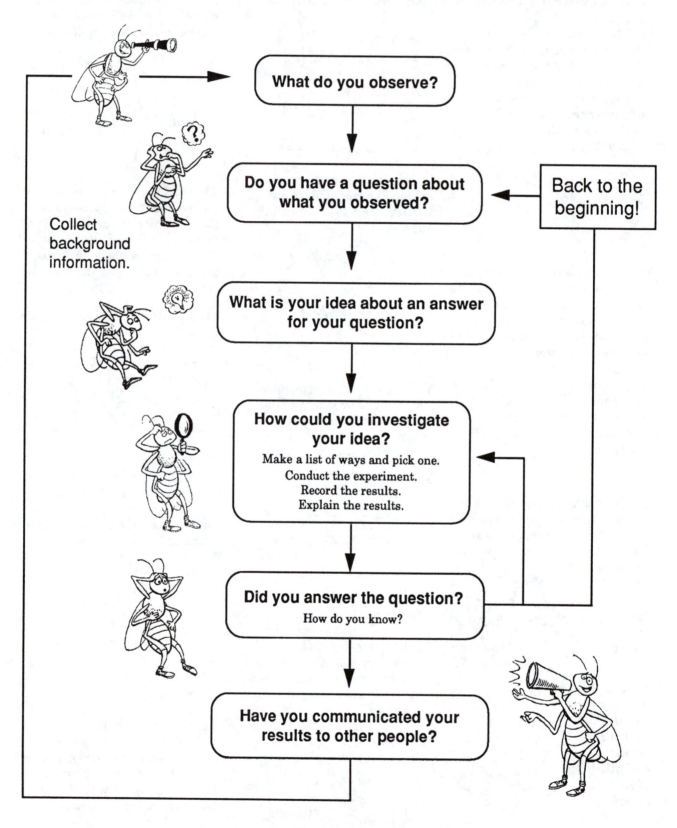

Collect background information.

**What do you observe?**

**Do you have a question about what you observed?**

Back to the beginning!

**What is your idea about an answer for your question?**

**How could you investigate your idea?**
Make a list of ways and pick one.
Conduct the experiment.
Record the results.
Explain the results.

**Did you answer the question?**
How do you know?

**Have you communicated your results to other people?**

## What Is A Flower?

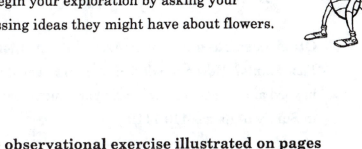

| Making observations |
| --- |

**Some preliminary questions:** Begin your exploration by asking your
students some questions and discussing ideas they might have about flowers.

- Why do flowers exist?
- What do they do?
- Why are flowers colorful?

**As you conduct the appropriate observational exercise illustrated on pages
75 and 77,** your students will observe the various parts of the flower, four sepals,
four petals, six stamens with yellow anthers on top, a central pistil with a stigma,
style and carpels (ovaries) containing the ovules or eggs. Younger students build a
model flower. Older students look for the nectaries at the base between the petals
and the stamens and dissect their flower.

**Accompanying activities:**

- Flower models. For homework or in class, students make a model of a brassica plant. See "Brassica Plant Model" (page 230). After models have been
  made, the students can evaluate their classmates' models and review flower
  parts using the "Brassica Flower Model Evaluation" worksheet (page 84).
- Use riddles and matching games to encourage mastery of flower parts and
  concepts, e.g., have groups of students prepare flower parts flash cards and
  quiz another group of students. Examples include the "Brassica Word
  Match" and "Brassica Bingo," found in the Section 7 (pages 221-242).
- Play the "Build a Brassica" game (page 236). Team competition requires only
  the blackboard.
- Make plant presses (page 74).
- Try the Nectar Quest (page 83).

| Asking questions |
| --- |

**What questions have your students raised from observing?** The
students should be curious about some of the things they have observed. A
class discussion should generate questions. Have your students make a list
of questions. Prompt them with the words **"What if."**

**Example questions derived from the observation:**

● Do all flowers have the same number of flower parts as Fast Plants? (Investigation #1)

▲ Do stamens outnumber petals? (Investigation #2)

■ Do all flowers have stamens and pistils? (Investigation #3)

**Other possible questions:** Are petals on other flowers arranged the same as on Fast Plants? How often does a plant produce flowers? Why do some anthers face inward and some face outward? For insight, see "Bees and Brassicas: A Partnership in Survival" (pages 110-111).

| Forming a hypothesis |

**What are your students' ideas about answers for their questions?** Following the discussion of observations, students can turn their questions into statements and write them down as hypotheses.

**Example hypotheses derived from questions:**

● All flowers have 6 stamens and 4 petals. (Investigation #1)

▲ Flowers have more stamens than petals. (Investigation #2)

■ Flowers contain both stamens and a pistil. (Investigation #3)

**Tips and suggestions:** Have the students check the Science Exploration Flow-chart to see what the next steps need to be in their science problem solving.

| Testing the hypothesis |

**How could your students investigate their ideas?** Design an experiment. Devise ways to test the hypothesis, choose the best one and carry it out. Refer to worksheet "Setting Up An Experiment" (pages 41-43) for help in designing the experiment/s.

**Control Experiments:** A *control* serves as a standard of comparison for verifying the results of an investigation. By controlling the variable factors of the experiment, the effects of changing one variable at a time are easily observed.

**Examples of ways to test hypotheses:**

● Provide a variety of flowers to study and dissect. Have students bring in flowers. Florists are a source of discarded flowers. Contact a flower shop several weeks before students will be observing Fast Plants flower parts and ask the florist to save flowers that would otherwise be thrown out. Commonly available flowers with easily observable flower parts are: lily, gladiolus, snapdragon, alstroemeria and geranium. Another source of flowers would be a field trip. Some suggested spring flowers would be daffodils, crocus, tulips, apple blossoms and violets. Observe, but do not pick, wildflowers. African violets and geraniums provide good flowers for dissection. Identify, count and compare parts of other flowers with those of Fast Plants. (Investigation #1)

**Management strategy:** It will take 15-16 days from the time of planting to complete these investigations. Contact a flower shop when the Fast Plants are planted and ask the florist to save flowers for you for the next two weeks. When the Fast Plants begin flowering, pick up the other flowers for this investigation. You will need hand lenses, toothpicks or tweezers. Allow 50 minutes for examining various flowers and comparing with Fast Plants.

▲ Use the same tests as described above in ●. (Investigation #2)

■ In the spring, observe aspen, willow, birch, maple trees or evergreens, such as spruce or pine. In fall and summer, observe grasses. (Investigation #3)

**Management strategy:** Take the time for an outdoor field trip to compare the experimental Fast Plants flowers with native plants in your area.

**Collect data:** See "Keeping Track of Things" (pages 23-26).

**Analyze the data:** Have the students explain the results. For example:

● Members of different families have different numbers of each flower part: sepals, petals, stamens and pistils. The number is usually constant within a family. (Investigation #1)

▲ Carnations from the florist have been bred to have many petals and may lack anthers. (Investigation #2)

■ Some plants have male and female parts in separate flowers on the same plant, e.g., cucumbers and melons. Many trees and grasses are wind pollinated and lack petals and sepals in their flowers. Other species such as spinach and some trees have male and female plants. (Investigation #3)

## Evaluating the hypothesis

**Was the hypothesis verified?** How do your students know that they know? For example: Was the test fair? Did they answer the question? Are they sure?

## Communicating the results

**Have your students communicated their results to others?** *No science investigation is complete until it is communicated in writing.* In addition, it can be communicated orally. Students can write their conclusions very simply, but the report should be understandable to anyone reading it, peers and teacher.

## References

### Books

Dowden, A. O. 1984. *From Fruit to Flower.* New York: Thomas Y. Crowell Co. A look at the amazing variety of fruits made by flowering plants, with interesting botany text and color botanical illustrations.

Dowden, A. O. 1963. *Look at a Flower.* New York: Thomas Y. Crowell Co. Explains the purposes of the parts that make up a flower.

Heller, R. 1986. *The Reason for a Flower.* New York: Grosset and Dunlap. A clear and colorfully illustrated view of the angiosperm life cycle, from flower to pollination to seed to plant. Some basic facts about plants and their importance are also included.

Hunken, J. and The New England Wild Flower Society. 1989. *Botany for All Ages.* Chester, CT: Globe Pequot Press. Activity-oriented botany for inquisitive children and adults, approached from the principles of observation and experimentation.

Lerner, C. 1989. *Plant Families.* New York: Morrow Junior Books. Concise, informative text explains how to recognize characteristics shared by the 12 largest plant families, accompanied by detailed color illustrations.

Selsam, M. E. and J. Hunt. 1977. *A First Look at Flowers.* New York: Walker and Co. Comprehensive text which addresses young readers and asks questions to engage them.

Selsam, M. E. 1984. *Tree Flowers.* New York: William Morrow and Co., Inc. A sampling of twelve familiar tree flowers with concise, readable text. Water color illustrations by Carol Lerner.

Stockley, C. 1986. *Dictionary of Biology (Usborne Illustrated).* London: Usborne Publishing, Ltd. A densely illustrated, clear guide to key terms and subject areas of plants and animals.

Suzuki, D. and B. Hehner. 1985. *Looking at Plants*. Toronto, Canada: Stoddart Publishing Co., Ltd. A tour through the plant world in clear and interesting language for students, plus short and long term projects.

Thielgaard Watts, M. 1955. *Flower Finder*. Berkeley, CA: Nature Study Guild.

**Films and videos**

*Many Worlds of Nature: Flowers*. 1977. Screenscope Films. Film - 12 minutes. Shows devices used by flowers to achieve cross-pollination, role of insects in pollination and basic flower parts. Appropriate for intermediate students.

*Flowering Plants From Seed to Seed*. 1979. International Film Bureau. Film - 11 minutes. Uses a tomato plant to illustrate the life cycle, showing the development of roots, stems, leaves, stamens, stigmas and ovaries. Seed dispersal is also discussed. Appropriate for both primary and intermediate students.

# The Nectar Quest

At the base of the two short anthers in the Fast Plants flowers are two or four dark green, glistening nectaries producing the nectar (glucose) that helps to attract the bee to the flower.

1. Take an 8 cm strip of 2 cm clear tape and stick its end to the back of a 4 x 6 index card. Place the card so that the sticky side of the tape is facing up (see Figure 1).

2. Pick a Fast Plants flower and press it onto the tape near the edge of the card.

3. Place a square of yellow glucose Tes-Tape®* on the sticky tape (Figure 1) and lightly moisten it.

4. With a toothpick, spread the flower parts, pressing them to the sticky tape, until you see the green nectaries and glistening nectar at the base of the pistil. Use a hand lens or microscope to view the flower.

5. Probe the nectaries with the toothpick, then touch the tip of the toothpick to the moist Tes-Tape®.

6. Is there a color change?

7. Voila! Green is proof of glucose!

8. To preserve the bee's treasure, fold and press the flower and tape onto the card.

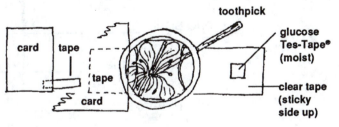

9. Find another flower in your environment and pursue the Nectar Quest again. What do you think pollinates this flower?

\* Glucose testing tape, sticks or strips are used by diabetics to check the glucose content of their urine and are available at pharmacies. If Tes-Tape® is not available, other similar products (such as Diastix®) can be substituted.

# Brassica Model Evaluation

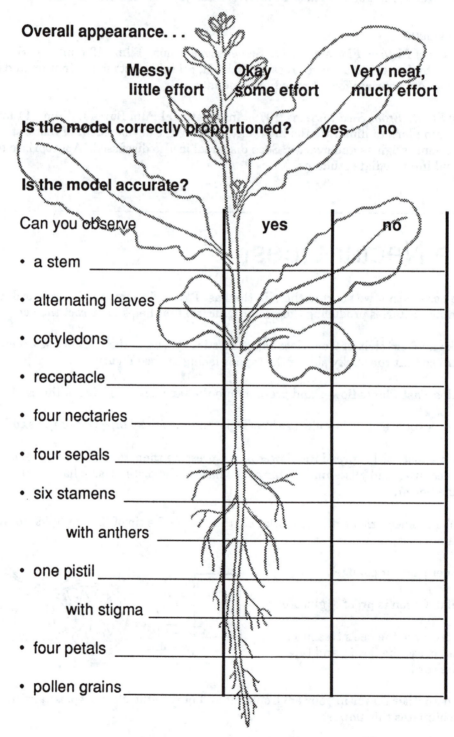

**Overall appearance. . .**

| **Messy**<br>little effort | **Okay**<br>some effort | **Very neat,**<br>much effort |
|---|---|---|

**Is the model correctly proportioned?**   yes   no

**Is the model accurate?**

| Can you observe | yes | no |
|---|---|---|
| • a stem | | |
| • alternating leaves | | |
| • cotyledons | | |
| • receptacle | | |
| • four nectaries | | |
| • four sepals | | |
| • six stamens | | |
| with anthers | | |
| • one pistil | | |
| with stigma | | |
| • four petals | | |
| • pollen grains | | |

signature of evaluator

_____

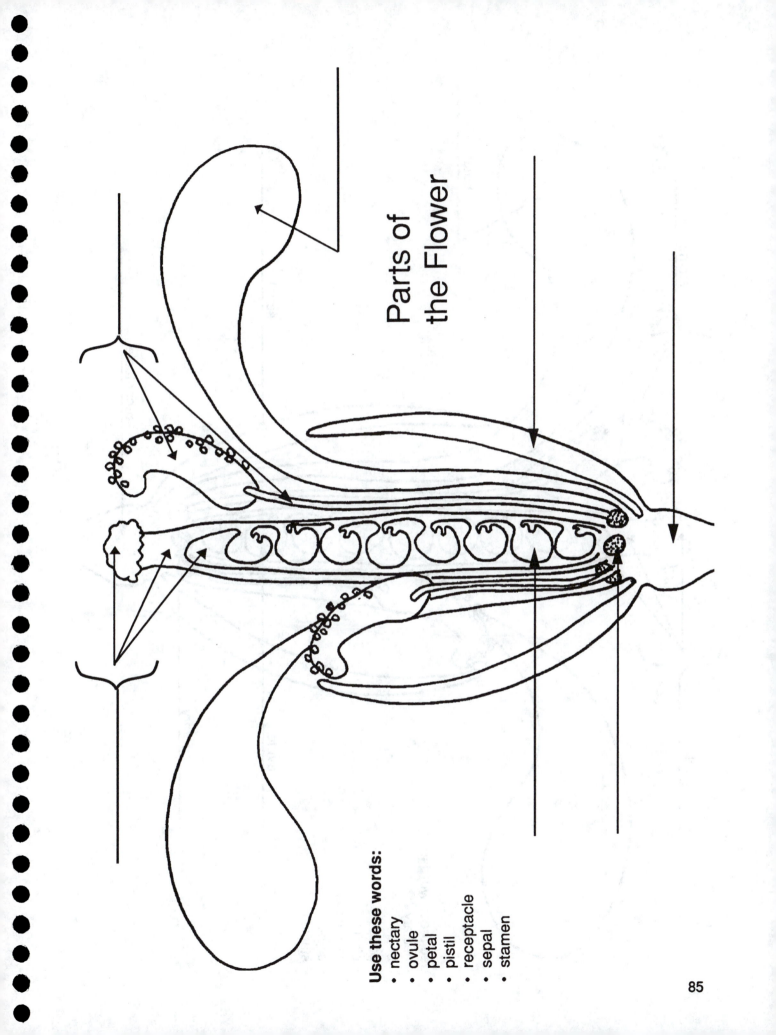

Parts of
the Flower

**Use these words:**
- nectary
- ovule
- petal
- pistil
- receptacle
- sepal
- stamen

85

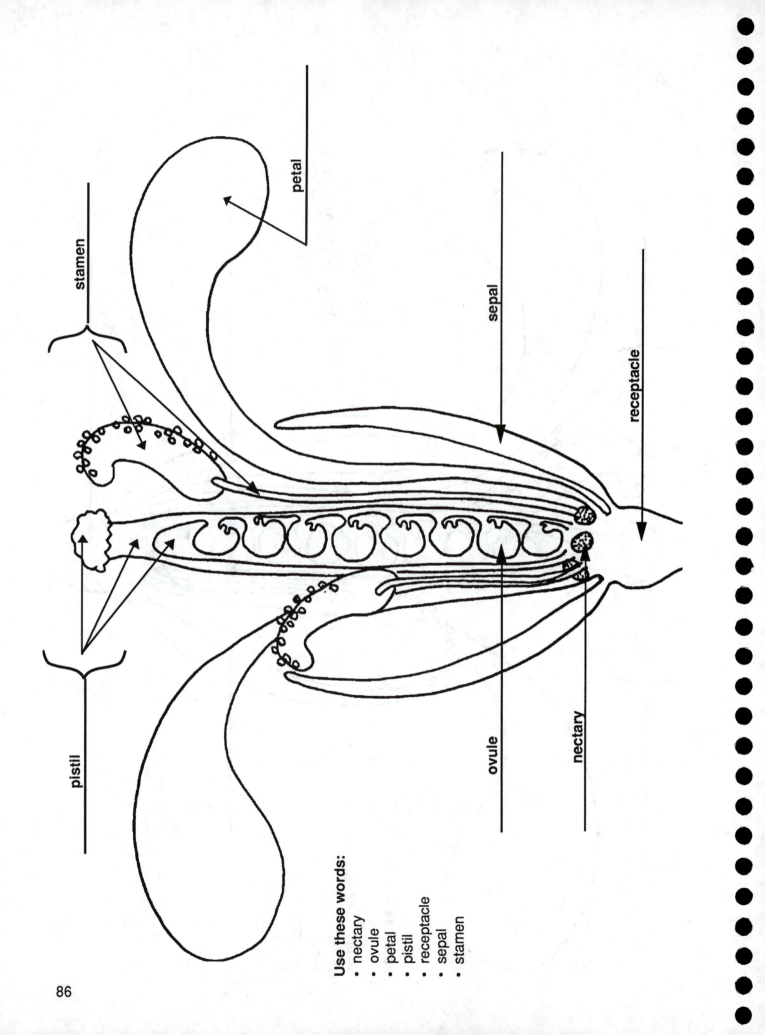

stamen

petal

pistil

sepal

receptacle

ovule

nectary

**Use these words:**
- nectary
- ovule
- petal
- pistil
- receptacle
- sepal
- stamen

86

# The Brassica Flower

Name _____

♀          ♂

**Use these words:**
- anther
- carpel
- filament
- nectary
- ovule
- petal
- pistil
- receptacle
- sepal
- stamen
- stigma
- style

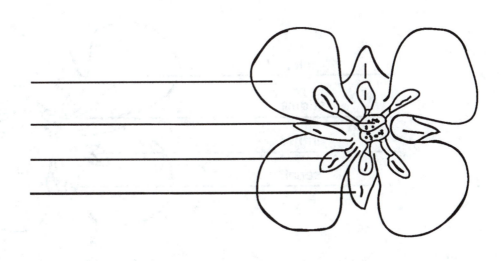

# The Brassica Flower (Key)

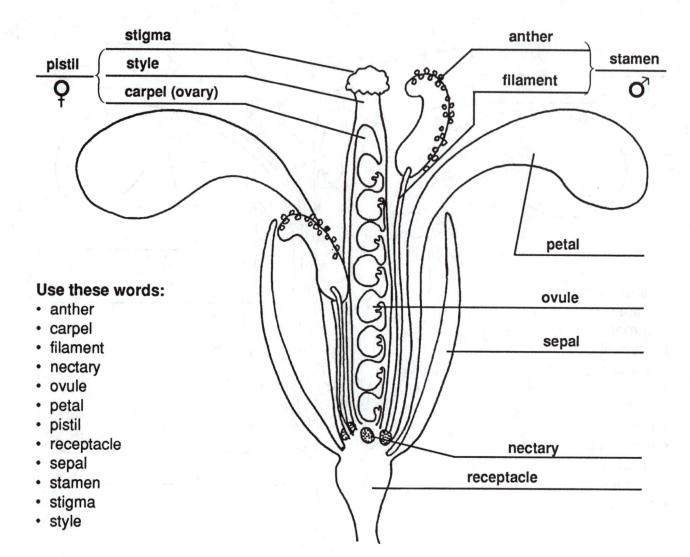

**pistil** ♀

**stigma**

**style**

**carpel (ovary)**

**anther**

**filament**

**stamen** ♂

petal

ovule

sepal

nectary

receptacle

**Use these words:**
- anther
- carpel
- filament
- nectary
- ovule
- petal
- pistil
- receptacle
- sepal
- stamen
- stigma
- style

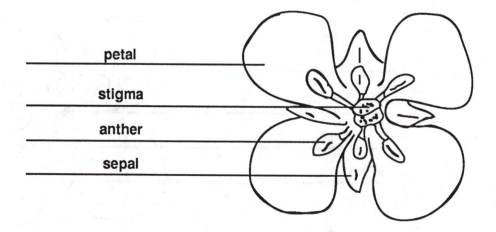

petal

stigma

anther

sepal

# Comparing Flower Parts

**Geranium flowers** have their parts in sets of five.

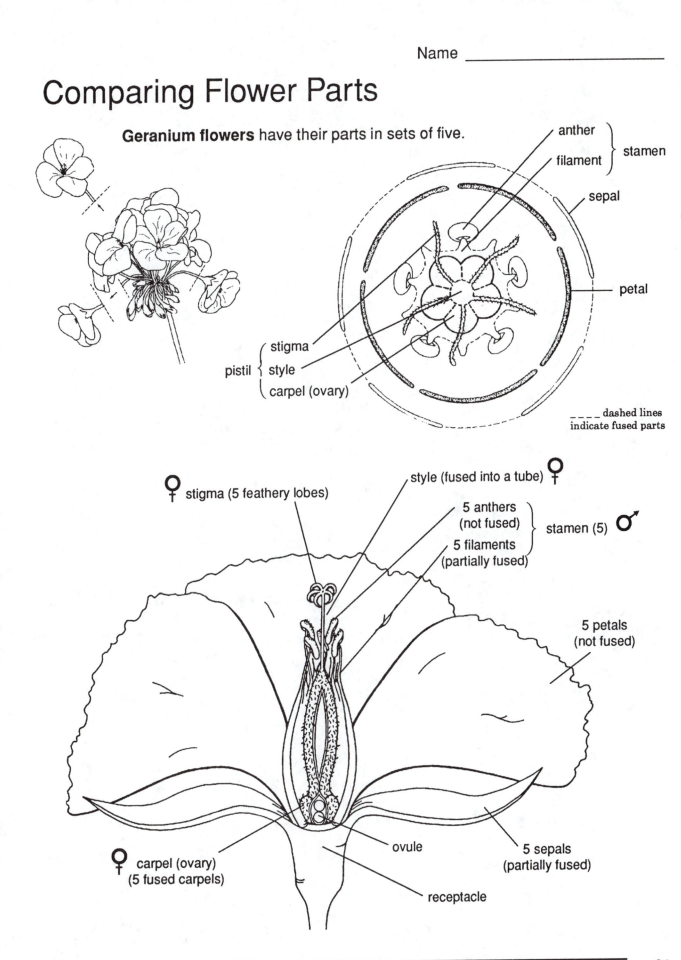

anther
filament
} stamen

sepal

petal

stigma
pistil { style
carpel (ovary)

_ _ _ _ dashed lines
indicate fused parts

♀ stigma (5 feathery lobes)

style (fused into a tube) ♀

5 anthers
(not fused)
5 filaments
(partially fused)
} stamen (5) ♂

5 petals
(not fused)

ovule

5 sepals
(partially fused)

♀ carpel (ovary)
(5 fused carpels)

receptacle

# Chapter 4: Pollination

**The students will explore a honeybee's body structure and its ability to transfer pollen.** Further investigations look at self-pollination, cross-pollination and various methods of artificial pollination. This can be a stand-alone observational exercise. The steps of each chapter are consistent with the boxed steps of the Science Exploration Flowchart. You can develop a complete scientific investigation using the questions your students ask as a result of this observational exercise. Some examples for complete scientific investigations are provided and identified by following specific icons; ●, ▲, ■ and ◆. If you don't have time to complete a full investigation, you might plan to continue with it later in the year.

## Background Information for the Teacher

The flower is the means by which the plant sexually reproduces via the process of *pollination*. Brassica *pollen* is too heavy and sticky to be carried by the wind. Bees are attracted to the brightly-colored petals and sweet scent of brassicas and, in the process of gathering nectar and pollen, pollinate the flower. See "Bees and Brassicas: A Partnership in Survival" (pages 110-111). Pollen from the anthers is picked up by the bee's hairy body parts.

As the bee moves to various flowers, some pollen grains are deposited on the sticky surface of each stigma. The pollen (which contains the male reproductive cell) adheres to the sticky stigmas of the flowers and each pollen grain sends a tube through the

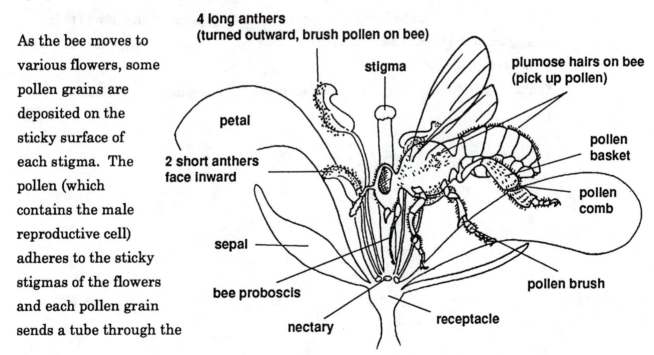

**4 long anthers**
**(turned outward, brush pollen on bee)**

stigma

**plumose hairs on bee**
**(pick up pollen)**

petal

pollen
basket

**2 short anthers**
**face inward**

pollen
comb

sepal

bee proboscis

pollen brush

nectary

receptacle

style to an ovule (which contains the female reproductive cell) to complete fertilization. Within three to five days after the fusion of these reproductive cells, petals drop and the pistil begins to elongate and form a pod as the seeds develop inside.

Pollen grains will fertilize ovules inside the carpels (ovaries) only if the pollen is *compatible* with this plant. In rapid-cycling brassicas, the pollen transferred from flower to flower on the same plant is not able to fertilize ovules and will abort, meaning that the plants are *self-incompatible*. Therefore the pollen must be carried from one plant to flowers on another plant (*cross-pollination*) for successful pollination and subsequent fertilization. Bees take care of this problem naturally as they move from plant to plant in search of nectar and pollen.

## Teaching Concepts

**Beginning concepts:**
- Pollination is the transfer of pollen from the anther to the stigma.
- Insects, especially bees, aid in pollination.

**Advanced concepts:**
- Fast Plants need to be cross-pollinated to produce seeds.
- Cross-pollination is the transfer of pollen from the anther of one plant to the stigma of the flower of another plant.
- Self-pollination is the transfer of pollen from the anther of one flower to the stigma of the same flower or another flower of the same plant. Fast Plants do not self-pollinate.
- Pollen germinates on the stigma and grows through the style to reach the egg.

# Pollination Observational Exercise

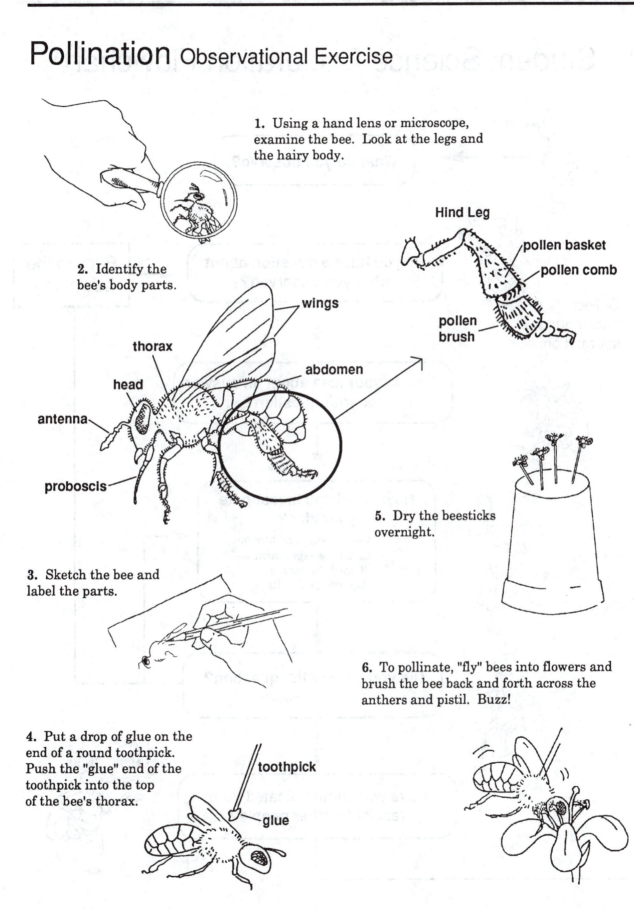

1. Using a hand lens or microscope, examine the bee. Look at the legs and the hairy body.

**Hind Leg**

pollen basket

pollen comb

pollen brush

2. Identify the bee's body parts.

wings

thorax

abdomen

head

antenna

proboscis

5. Dry the beesticks overnight.

3. Sketch the bee and label the parts.

6. To pollinate, "fly" bees into flowers and brush the bee back and forth across the anthers and pistil. Buzz!

4. Put a drop of glue on the end of a round toothpick. Push the "glue" end of the toothpick into the top of the bee's thorax.

toothpick

glue

# Student Science Exploration Flowchart

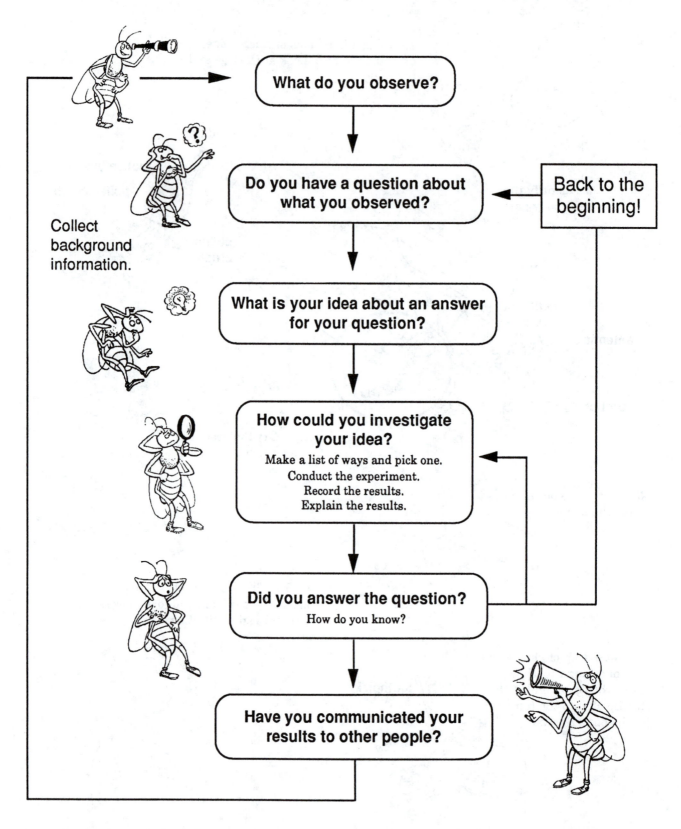

What do you observe?

Do you have a question about what you observed?

Back to the beginning!

Collect background information.

What is your idea about an answer for your question?

How could you investigate your idea?

Make a list of ways and pick one.
Conduct the experiment.
Record the results.
Explain the results.

Did you answer the question?
How do you know?

Have you communicated your results to other people?

## Preparation and Planning for Observational Exercise

**Time required:** 45 minutes.

**Tips and suggestions:**

- An alternative method for making beesticks is to use just the thorax of dissected (or broken) bees to pollinate (see Figures 1, 2 and 3 below).

<br>

**Materials needed per student/team:**
- hand lenses
- materials for making beesticks — dried bees, round toothpicks, Elmer's glue, bee worksheet, pollen/bee photo (1,000X magnification, page 107).

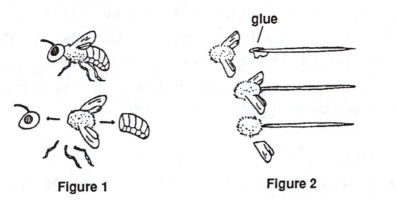

**Figure 1**     **Figure 2**     **Figure 3**

- When making beesticks with whole bees as shown in the illustrated instructions, they may be very dry and brittle. The night before making beesticks, place bees in an airtight container overnight with a little moist paper toweling. [Separate the bees from the paper with a piece of transparency film (see illustration)]. This will make the bees less brittle and easier for students to work with.

You can also put a moist piece of paper toweling in a film can with a hole in the lid. Place the can into the container of bees.

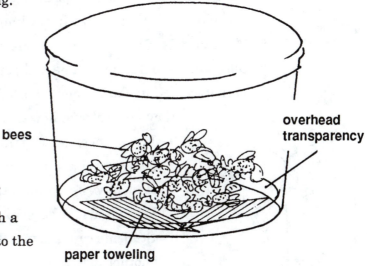

bees

overhead transparency

paper toweling

## Exploring Pollination

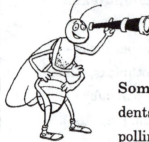

| Making observations |
| --- |

**Some preliminary questions:** Begin your exploration by asking your students some questions and discussing ideas they might have about bees and pollination.

**As you conduct the observational exercise illustrated on page 93**, your students will observe the bee's three body parts, head, thorax and abdomen, and three pairs of legs. Students should find the special adaptations on the legs for collecting pollen. Bees have two pairs of wings, attached to each other by little hooks. Notice the hair all over the body, including the eyes. The proboscis (tube-like mouth parts) is used to sip nectar. As your students pollinate, they should notice how much pollen collects on the hairy body.

Accompanying activities:
- Let the students read the story, "Speedy Bee and the Brassica Morning" (pages 225-227). This would be a good time to look at the diagram of the bee on the brassica flower (page 91) to see the relationship of the bee's body to the flower parts. Look at the photograph of pollen caught on the plumose hairs of the bee at 1,000X magnification (page 107).
- Have a beekeeper come to speak to the class about what he/she does and show the equipment that is used in working with bees. Taste honey!
- Make models of bees. See the "Honeybee Model" (page 231).
- Observe bees outdoors, if time and place permit, without disturbing their activities. (Hint: dandelions.) Look for pollen on body hairs and on legs as they visit colorful flowers in fields and gardens.
- Make a beestick folder. As a bridge of learning from school to home, make a small, construction paper folder. Have each student write up what the class has been doing with bees and Fast Plants. A beestick can be taped inside the folder.
- Students can design a flower as a landing strip for a bee or another insect.

### Asking questions

**What questions have your students raised from observing?** The students should be curious about some of the things they have observed. A class discussion should generate questions. Have your students make a list of questions. Prompt them with the words **"What if."**

**Example questions derived from observations:**
- ● What would happen if you didn't pollinate Fast Plants? (Investigation #1)
- ▲ What happens if you pollinate only one plant? (Investigation #2)
- ■ Are flowers pollinated by other means? (Investigation #3)

**Other possible questions:** Do bees pollinate all flowers? (Hint: Watch *Pollination*, a film listed in the references at the end of this chapter.)

### Forming a hypothesis

What are your students' ideas about answers for their questions? Following the discussion of observations, students can turn their questions into statements and write them down as hypotheses.

**Example hypotheses derived from questions:**
- ● All Fast Plants must be pollinated to produce seed. (Investigation #1)
- ▲ All Fast Plants must be cross-pollinated to produce seed. (Investigation #2)
- ■ Beesticks are the best pollination tools for Fast Plants. (Investigation #3)

**Tips and suggestions:** Have the students check the Science Exploration Flowchart to see what the next steps need to be in their science investigation.

### Testing the hypothesis

**How could your students investigate their ideas?** Design and experiment. Devise a way to test the hypothesis, choose the best one and carry it out. Refer to worksheet "Setting Up An Experiment" (pages 41-43) for help in designing the experiment/s.

**Control Experiments:** A *control* serves as a standard of comparison for verifying the results of an investigation. By controlling the variable factors of the experiment, the effects of changing one variable at a time are easily observed. Cross-pollinating Fast Plants is the standard or "control" situation.

**Example of ways to test hypotheses:**

● Students can set up an experiment where some plants are not pollinated at all and others are cross-pollinated (control). Hint: Before the flowers open, make a divider (see illustrations below) with 5" x 8" index cards to keep plants from brushing against each other. (Investigation #1)

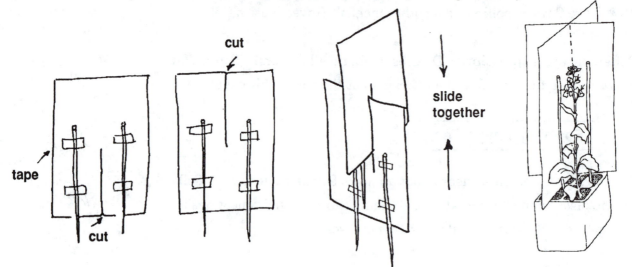

▲ Self-pollinate some plants and cross-pollinate others (control). Hint: In self-pollinations, plants should all be separated from each other with a divider as in #1. Each plant should be pollinated only with its own beestick to prevent pollen contamination from another plant. (Investigation #2)

■ Compare cross-pollination results using devices the students suggest such as Q-tips, pipe cleaners, or camel hair brushes, to those found when using beesticks (control). Hint: The proof will be in the number of pods and amount of seed produced using each technique. (Investigation #3)

**Tips and suggestions:**

· Pollinate with beesticks for about 4 days, generally Days 14-18.

· Gently rotate the beestick in the flowers to pick up and distribute pollen.

· Flowers being pollinated should be fresh (brightly colored with no signs of withering). A new flower opens approximately every eight hours.

- During cross-pollination activities, after students have collected pollen from their own plants, let them move quietly around the room, pollinating other students' plants. They can "buzz" quietly while they're doing this. This simulates the random cross-pollination of bees: the bees are moving, the plants remain on the desks.

- If pollination has been successful and fertilization has taken place, within two days the pistils will begin to elongate and the petals of the flowers will fall off as the process of seed development (embryogenesis) begins.

**Collect data:** See "Keeping Track of Things" (pages 23-26).

**Analyze the data:** Have students explain the results. For example:

- ● Seed has been produced on plants that were not pollinated. Hint: Possible contamination, flies in the room moving the pollen. (Investigation #1)

- ▲ Self-pollinated plants produced no seed. Results support the hypothesis that Fast Plants must be cross-pollinated. (Investigation #2)

- ■ What did you find out? (Investigation #3)

### Evaluating the hypothesis

**Was the hypothesis verified?** How do your students know that they know? For example: Was the test fair? Did they answer the question? Are they sure?

### Communicating the results

**Have your students communicated their results to others?** *No science investigation is complete until it is communicated in writing.* In addition, it can be communicated orally. Students can write their conclusions very simply, but the report should be understandable to anyone reading it, peers and teacher.

# References

## Books

Burne, D. 1989. *Eyewitness Books, Plant.* New York: Alfred A. Knopf. A photoessay introducing the world of plants including life cycles, plant defenses, plant uses and plant collectors.

Dowden, A. O. 1990. *The Clover and the Bee.* New York: Thomas Y. Crowell Co. The extraordinary process of pollination and the interdependence of plants with animals and insects is detailed with exquisite illustrations and clear text.

Echols, J. C. 1987. *Buzzing a Hive.* Berkeley, CA: Lawrence Hall of Science, University of California-Berkeley. A teacher's guide to the bee. Each lesson contains activities and black line masters.

Hunken, J. and The New England Wild Flower Society. 1989. *Botany for All Ages.* Chester, CT: Globe Pequot Press. Activity-oriented botany for inquisitive children and adults, approached from the principles of observation and experimentation.

Lauber, P. 1981. *From Flower to Flower, Animals and Pollination.* New York: Crown Publishers, Inc. A close-up view of the way flowers advertise, of their insect and animal helpers. Excellent photography by Jerome Wexler.

Parker, S. 1985. *Do You Know How Plants Grow?* New York: Warwick Press. Chapter 8 explains not only the relationship between bees and flowers, but explores other means of pollination such as wind, beetles, animals and birds.

von Frisch, K. 1953. *The Dancing Bees.* New York: Harvest/Harcourt Brace Janovich. The life and senses of the honeybee.

## Films and videos

*The Magic School Bus Goes to Seed.* 1994. Scholastic's The Magic School Bus (tel: 212-780-9830). Video - 30 minutes. Ms. Frizzle shrinks the Magic School Bus to the size of a ladybug and the class is off to find a plant. The bus then shrinks to the size of a pollen grain and travels down the pistil of a flower to find an ovule. Appropriate for both primary and intermediate students.

*Many Worlds of Nature: Flowers.* 1977. Screenscope Films. Film - 12 minutes. Shows devices used by flowers to achieve cross-pollination, role of insects in pollination and basic flower parts. Appropriate for intermediate students.

*Pollination.* 1983. National Geographic Society. Film - 23 minutes. Reproductive parts of a flower are displayed in close-up view, self- and cross-pollination are described, coevolution of insects and flowers discussed and wind and water pollination differentiated. Appropriate for both primary and intermediate students.

*Sexual Encounters of the Floral Kind.* 1984. From the "Nature" series, WNET, New York. Film - 55 minutes. About pollination, includes unusual mechanisms of pollination, excellent photography. Appropriate for intermediate students.

# The Honeybee

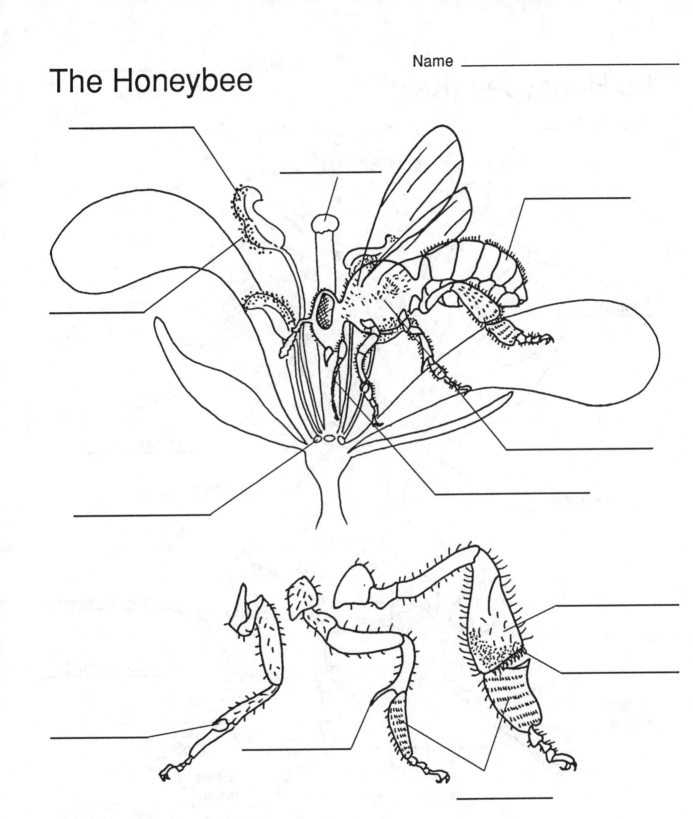

**Use these words to identify important bee and flower parts used during pollination:**

- abdomen
- antenna cleaner
- anther
- nectary

- pollen
- pollen basket
- pollen brush
- pollen comb

- proboscis
- spur
- stigma
- thorax

# The Honeybee (Key)

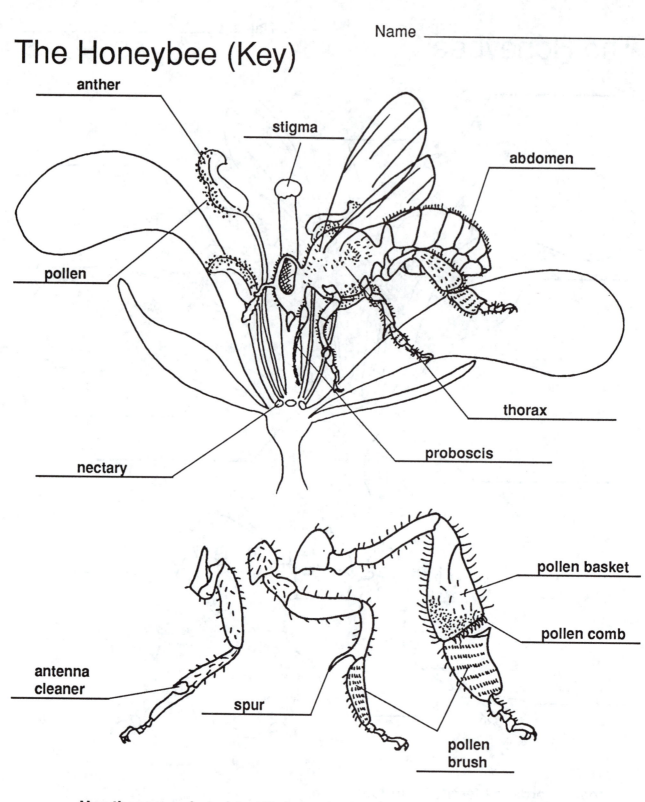

anther

stigma

abdomen

pollen

nectary

thorax

proboscis

pollen basket

pollen comb

antenna cleaner

spur

pollen brush

**Use these words to identify important bee and flower parts used during pollination:**

- abdomen
- antenna cleaner
- anther
- nectary

- pollen
- pollen basket
- pollen brush
- pollen comb

- proboscis
- spur
- stigma
- thorax

102

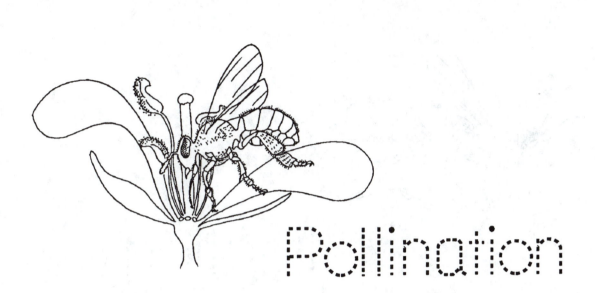

# Pollination

Cut out the sentences and glue them on another piece of paper in the proper order to show what happens when pollination takes place.

- - - - - - - - - - - - - - - - - - - - - - - - - - - - - - - - - - -

The bee goes to another flower on another plant.

- - - - - - - - - - - - - - - - - - - - - - - - - - - - - - - - - - -

The bee gets nectar from a flower and some pollen sticks to the bee.

- - - - - - - - - - - - - - - - - - - - - - - - - - - - - - - - - - -

After pollination new seeds form.

- - - - - - - - - - - - - - - - - - - - - - - - - - - - - - - - - - -

Some pollen from the bee sticks to the stigma of the new flower.

- - - - - - - - - - - - - - - - - - - - - - - - - - - - - - - - - - -

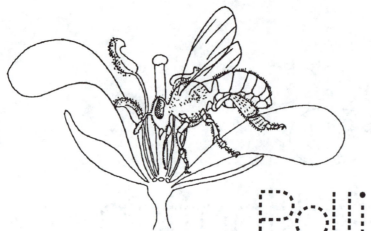

# Pollination (Key)

Cut out the sentences and glue them on another piece of paper in the proper order to show what happens when pollination takes place.

---

The bee goes to another flower on another plant.  2

---

The bee gets nectar from a flower and some pollen sticks to the bee.  1

---

After pollination new seeds form.  4

---

Some pollen from the bee sticks to the stigma of the new flower.  3

---

# Pollination

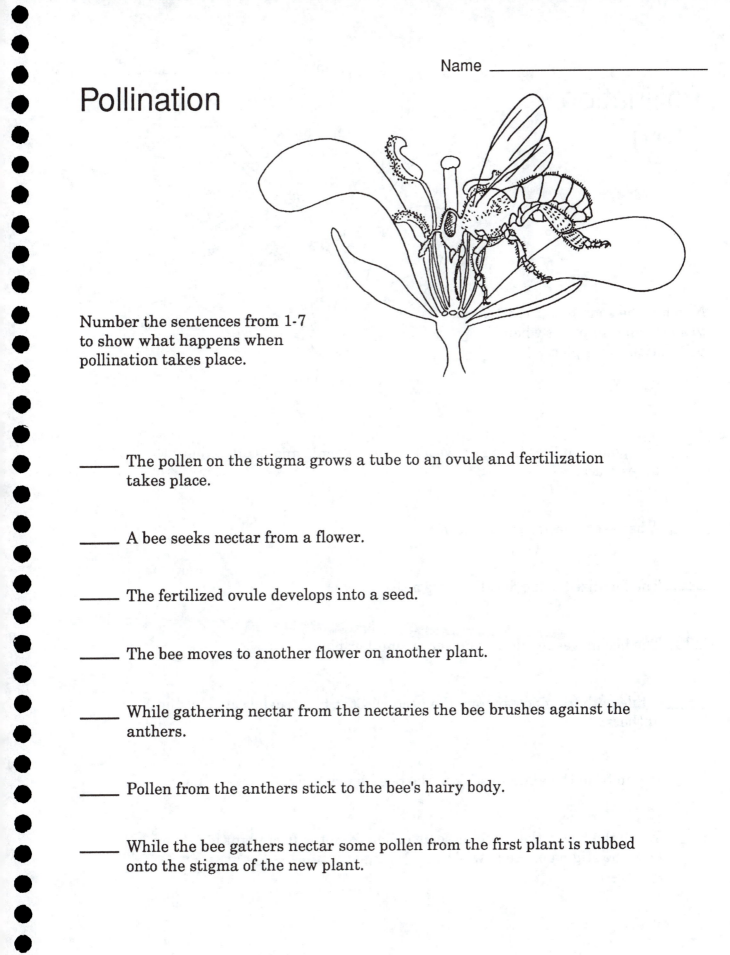

Number the sentences from 1-7
to show what happens when
pollination takes place.

_____ The pollen on the stigma grows a tube to an ovule and fertilization
takes place.

_____ A bee seeks nectar from a flower.

_____ The fertilized ovule develops into a seed.

_____ The bee moves to another flower on another plant.

_____ While gathering nectar from the nectaries the bee brushes against the
anthers.

_____ Pollen from the anthers stick to the bee's hairy body.

_____ While the bee gathers nectar some pollen from the first plant is rubbed
onto the stigma of the new plant.

# Pollination
# (Key)

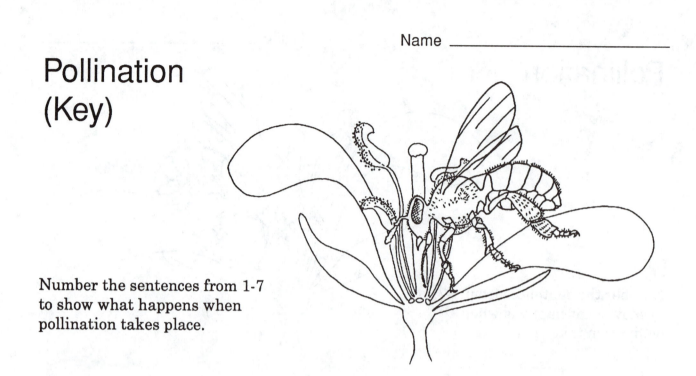

Number the sentences from 1-7
to show what happens when
pollination takes place.

**6** The pollen on the stigma grows a tube to an ovule and fertilization
takes place.

**1** A bee seeks nectar from a flower.

**7** The fertilized ovule develops into a seed.

**4** The bee moves to another flower on another plant.

**2** While gathering nectar from the nectaries the bee brushes against the
anthers.

**3** Pollen from the anthers stick to the bee's hairy body.

**5** While the bee gathers nectar some pollen from the first plant is rubbed
onto the stigma of the new plant.

# Construct . . .

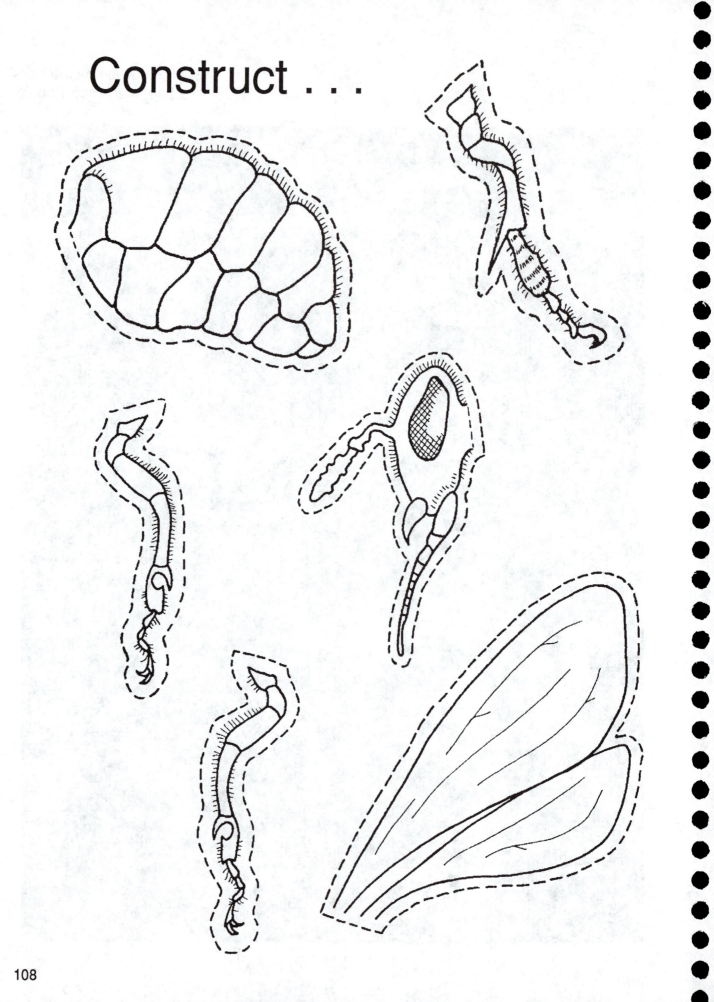

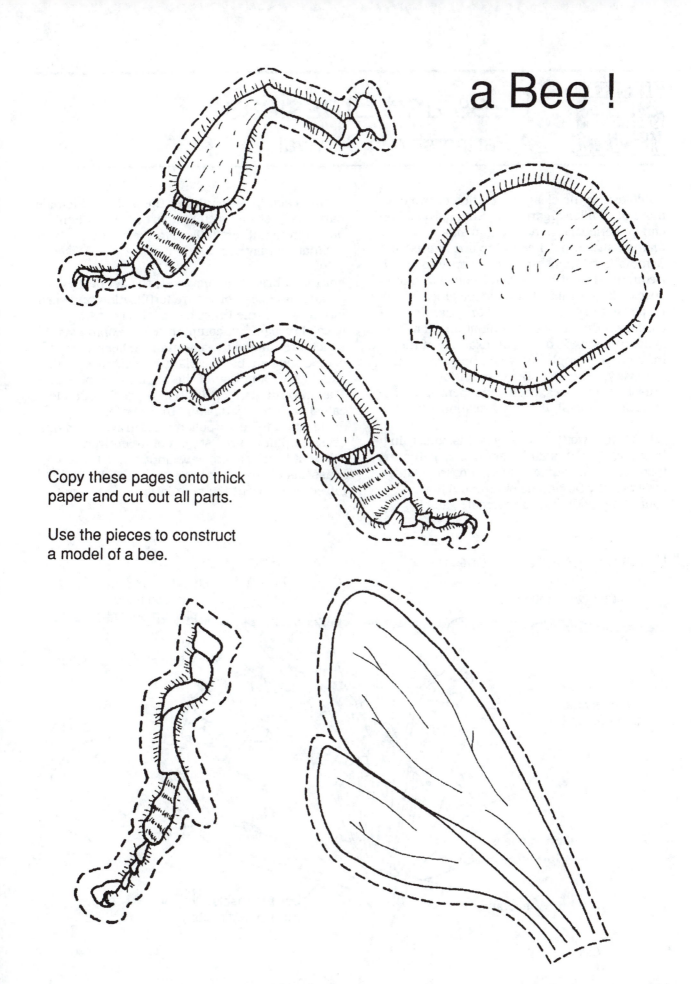

# a Bee !

Copy these pages onto thick
paper and cut out all parts.

Use the pieces to construct
a model of a bee.

# Bees and Brassicas:
## A Partnership in Survival

*Symbiosis* is the close association of two or more dissimilar organisms. Such associations can be beneficial to both organisms *(mutualistic)* or detrimental to one *(parasitic)*. Symbiotic relationships among species occur frequently in nature. When the two or more species in a symbiosis evolve reciprocally, in response to each other, they are said to *coevolve*. Under close examination each symbiosis stands out as an example of the miraculous complexity which has evolved in our everyday world. The coevolution of brassicas and bees, each dependent upon the other for survival, is such a relationship.

What is a flower? In our eyes it is something to enjoy. For bees and other nectar-gathering insects, it is a source of food. For the plant, flowers are vital organs of reproduction containing both male and female gametes.

Within each brassica flower the male and female parts are just millimeters apart so that when pollen from anthers falls onto the stigma, pollination may occur.

For many brassicas, however, the act of pollination does not insure fertilization and seed formation. Some brassica species contain special recognition compounds, *glycoproteins*, which are unique to each plant. These compounds enable the plant to recognize "self," causing the abortion of the plant's own pollen. The prevention of fertilization of "self" pollen is called *self-incompatibility*. In order for fertilization to occur pollen must travel from one brassica plant to the stigma of an entirely different brassica *(cross-pollination)*. In this way brassicas ensure that their genes will be well mixed throughout the population.

## Brassica Flower and Honeybee

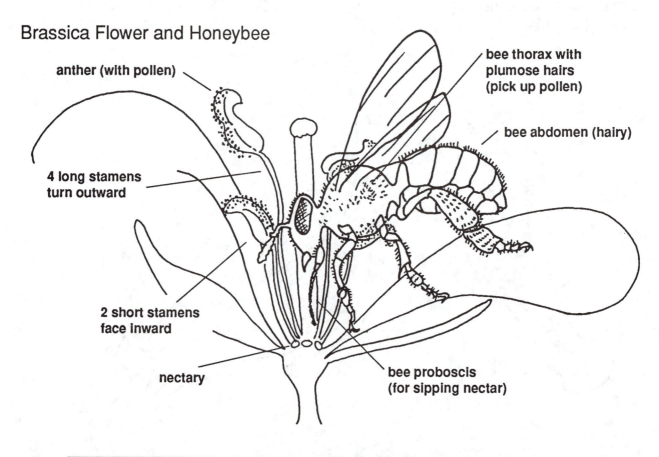

anther (with pollen)

bee thorax with plumose hairs (pick up pollen)

bee abdomen (hairy)

4 long stamens turn outward

2 short stamens face inward

nectary

bee proboscis (for sipping nectar)

The pollen itself is heavy and sticky — unable to be easily wind-borne. For brassica plants, bees are marvelously coevolved pollen transferring devices. Bees are members of the insect family Apidae, which are unique in that their bodies are covered with feather-like hairs. The bright yellow flower petals act as both beacon and landing pad for the bees, attracting them to the flower and guiding them to the nectaries. The bee drives its head deep into the flower to reach the sweet liquid (nectar) secreted by the nectaries and brushes against the anthers and stigma. Quantities of pollen are entrapped in its body hairs. As the bees work the brassica fields, moving from plant to plant, cross-pollination occurs and genetic information is widely transferred.

Bees depend on the flower for their survival. Sugars in the nectar provide carbohydrates to power flight and life activities. Pollen is the primary source of proteins, fats, vitamins, and minerals to build muscular, glandular, and skeletal tissues. The average colony of bees will collect 44 to 110 pounds of pollen in a season. *Royal jelly*, a glandular secretion of the workers, rich in pollen protein is fed to the young larvae and to the queen.

A worker bee foraging for pollen will hover momentarily over the flower as she uses her highly adapted legs for pollen collection. The fore leg is equipped with the *antenna cleaner*, a deep semicircular notch with a row of small spines. This is quickly passed over the antenna. Using the large flat *pollen brushes* on the midlegs, the bee quickly brushes the sticky pollen from her head, thorax and forelegs. The pollen is transferred to *pollen baskets* by special adaptive features of the hind legs. First the pollen captured on the midleg brushes is raked off by the *pollen combs* onto the *pollen press*. This press is a deep notch located in the joint just below the pollen basket. Flexing the leg, the bee packs the pollen into the baskets which are enclosed spaces on the upper hind leg formed by a concave outer surface fringed with long curved hairs. When the baskets are filled, the worker bee returns to the hive with her supplies to feed the colony—nectar in her honey stomach, pollen in her baskets. In the process the continuation of a new generation of brassicas is ensured through her pollination activities.

## Honeybee Legs

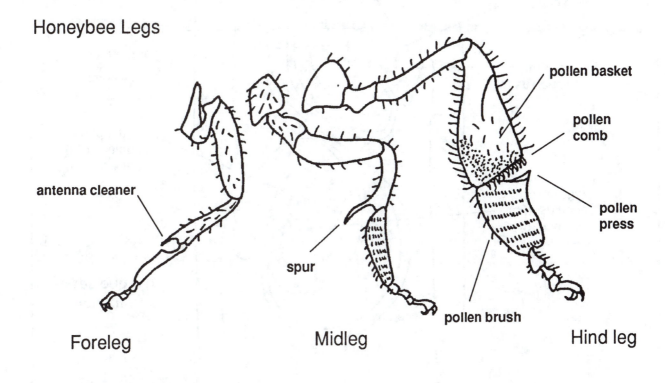

Foreleg      Midleg      Hind leg

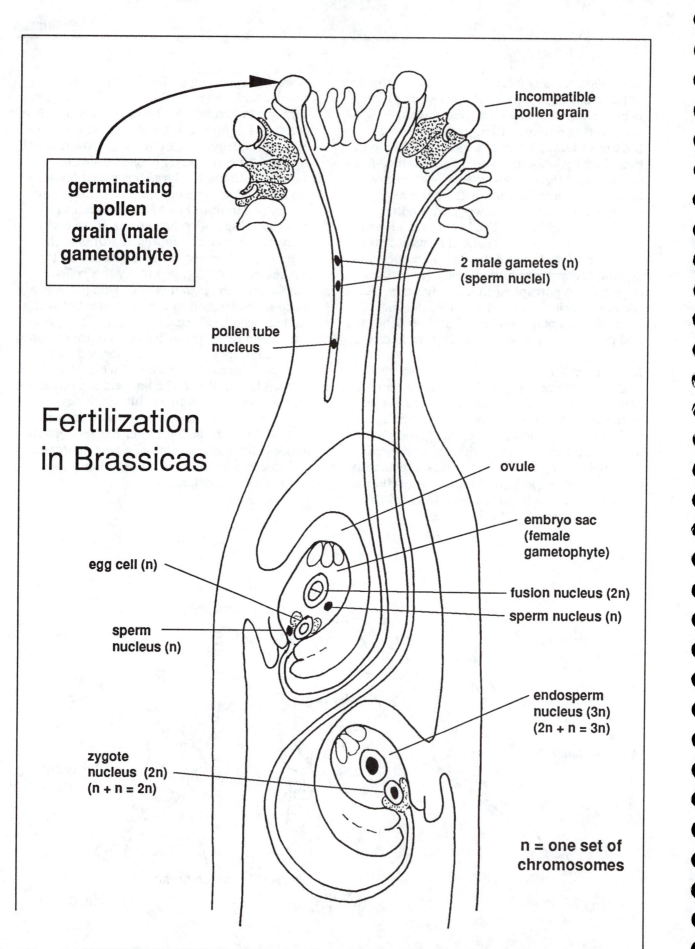

germinating pollen grain (male gametophyte)

incompatible pollen grain

2 male gametes (n) (sperm nuclei)

pollen tube nucleus

Fertilization in Brassicas

ovule

embryo sac (female gametophyte)

egg cell (n)

fusion nucleus (2n)

sperm nucleus (n)

sperm nucleus (n)

endosperm nucleus (3n) (2n + n = 3n)

zygote nucleus (2n) (n + n = 2n)

n = one set of chromosomes

# Chapter 5: Double Fertilization and Seed Pod Development

**In this exploration, students will investigate ovule development.** Further investigations explore the development of seeds in the pods. This can be a stand-alone observational exercise. The steps of each chapter are consistent with the boxed steps of the Science Exploration Flowchart. You can develop a complete scientific investigation using the questions your students ask as a result of this observational exercise. Some examples for complete scientific investigations are provided and identified by following specific icons; ●, ▲, ■ and ◆. If you don't have time to complete a full investigation, you might plan to continue with it later in the year.

## Background Information for the Teacher.

After pollination, each compatible pollen grain adhering to the stigma sends through the style a pollen tube which carries two male *gametes* (sperm cells) to the ovule, where the *egg* and other *cell nuclei* are housed in the embryo sac. One sperm (n) unites with the egg cell (n) to produce a zygote (2n) which becomes the *embryo* (2n).

The second sperm (n) unites with the diploid fusion nucleus (2n) to form the triploid *endosperm* (3n), the food source for the developing embryo. This process is known as *double fertilization*. Gametes are the sex cells which contain one set of chromosomes. One set of chromosomes is n (n = haploid). Cells of most plants and other organisms contain two sets of chromosomes (2n = diploid). Endosperm first grows as a liquid tissue, filling the enlarging ovules. The embryo's development is then nourished by the endosperm. Within 2-3 days after fertilization, the pistil elongates and swells to become the seed pod. The sepals and petals wither and drop off, having completed their functions. See "Embryogenesis" (pages 123-124).

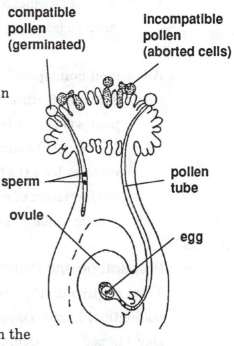

compatible pollen (germinated)

incompatible pollen (aborted cells)

sperm

pollen tube

ovule

egg

**fertilization**

Days 17-35 in the Fast Plants growth cycle is the stage when the embryos develop into seeds. The embryos go through a series of developmental stages, known as *embryogenesis*, enlarging to occupy the space taken by the endosperm. In *Brassica*, in the latter stages of embryo development the nutrient reserves in the endosperm are used by the developing embryo and the space that was filled by the endosperm is occupied by the enlarging embryo. In cereal crops, such as wheat, rice and corn, endosperm is not used by the enlarging embryo and remains a major portion of the seed as a starchy energy source for germination. Through the development of the seed, the plant has solved the problem of packaging its new generation (embryo) to survive until favorable conditions for growth (germination) return. As the seed matures, the walls of each ovule develop into a protective seed coat and the entire ovary becomes a fruit (seed pod). Embryos mature into seeds in 20 days.

## Teaching Objectives

**Beginning concepts:**

- Fertilization is the union of male (sperm) and female (egg) reproductive cells (gametes) in the ovule.
- Fertilization occurs within 24 hours of pollination.
- Within 3-5 days of fertilization, the flower petals drop and the pistil swells and elongates.
- The fertilized egg develops through various stages over the next twenty days until it becomes a mature embryo (seed).

---

**Materials needed per student/team:**

- Fast Plants with developing pods
- pins
- hand lenses

---

**Advanced concepts:**

- A unique feature of higher plants is double fertilization.
- Double fertilization in plants involves both the formation of an embryo (which will be the new plant) and the formation of a special food source (endosperm).
- A pollen tube forms to allow the male gametes (sperm) to reach the ovule.

## Preparation and Planning for Observational Exercise

**Time required:** $1^1/_2$ weeks, 3 hours actual time. Day 1: pistil observation and pollination, 1 hour; Days 4-14: measuring and recording, every other day, $^1/_2$ hour; Day 14: pod dissection, 1 hour.

# Double Fertilization and Seed Pod Development   Observational Exercise

**1.** Observe the pistils on the unpollinated flowers.

**2.** When several flowers are open, pollinate them.

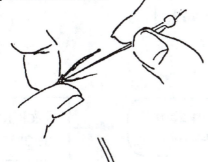

**3.** Three days later, look for signs of pistil elongation. Observe the flower petals. Are they withering? Make a drawing of your plant.

**4.** Measure the length of each pistil. Write the measurement next to the picture of each pistil.

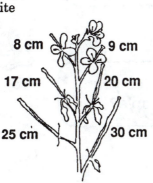

8 cm    9 cm

17 cm    20 cm

25 cm    30 cm

**5.** Repeat the drawing and measurements twice a week for two weeks.

**6.** Carefully strip off a seed pod. Use a strong pin to open (dissect) the pod. Observe the size of the ovules.

**7.** Examine seed development along the length of the pod with a hand lens or microscope.

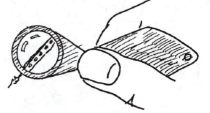

**8.** Illustrate and label what you see inside the pods. Date the drawings.

**9.** Prick the ovule and squeeze out the developing embryo. Look carefully with your hand lens. What do you see?

# Student Science Exploration Flowchart

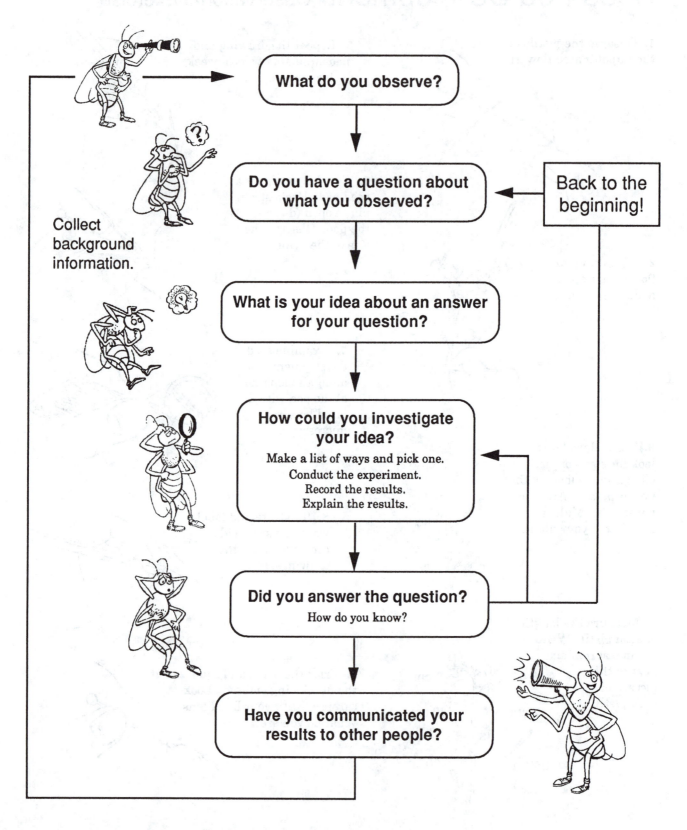

**What do you observe?**

Collect background information.

**Do you have a question about what you observed?**

Back to the beginning!

**What is your idea about an answer for your question?**

**How could you investigate your idea?**

Make a list of ways and pick one.
Conduct the experiment.
Record the results.
Explain the results.

**Did you answer the question?**

How do you know?

**Have you communicated your results to other people?**

**Tips and suggestions:**

- Signs of pistil elongation (the seed pod beginning to grow) should be visible within 2-3 days after successfully pollinating a flower. The ovules enlarge within the first week, filling with liquid endosperm.

- As the pods develop, have students discuss their recorded observations and predict what their pods and seeds will look like in 2 days, 4 days, 6 days, etc.

- If there is a concern about using the sharp end of a pin, push the pin into the blunt end of a pencil and use the side of the pin head to slit the seed pod.

## Where Seeds Come From

| Making observations |
|---|

**Some preliminary questions:** Begin your exploration by asking your students some questions and discussing ideas they might have about seeds and where they come from.

**As you conduct the observational exercise illustrated on page 115,** your students will observe how the pistils begin to elongate even before the petals wither. Accuracy and care will be required in measuring the length of the pistils. Students will dissect a developing seed pod, notice how the ovules lie within the ovary. If they are successful in opening an ovule, they will notice liquid endosperm and a tiny green embryo.

**Accompanying activities:** Modeling the fertilization process. See "Fertilization Model" (page 232).

| Asking questions |
|---|

**What questions have your students raised from observing?** The students should be curious about some of the things they have observed. A class discussion should generate questions. Have your students make a list of questions. Prompt them with the words **"What if."**

**Example questions derived from observations:**

- ● Why is the pistil growing longer? (Investigation #1)
- ▲ Do the biggest seed pods produce the most seed? (Investigation #2)
- ■ Do unpollinated flowers produce seed? (Investigation #3)

**Other possible questions:** How long can a seed pod grow to be?

---

### Forming a hypothesis

**What are your students' ideas about answers for their questions?** Following the discussion of observations, students can turn their questions into statements and write them down as hypotheses.

**Example hypotheses derived from questions:**

- ● Seeds are developing in the carpels. (Investigation #1)
- ▲ The more the pistil swells, the more seeds will be made in the pod. (Investigation #2)
- ■ Unpollinated flowers don't produce seeds. (Investigation #3)

**Tips and suggestions:** Have the students check the Science Exploration Flowchart to see what the next steps need to be in their science problem solving.

---

### Testing the hypothesis

**How could your students investigate their ideas?** Design and experiment. Devise ways to test the hypothesis, choose the best one and carry it out. Refer to the worksheet "Setting Up An Experiment" (pages 41-43) for help in designing the experiment/s.

**Control Experiments:** A *control* serves as a standard of comparison for verifying the results of an investigation. By controlling the variable factors of the experiment, the effects of changing one variable at a time are easily observed.

**Examples of ways to test the hypotheses:**

- ● Dissect developing seed pods at two day intervals during the 2nd and 3rd weeks after pollination. (Investigation #1)

- Measure the length of the developing pod.
- Count the number of ovules (record date of the drawing).
- Look for embryos in the ovules. Hint: The seed pods are lengthening because the embryos are enlarging.
- The control would be the unpollinated flowers.

**Management Strategy:** You will need hand lenses and/or dissection microscopes, needles/probes or toothpicks and tweezers. Looking for embryos can be a time-consuming process. Allow 30 minutes for this activity. Dissection microscopes are necessary for viewing the globular, heart and torpedo stages (see page 124). The older the embryo, the easier it is to locate and view under the microscope. Globular embryos are difficult to view intact because the suspensor often breaks up and you are left with only the embryo. Viewing with a dissection scope may be more successful if you adjust the lighting of the microscope to give a dark background (dark field microscopy).

▲ Have students measure and record the length of specific developing seed pods. (Investigation #2)

- Predict how many seeds different pods on one Fast Plant will have.
- Mark each pod with a colored piece of yarn or Magic marker so predictions can be revised and confirmed as the pod matures.
- The log or chart should include illustrations of the developing pod.
- This activity should be repeated every other day for two weeks.
- Finally, count the number of seeds produced/pod.
- As a class, plot a distribution showing number of seeds versus pod length.

■ Don't pollinate the flowers on one plant. Observe the development of those pods. Measure and record pod length and seed numbers. (Without pollination, mature pods will not develop. An empty, shriveled pod will develop, being only slightly larger in diameter than the stem.)
Hint: Make a divider as illustrated with 5" x 8" index cards to keep the plants from brushing against each other (see page 98). The control is a plant with pollinated flowers, which is the reverse of Investigation #1. (Investigation #3)

**Collect data:** See "Keeping Track of Things" (pages 23-26).

**Analyze the data:** Have the students explain the results. For example:

● The embryos did increase in size and become seeds. (Investigation #1)

▲ There were more seeds in the larger pods. (Investigation #2)

■ The pistils elongated for a few days, then stopped and remained thin. No seeds developed in the pods. (Investigation #3)

## Evaluating the hypothesis

**Was the hypothesis verified?** How do your students know that they know? For example: Was the test fair? Did they answer the question? Are they sure?

## Communicating the results

**Have your students communicated their results to others?** No science investigation is complete until it is communicated in writing. In addition, it can be communicated orally. Students can write their conclusions very simply, but the report should be understandable to anyone reading it, peers and teacher.

## References

### Books

Bjork, L. and L. Anderson. 1978. *Linnea's Windowsill Garden.* New York: Farrar, Straus & Giroux. A tour of a young girl's indoor garden. Includes conversations about what keeps plants satisfied and what to do when plants are attacked by insect pests. Ideas for a "plant olympics," a plant problem chart, etc.

Dowden, A. O. 1984. *From Fruit to Flower.* New York: Thomas Y. Crowell Co. A look at the amazing variety of fruits made by flowering plants, with interesting botany text and color botanical illustrations.

Stockley, C. 1986. *Dictionary of Biology (Usborne Illustrated).* London: Usborne Publishing, Ltd. A densely illustrated, clear guide to key terms and subject areas of plants and animals.

### Films and videos

*Seeds and Seasons.* 1987. Churchill Farms. Video - 10 minutes. Primary presentation of a sunflower from seed to maturity, shows the effects of weather and insects on the plant. Uses time-lapse photography. Appropriate for primary students.

# Double Fertilization and Seed Pod Development

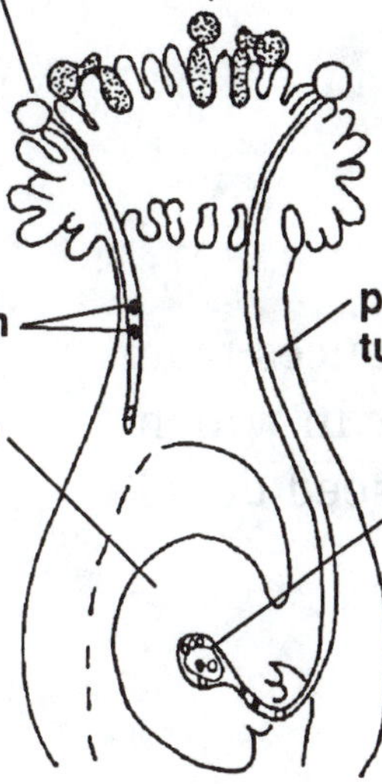

compatible pollen (germinated)

incompatible pollen (aborted cells)

sperm

pollen tube

ovule

egg

**fertilization**

Number the sentences from 1 to 6 in the order in which fertilization and seed development occurs.

_____ The pistil elongates and swells.

_____ A sperm (n) unites with the egg (n) to form an embryo (2n).

_____ Sepals and petals wither and fall off.

_____ A pollen tube grows from the stigma to the ovule.

_____ A sperm (n) unites with the fusion nucleus (2n) to form the endosperm (3n).

_____ The pistil becomes a seed pod.

# Double Fertilization and Seed Pod Development (Key)

Number the sentences from 1 to 6 in the order in which fertilization and seed development occurs.

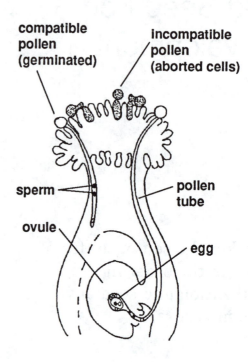

**fertilization**

_____4_____ The pistil elongates and swells.

_____2_____ A sperm (n) unites with the egg (n) to form an embryo (2n).

_____5_____ Sepals and petals wither and fall off.

_____1_____ A pollen tube grows from the stigma to the ovule.

_____3_____ A sperm (n) unites with the fusion nucleus (2n) to form the endosperm (3n).

_____6_____ The pistil becomes a seed pod.

# Embryogenesis

What happens between fertilization and seed harvest? Many current biology texts do not discuss the stages of embryo development, or *embryogenesis*. Texts skip to seed structure once fertilization and the formation of zygote and endosperm are presented. You and your students can explore the development of the plant embryo from a fertilized egg to a mature seed with Wisconsin Fast Plants.

To set the scene...Fifteen days ago, your students began to explore the life cycle of rapid-cycling *Brassica rapa* by planting Wisconsin Fast Plants (Rbr) seeds. For three days, "buzzing" students have moved beesticks from plant to plant, carrying pollen from stamen to pistil. Today, students observe swelling and elongating pistils, evidence that double fertilization has taken place.

Following *double fertilization* (a characteristic of higher plants), four complex processes are triggered. First, the ovary wall and related maternal structures rapidly grow to become the fruit tissue surrounding the developing seeds. The ovules within the fruit enlarge to accommodate the developing endosperm and embryos. The various outer cell layers of the ovule (integuments) eventually become the seed coat. Within the embryo sac, the triploid endosperm nuclei, which resulted from the fusion of the diploid endosperm nucleus in the central cell and one of the two male sperm nuclei, divides to form the liquid endosperm. The liquid endosperm provides nutrients to the developing embryo. Finally, the diploid zygote cell divides and develops into the embryo.

During the next three weeks, explore the stages of embryogenesis. You will need: a dissecting microscope with 20-40X magnification, dissection needles, glass slides, dropper bottles with water, and pods (siliques) from the Fast Plants.

The different stages in embryogenesis are illustrated on page 124. Six days after the last pollination with beesticks, remove a pod from a plant. Place the pod on a glass slide and observe it with the dissecting microscope. Use dissection needles to open the pod along its "seam," the fusion line of the two carpels. Carefully remove the ovules and set them aside in a drop of water on the slide. With a sharp needle, rupture an ovule and tease out the young embryo. The fine granular liquid that spills out of the ovule with the embryo is the starchy endosperm. Try staining the starch with iodine solution.

Look for the developing embryo. Observing the *globular* stage in the embryonic development is a challenging task at the microscope. (More mature stages are easier to observe.) Since fertilization, the zygote has undergone several mitotic divisions. The first few divisions produced a strand of eight cells known as the *suspensor*. The suspensor orients the developing embryo within the ovule and is thought to serve as an "umbilical cord," as its cells pass nutrients from the endosperm to the embryo cells. The basal cell of the suspensor anchors the developing embryo and orients the embryonic root tip near the micropyle, the hole in the integuments where the pollen tube entered. At the tip of the suspensor, opposite the basal cell, repeated divisions give rise to the young globular embryo.

By Day 9, the embryo becomes flattened and bilaterally symmetric with two lobes which will become the cotyledons. This is the *heart* stage. As development continues, the axis of the embryo elongates into the *torpedo* stage, the embryo develops chlorophyll and becomes green. Elongation of the embryonic hypocotyl axis separates the root apex from the shoot meristem hidden between the cotyledons. In the latter stages of embryogenesis, the nutrient reserves in the endosperm are used by the developing embryo and the space that was filled by the endosperm is occupied by the enlarging embryo. To package the enlarging embryo, the cotyledons are folded around the hypocotyl axis, now curved within the ovule integuments. This is the *walking stick* stage. By Day 20, the walls of the ovule have formed a seed coat and the seed and pod begin the maturation process.

Between Days 11 and 20, continue to remove pods and repeat this procedure to observe the developing embryo stages. How good are your observational, dissecting and microscope skills? Is there any difference in the stages of development in the embryos at one end of the pod from the other? There are many questions that remain unanswered in developmental embryology—perhaps your students can answer some of them!

## References

Williams, P. H. 1985. CrGC Resource Book. Department of Plant Pathology, University of Wisconsin-Madison.

Williams, P. H. 1986. Rapid Cycling Populations of Brassica. Science 232:1385-1389.

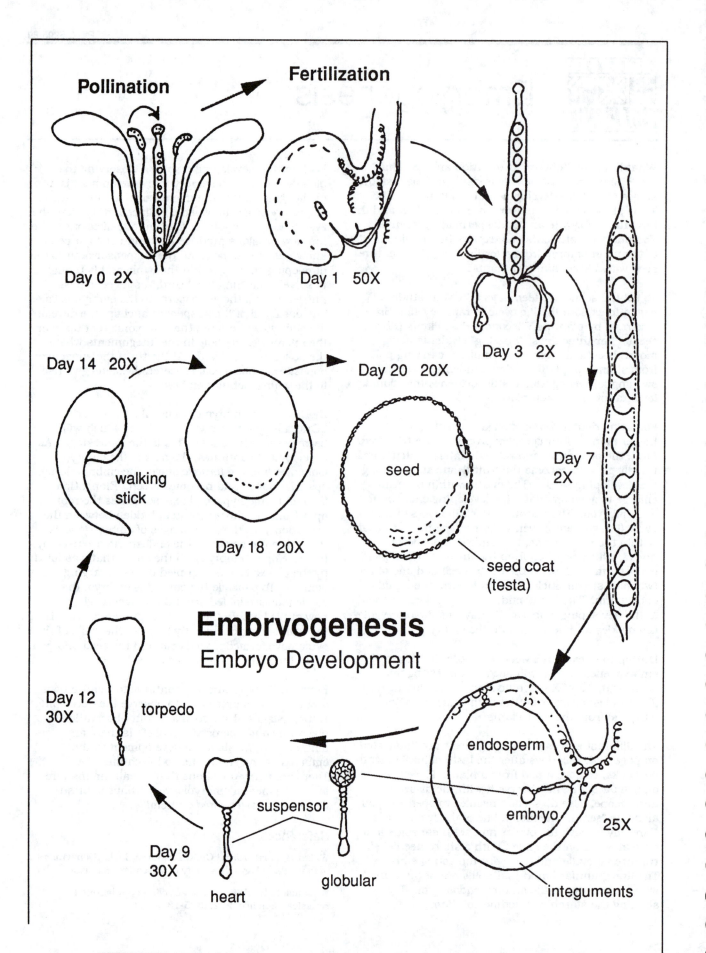

Pollination

Fertilization

Day 0  2X

Day 1  50X

Day 3  2X

Day 7  2X

Day 14  20X

Day 20  20X

walking stick

seed

Day 18  20X

seed coat (testa)

# Embryogenesis
## Embryo Development

Day 12  30X

torpedo

endosperm

embryo

25X

suspensor

Day 9  30X

heart

globular

integuments

124

# Chapter 6:  Seed Maturation and Dispersal

**The students will harvest Fast Plants seeds and will observe the variability among seeds.** This can be a stand-alone observational exercise. The steps of each chapter are consistent with the boxed steps of the Science Exploration Flowchart. You can develop a complete scientific investigation using the questions your students ask as a result of this observational exercise. Some examples for complete scientific investigations are provided and identified by following specific icons; ●, ▲, ■ and ◆. If you don't have time to complete a full investigation, you might plan to continue with it later in the year.

## Background Information for the Teacher

Through the development of the seed, the plant has solved the problem of packaging its new generation (embryo) to survive until favorable conditions for growth (germination) return. After cross-pollination of the Fast Plants has been completed, the plants will continue to produce new flower buds.

**pinching off buds**

These new flower buds should be pinched or cut off after they form. The plant will then direct its resources into the developing seed pods. With Fast Plants, the embryos in the developing ovules will mature in about 20 days following pollination. Twenty days after the last pollination, the plants should be removed from the water mat and allowed to dry for 5 days. Dried seed pods can then be gently opened or crushed and the seeds collected. The seed pod has developed *weakened seams* along the length of the ovary wall which split open in nature to release the seed.

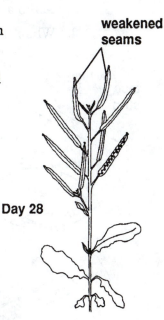

**weakened seams**

**Day 28**

## Teaching Objectives

**Beginning Concepts:**

- Seeds mature approximately 20 days after fertilization.
- Seeds are harvested after plants and pods are dried.
- Seeds vary in size, shape, color and viability.
- Seeds have stored energy to grow new plants under the right conditions.

## Preparation and Planning for Observational Exercise

**Time required:** 1 class hour.

---

**Materials needed per student/team:**
- paper toweling
- scissors
- dried Fast Plants with pods
- seed envelope
- marking pen

---

**Tips and suggestions:**

- Snip off the pod with a scissors. Gently roll the dry pod between your fingers or carefully break it open along the seam. The seeds are tiny and easily scatter.
- Place seeds in a paper envelope and store in a cool, dry place.
- The suggested hypotheses provide ideas for the next generation of Fast Plants in your classroom.

- **Optional Seed Harvesting Method**
  1. Cut a 6" strip of transparent tape (Figure 1). Fold back each end of the tape $1/_2$", sticky side in.
  2. Make a loop of tape with sticky side out.
  3. When harvesting, drop seed onto tape loop (Figure 2).
  4. Open loop and put sticky sides together to protect seed until needed.
  5. Label tape with student name, seed type and date (Figure 3).
  6. Store (for example, in an envelope) until needed.

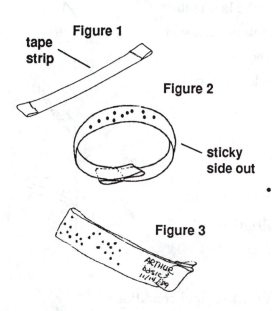

Figure 1
tape strip

Figure 2
sticky side out

Figure 3

- **Option to Harvesting Seed**

  As an alternative to immediately harvesting the seeds, the seed pods themselves can be cut from the plant and stored as pods, so that next year's students begin harvesting the seed, rather than just planting it. This approach reinforces the concept of the pod as the "mother" and the seeds as half-siblings. See "What can you teach with a seed pod" (page 132), and "Fast Plants and Families" (pages 193-198) for complete instructions and background information.

- **Seed Storage**

  Fast Plants seed will store for many years without losing germinability or vigor when stored dry and cold. Seeds and/or harvested pods are best stored in a sealed glass or plastic jar with a few grams of silica gel desiccant (available from a pharmacist or photo shop).

# Seed Maturation and Dispersal
## Observational Exercise

**3.** Count and record the number of seeds and note any variations in the seeds.

**1.** Remove one pod at a time by snipping the pod from the plant with scissors.

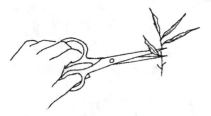

**4.** Transfer the seeds to an envelope labeled with names, date and type of seed. Repeat steps 1-4 for each pod of the plant.

**2.** Roll the pod between finger and thumb over a paper towel until all seeds are removed from the pod.

**5.** Collect class data on the number of seeds per plant.

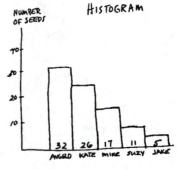

**6.** Make a histogram or graph of the number of seeds harvested from the plants.

# Student Science Exploration Flowchart

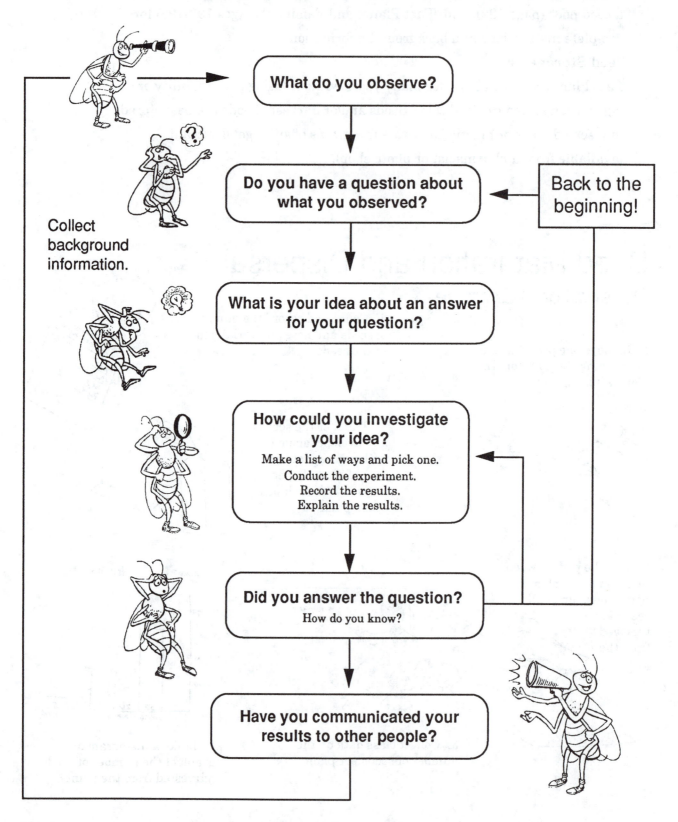

Collect background information.

**What do you observe?**

**Do you have a question about what you observed?**

Back to the beginning!

**What is your idea about an answer for your question?**

**How could you investigate your idea?**

Make a list of ways and pick one.
Conduct the experiment.
Record the results.
Explain the results.

**Did you answer the question?**
How do you know?

**Have you communicated your results to other people?**

## What Happens To Seeds

### Making observations

**Some preliminary questions:** Begin your exploration by asking your students some questions and discussing ideas they might have about seeds and harvesting.

**As you conduct the observational exercise illustrated on page 127,** your students will observe how the seed pod splits open along the seams. Some seeds may still be attached to the wall of the ovary (or carpel). Others will fall out. Observe seeds for variation in size, shape, color, etc.

**Accompanying activities:** Discuss the meaning of life cycles to plants now that one cycle has been completed. Students might write about the life cycle from the view point of a plant that is being "reared" by a student.

### Asking questions

**What questions have your students raised from observing?** The students should be curious about some of the things they have observed. A class discussion should generate questions. Have students make a list of questions. Prompt them with the words **"What if."**

**Example questions derived from the observation:**
- ● Will large seeds germinate better than small ones? (Investigation #1)
- ▲ Why did some pods have lots of seeds and others have few? (Investigation #2)

**Other possible questions:** Do other plants produce more seeds per pod than Fast Plants?

### Forming a hypothesis

**What are your students' ideas about answers for their questions?** Following the discussion of observations, students can turn their questions into statements and write them down as hypotheses.

**Example hypotheses derived from questions:**

● Big round seeds germinate better than little flat ones. (Investigation #1)

▲ The more times a flower is pollinated, the more seeds per pod it produces. (Investigation #2)

**Tips and suggestions:** Have the students check the Science Exploration Flow-chart to see what the next steps need to be in their science problem solving.

> ### Testing the hypothesis

**How could your students investigate their ideas?** Design an experiment. Devise ways to test the hypothesis, choose the best one and carry it out. Refer to worksheet "Setting Up An Experiment" (pages 41-43) for help in designing the experiment/s.

**Control Experiments:** A *control* serves as a standard of comparison for verifying the results of an investigation. By controlling the variable factors of the experiment, the effects of changing one variable are easily observed.

**Examples of ways to test hypotheses:**

● Germinate harvested seeds which have been sorted by size. Test the germination of the seeds, following the procedure illustrated on page 47. Germination is a continual process. You and your students will decide when to record

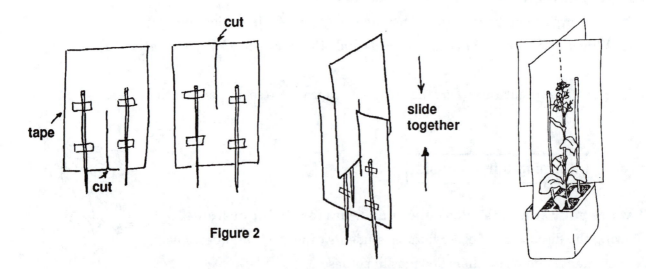

Figure 2

germination. An easy time for comparison would be after 48 hours when roots and cotyledons have emerged. See Germination chapter (pages 45-56). (Investigation #1)

**Management Strategy:** Allow approximately 5 days for this germination test. You may want to grow the plants for the entire life cycle and see if the seed size affects plant size, number of flowers, etc. You will need the same materials as in the germination investigation (page 47).

▲ Grow another cycle. Control the number of pollinations for different groups of plants. For example, pollinate one group on only one day, pollinate the second group two days in a row, etc. The third group, the control, can be pollinated for three days. Hint: Make a divider (Figure 2) with 5" x 8" index cards to keep plants from brushing against each other. (Investigation #2)

**Collect data:** See "Keeping Track of Things" (pages 23-26).

**Analyze the data:** Have students explain the results. For example:
- More big round seeds germinated than small flat ones. (Investigation #1)
- ▲ The plants that were pollinated most produced the most seeds per pod. (Investigation #2)

### Evaluating the hypothesis

**Was the hypothesis verified?** How do your students know that they know? For example: Was the test fair? Did they answer the question? Are they sure?

### Communicating the results

**Have your students communicated their results to others?** *No science investigation is complete until it is communicated in writing.* In addition, it can be communicated orally. Students can write their conclusions very simply, but the report should be understandable to anyone reading it, peers and teacher.

### References

#### Books

Heller, R. 1986. *The Reason for a Flower*. New York: Grosset and Dunlap. A clear and colorfully illustrated view of the angiosperm life cycle, from flower to pollination to seed to plant. Some basic facts about plants and their importance are also included.

Suzuki, D. and B. Hehner. 1985. *Looking at Plants*. Toronto, Canada: Stoddart Publishing Co., Ltd. A tour through the plant world in clear and interesting language for students, plus short and long term projects.

#### Films and videos

*Flowering Plants From Seed to Seed*. 1979. International Film Bureau. Film - 11 minutes. Uses a tomato plant to illustrate the life cycle, showing the development of roots, stems, leaves, stamens, stigmas and ovaries. Seed dispersal is also discussed. Appropriate for primary and intermediate students.

---

# What can you teach with a seed pod?

A family approach to investigating Fast Plants*

- variation
- maternal inheritance
- paternity
- pedigrees/lineage
- genetics vs. environment

> the pod (part of the maternal parent) = mother
>
> the seeds (offspring of a common maternal parent) = siblings

### Ideas

1. **observe, measure, record**
   - characteristics of each pod (mother)
   - each family of pods

2. **compare**
   - pods from one family (mother plant) with other families as to length, # of seeds per pod, condition of the seed, length of the style

3. **consider parentage**
   - do all the siblings have the same father?
   - could the mother be the father?
   - could all the siblings have the same father?

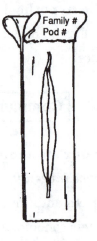

Family #
Pod #

4. **evaluate siblings**
   - is there variation among the sibling plants from one pod?
   - are they more like each other than like progeny from other plants?

5. **correlate: is there a relationship...**
   - between pod length and the number of seeds it produces?
   - between the length of a seed pod and its position on the maternal plant?
   - between the # of seeds in a pod and the position of the pod on the plant?

**\* See "Fast Plants and Families" (pages 193-198) for the complete investigation.**

# Seed Pods

Choose four seed pods. **Estimate** the number of seeds in each pod. Now open and carefully **count** the number of seeds in each pod. **Subtract** to find out how many seeds you were off in your estimation.

| | Estimate | Count | Difference Subtract to find the difference between your estimate and your count |
|---|---|---|---|
| Pod 1 | | | |
| Pod 2 | | | |
| Pod 3 | | | |
| Pod 4 | | | |

# Seed Harvest Data

Name _____

Count the number of pods on one of your plants.
Color one of the pods below for each one on your plant.

My plant has _____ pods.

Open one large pod from your plant.
Draw one seed in this pod for each seed you count in the pod from your plant.

My pod had _____ seeds in it.

From these seeds new _____ will grow.

# Pod Harvest Data

1. Count the pods on each plant from your quad.

   Number on plant 1: _____

   Number on plant 2: _____

   Number on plant 3: _____

   Number on plant 4: _____

   Total number of pods: _____

2. Determine the range of pods for each quad.

   Highest number of pods from one plant: _____

   Lowest number of pods from one plant: _____

   Subtract _____ = range of pods for quad

3. Find the average number of pods per plant for your quad.

   Divide the total number of pods ( _____ ) by the

   number of plants in your quad ( _____ ).

   _____ ÷ _____ = _____
   total number of pods    number of plants    average number of
                                               pods per plant

4. Graph the results of your computations on the class graph.

   Compare your total, range and average with others in your class.

   Do you and your partner have a "green thumb?"

5. Explain what factors may have caused your plant to have high, average, or low production.

# The Influence of the Environment on Plant Growth

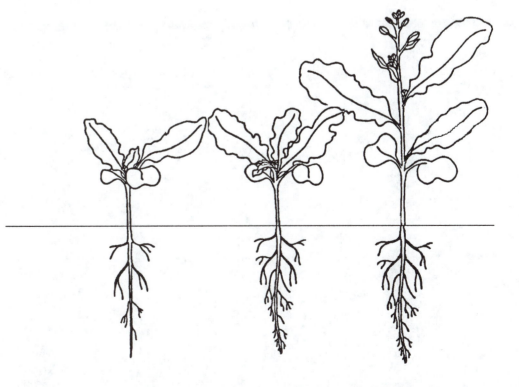

# Concepts: The Influence of the Environment on Plant Growth

Fundamental to biology is understanding the role that environment plays in the functioning and appearance (phenotype) of individual organisms. The phenotype of an individual is the result of the genetic makeup (genotype) of that organism being expressed in the environment in which the organism exists.

Components of the environment are physical (temperature, light, gravity), chemical (water, elements, salts, complex molecules), and biotic (microbes, animals and other plants). Environmental studies explore the influence of one or more components of the environment on the growth, behavior and reproduction of the organism/s under study.

## Accessing Resources for Growth

Plants access and respond to light, gravity, water, elements, and complex molecules. The energetic, catalytic, structural and solvent properties of these resources underlie life processes.

### Nutrition

Using specialized structures (roots, root hairs, leaves and stems) the plant accesses light, water, minerals and complex molecules for growth and development. Limiting the quantities of one or more essential components for growth will reduce the growth of a plant. Plants compete for essential growth components.

- *What is "food" for plants?*
- *How does limiting essential growth components affect plant growth?*
- *How does proximity (population density) influence competition for essential growth components?*
- *Are plants capable of growth without light?*

### Bioassays with Fast Plants

A bioassay is an experimental method for determining the influence of an environmental component on an organism. Inferences are drawn from the results of a bioassay and extrapolated to predict the effects of the component on other organisms and populations.

- *How are bioassays used to generate information?*

### Tropisms

Rooted in the ground, plants, unlike most animals, are unable to move or relocate themselves in their environment from their fixed position. They are, however, capable of orienting themselves so as to optimize their capacity to access the environmental components essential to their life. How plants orient themselves to light and gravity is called tropism. Plants use guidance systems which sense and respond to gravity (gravitropism) ensuring that roots anchor plants and access water and that shoots emerge into the light. Plants then use light to activate energy-capturing photosynthesis. Light also guides the development of leaf expansion (photomorphogenesis), stem bending and elongation (phototropism), and pigment (chlorophyll and anthocyanin) production.

- *How does a plant grow up?*
- *Why does the shoot grow up and the root down?*
- *How do leaves expand?*

# Health and Wellness

Health or wellness of an individual exists when that individual is growing optimally within its environment. Deviations in the environment from optimum can lead to disease in an organism. Modification in the atmospheric, terrestrial or biotic environment of the plant frequently stress the plant, resulting in less than optimal growth.

- *How does modifying components of the atmosphere influence plant growth and reproduction?*
- *How does modifying components of the terrestrial or aquatic environment influence plant growth and reproduction?*

### Modifying the Atmosphere
### Salt Effects on Plants

# Chapter 7: Nutrition

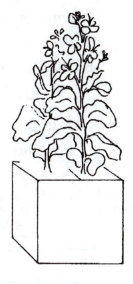

**The students will observe Fast Plants grown with various amounts of fertilizer pellets and explore both the necessary amount of mineral nutrient for a healthy plant and the effect of nutrient on seed production.** This can be a stand-alone observational exercise. The steps of each chapter are consistent with the ⬚boxed⬚ steps of the Science Exploration Flowchart. You can develop a complete scientific investigation using the questions your students ask as a result of this observational exercise. Some examples for complete scientific investigations are provided and identified by following specific icons; ●, ▲, ■ and ◆. If you don't have time to complete a full investigation, you can continue with it later in the year.

## Background Information for the Teacher

Fast Plants have been selectively bred to grow under specific light, moisture, soil, space and nutrient conditions. They grow best with continuous fluorescent light of a certain intensity, a constant water supply, a sterilized potting mix medium and fertilizer, e.g., three to four fertilizer pellets per cell.

The three to four fertilizer pellets provide the optimum amount of *nitrogen* (N), *phosphorus* (P) and *potassium* (K). Fewer pellets produce shorter plants with pale yellow or reddish leaves and few flowers. Addition of six to eight pellets produces taller plants with more foliage, lateral branching and slightly delayed flower production. Addition of sixteen or more pellets can result in a severely stunted plant or death due to the buildup of toxic salt concentrations in the soil. Plants will produce a maximum yield of seed under optimum conditions with nutrient (fertilizer).

## Teaching Objectives

**Beginning Concept:** Specific amount of nutrients (nitrogen, phosphorus and potassium) are needed for optimal growth of plants.

**Advanced Concept:** The absence or excess of essential nutrients may prevent plants from completing their life cycle (forming viable seeds).

## Preparation and Planning for Observational Exercise

**Time required**: 18 days advance preparation of plants by teacher, and 30 minutes observation and discussion.

---

**Materials needed per student/team:**
- Grown in advance by the teacher: four quads of 18-day old Fast Plants, two grown with 0 fertilizer pellets per cell, and two grown with 4 pellets per cell
- metric rulers

---

**Tips and suggestions:**
- Plant separate quads of each fertilizer treatment.
- Tell students that the lighting, moisture and potting mix is the same in all quads.
- Alternatively, students may make observations and measurements on Days 7, 14 and 21 after seeding.

## How Much Is Enough?

| Making observations |
| --- |

**Some preliminary questions:** Begin your exploration by asking your students some questions and discussing ideas they might have about plants and nutrition.

**As you conduct the observational exercise illustrated on page 141,** your students will observe that plants grown with no fertilizer pellets appear shorter, have fewer flowers or pods, and their cotyledons and leaves will be more yellow-green than those grown with four fertilizer pellets.

# Nutrition Observational Exercise

**1. Measure and record plant height in the 4 quads.**

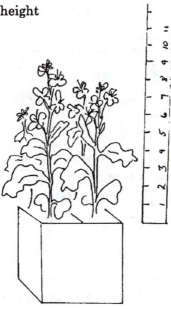

**3. Measure and record leaf length on plants in each quad.**

**2. Count and record the number of flowers per plant in each quad.**

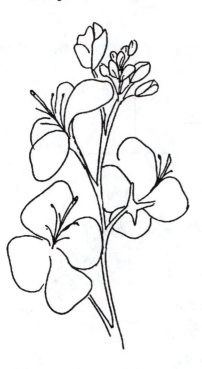
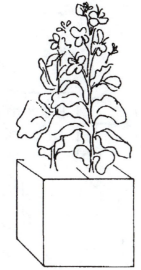

**4. Observe and record the color and condition of the leaves.**

DAILY SCIENTIST RECORD

| | QUAD 1 | QUAD 2 | QUAD 3 |
|---|---|---|---|
| Name — | | | |
| Date — | | | |
| Plant height | | | |
| Leaf length | | | |
| Numbers of flowers | | | |
| Color and condition of leaf | | | |

DAILY SCIENTIST RECORD

Name ———
Date ———

I think that the plants in the quads are different because ......

**5. List reasons for differences in appearance among the quads.**

# Student Science Exploration Flowchart

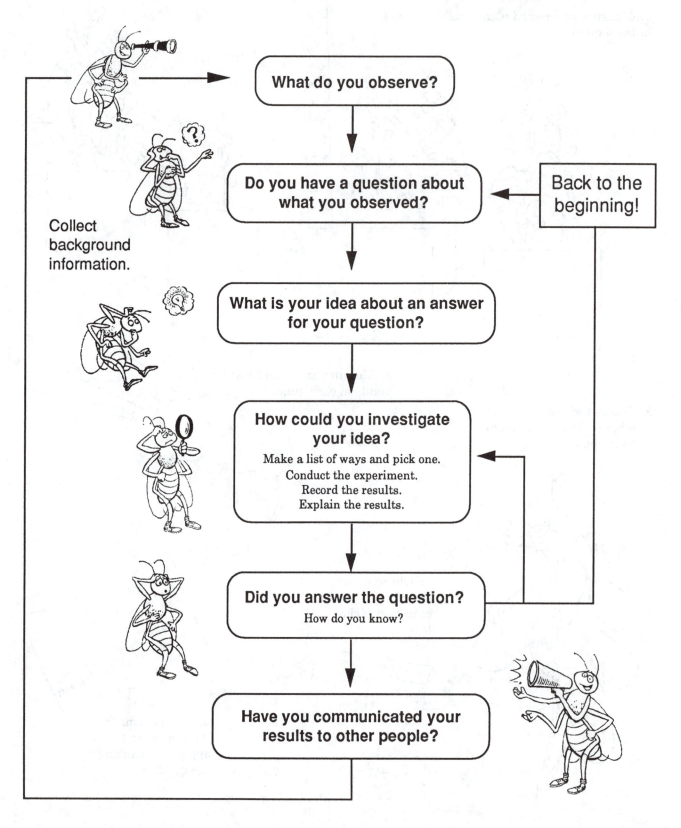

Collect background information.

What do you observe?

Do you have a question about what you observed?

Back to the beginning!

What is your idea about an answer for your question?

**How could you investigate your idea?**

Make a list of ways and pick one.
Conduct the experiment.
Record the results.
Explain the results.

**Did you answer the question?**
How do you know?

Have you communicated your results to other people?

### Asking questions

**What questions have your students raised from observing?** The students should be curious about some of the things they have observed. A class discussion should generate questions. Have your students make a list of questions. Prompt them with the words **"What if."**

**Example questions derived from the observation:**

- ● What is the ideal amount of fertilizer pellets to add to Fast Plants? (Investigation #1)
- ▲ Will Fast Plants produce seed when lots of pellets are added? (Investigation #2)
- ■ How do Fast Plants grow with other fertilizer treatments instead of fertilizer pellets? (Investigation #3)
- ◆ What would happen if you increased the number of plants in your quad or growing container? (Investigation #4)

### Forming a hypothesis

**What are your students' ideas about answers for their questions?** Following the discussion of observations, students can turn their questions into statements and write them down as hypotheses.

**Example hypotheses derived from questions:**

- ● Six to eight fertilizer pellets per cell is the ideal amount to get optimum growth in Fast Plants. (Investigation #1)
- ▲ Plants given 24 fertilizer pellets per cell will produce lots of seeds. (Investigation #2)
- ■ Plants fertilized with cow manure will grow taller and produce more foliage than plants grown with the three fertilizer pellets per cell. (Investigation #3)
- ◆ Growing two or more plants where one normally grows will result in both plants being smaller. (Investigation #4)

**Tips and suggestions:** Ask students to check the Science Exploration Flowchart to see what the next steps need to be in their science investigation.

**Testing the hypothesis**

**How could your students investigate their ideas?** Design an experiment. Devise ways to test the hypothesis, choose the best one and carry it out. Refer to worksheet "Setting Up An Experiment" (pages 41-43) for help in designing the experiments.

**Control Experiments:** A *control* serves as a standard of comparison for verifying the results of an investigation. By controlling the variable factors of the experiment, the effects of changing one variable at a time are easily observed.

**Examples of ways to test hypotheses:**

● Grow Fast Plants with various amounts of fertilizer pellets. Try a range of pellets from one to 20 per cell. How should the control be set up? (Investigation #1)

**Management Strategy:** The fertilizer pellets are time-release pellets containing a balanced mixture of 14% nitrogen, 14% phosphate and 14% potassium.

**Accompanying activity:** Pollinate all plants carefully. See "Illustrated Growing Instructions" (pages 31-32). Harvest seed from plants from each fertilizer treatment separately and plant separately. Observe to see if nutrient level of parents has any influence on size and vigor of offspring.

▲ Grow plants with 24 fertilizer pellets, pollinate and count the seeds produced. Compare results with plants grown with the recommended number (3) of fertilizer pellets (control sample). (Investigation #2)

■ Compare growth of plants with cow manure and those with three pellets of fertilizer (control). Bags of dried cow manure can be purchased at a local garden store. (Investigation #3)

**Management Strategy:** Cow manure contains nitrogen. Quantify the amount of manure used with measuring spoons. Check the bag for any information regarding nitrogen content of the manure. Try other manures, such as sheep manure, if available.

◆ Grow two or more plants per cell of your quad, using three pellets per cell. The control will be a quad with one plant per cell. (Investigation #4)

**Collect data:** See "Keeping Track of Things" (pages 23-26).

**Analyze the data:** Have the students explain the results. For example:

- One fertilizer pellet resulted in early flowering. Hint: Limiting the fertilizer usually stresses the plant into flowering earlier. Eight to sixteen pellets resulted in more and bigger leaves. Hint: Larger amounts of fertilizer, up to a certain level, result in more vegetative growth. (Investigation #1)

▲ Plants did not survive to produce seed. Hint: Adding an excess of fertilizer to plants does not produce healthier plants, but may cause plants to die. Excess fertilizer salts can be toxic to the germinating seedlings. (Investigation #2)

■ The nutrients in cow manure may have caused plants to produce more foliage and grow taller but slowed the flowering process. Hint: Added nitrogen from the cow manure causes more growth of vegetation which delays the onset of flowering. (Investigation #3)

◆ Plants are smaller than the singly grown plants. Hint: One Fast Plant grown in the cell of a quad is already under considerable stress due to the limited amount of soil and space. (Investigation #4)

**Accompanying activity:** Instead of cow manure, use the compost generated from the "Biocolumn Composting" investigation (page 211-216).

> ### Evaluating the hypothesis

**Was the hypothesis verified?** How do your students know that they know? For example: Was the test fair? Did they answer the question? Are they sure?

> ### Communicating the results

**Have your students communicated their results to others?** *No science investigation is complete until it is communicated in writing.* In addition, it can be communicated orally. Students can write their conclusions very simply, but the report should be understandable to anyone reading it, peers and teacher.

## References

### Books

Cochrane, J. 1987. *Plant Ecology*. New York: Bookwright Press. One of a series of books on ecology. Examines plants and how they are affected by other factors in the world: the sun, water, bacteria. Looks at the place of plants in the ecological scene and their future.

Pranis, E. and J. Hale. 1988. *Grow Lab, A Complete Guide to Gardening in the Classroom*. Burlington, VT: National Gardening Association. Many ideas for investigating the mysteries of growth under fluorescent lights in the classroom and integrating gardening ideas into your curriculum.

Schumann, D. N. 1980. *Living with Plants, A Guide to Practical Botany*. Eureka, CA: Mad River Press, Inc. Excellent introductory chapter for background information entitled, "Introduction to a Plant," as well as other topics such as nutrients, soils and plant hormones.

Williams, P. H. 1993. *Bottle Biology*. Dubuque, IA: Kendall/Hunt Publishing Co. An idea book for exploring the world through plastic bottles and other recyclable materials.

WFPID 8-5995-91

# Exploring Photosynthesis with Fast Plants

Every day green plants capture sunlight and convert it into chemical energy necessary for them to live and grow. This amazing process, called *photosynthesis*, is the critical link between the energy of the sun and the food and fuel we consume in our daily lives.

Most teachers who work with the concept of photosynthesis use a textbook or curriculum lesson as a base, supplemented with favorite articles and their own materials. This activity offers a hands-on laboratory investigation which can be used to explore and demonstrate this difficult concept.

This investigation uses low cost, simple materials and seed leaves (cotyledons) from 3- or 4-day old Fast Plants. When plants photosynthesize they release *oxygen* into the atmosphere. This oxygen comes from water in the cells of leaves and is initially released into spaces inside leaves (see Figure 1). The oxygen then moves from leaves into the atmosphere through small holes on the leaf surface called *stomata* (singular: stoma). In this exercise the production of oxygen is used as a measure of the rate of photosynthesis. Plants also need carbon dioxide for photosynthesis. For this investigation carbon dioxide is provided by a baking soda solution.

## Materials

- 3- or 4-day old Fast Plants seedlings
- baking soda
- small straw
- 35 mm film can
- 5 ml syringe

## Tips

Do not use too much baking soda! Use just enough to barely cover the bottom of the film can. If you use too much, bubbling will occur. The resulting bubbles will stick to the leaf discs and keep them from sinking. Add a drop of liquid soap or detergent to the baking soda solution to reduce static.

After you have created a vacuum in the syringe, some of the leaf discs may still float. This is frequently caused by bubbles stuck to the discs. These bubbles can usually be removed by sharply rapping the syringe on the edge of a desk or with your finger.

While running your experiment, tap the syringe with your finger every 20-30 seconds to dislodge discs which are ready to float but stuck to the syringe.

Remember that photosynthesis is dependent on light. For your initial experiments you may want to have the discs rise quickly (3-5 minutes). This will require that your syringes be several centimeters from the light bank lights or in direct sunlight.

## Extensions

This investigation can also allow you to explore *respiration* through the measurement of oxygen consumption. Respiration is common to all plants, animals and other organisms which live in an aerobic environment. When plants are grown in the light they usually produce more oxygen through photosynthesis than they consume through respiration. However, when plants are grown in the dark, the trapping of light by photosynthesis can no longer occur, and more oxygen is usually consumed through respiration than is produced by photosynthesis. Thus, when the syringe in this experiment is put in a dark place, or covered by a black film can, it is possible to investigate plant respiration.

White light is composed of all of the colors of the spectrum. You can investigate which of these colors is necessary for photosynthesis by covering the syringe with cylinders of different colors of plastic film. We suggest you try at least the three primary colors: red, yellow and blue.

The green color in leaves is caused by *chlorophyll*, the main pigment involved in the light capturing machinery of photosynthesis. The role of chlorophyll in photosynthesis can be explored by running these leaf disc experiments with tissue from mutant yellow-green Fast Plants.

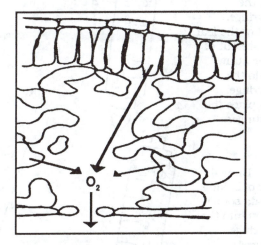

**Figure 1:** Cross section of a Fast Plants leaf

## Reference

Steucek, G. L. and R. J. Hill. 1985. Photosynthesis I: An Assay Utilizing Leaf Discs. The American Biology Teacher 47(2):96-99.

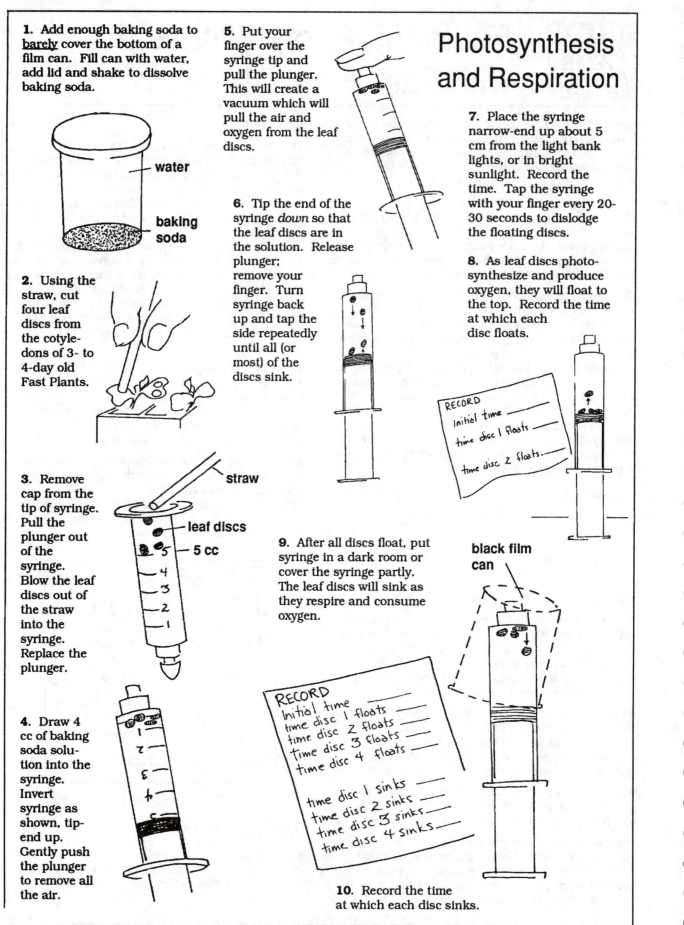

# Photosynthesis and Respiration

**1.** Add enough baking soda to <u>barely</u> cover the bottom of a film can. Fill can with water, add lid and shake to dissolve baking soda.

water

baking soda

**2.** Using the straw, cut four leaf discs from the cotyledons of 3- to 4-day old Fast Plants.

**3.** Remove cap from the tip of syringe. Pull the plunger out of the syringe. Blow the leaf discs out of the straw into the syringe. Replace the plunger.

straw

leaf discs

5 cc

**4.** Draw 4 cc of baking soda solution into the syringe. Invert syringe as shown, tip-end up. Gently push the plunger to remove all the air.

**5.** Put your finger over the syringe tip and pull the plunger. This will create a vacuum which will pull the air and oxygen from the leaf discs.

**6.** Tip the end of the syringe *down* so that the leaf discs are in the solution. Release plunger; remove your finger. Turn syringe back up and tap the side repeatedly until all (or most) of the discs sink.

**7.** Place the syringe narrow-end up about 5 cm from the light bank lights, or in bright sunlight. Record the time. Tap the syringe with your finger every 20-30 seconds to dislodge the floating discs.

**8.** As leaf discs photosynthesize and produce oxygen, they will float to the top. Record the time at which each disc floats.

RECORD
Initial time ____
time disc 1 floats ____
time disc 2 floats ____

**9.** After all discs float, put syringe in a dark room or cover the syringe partly. The leaf discs will sink as they respire and consume oxygen.

black film can

RECORD
Initial time ____
time disc 1 floats ____
time disc 2 floats ____
time disc 3 floats ____
time disc 4 floats ____

time disc 1 sinks ____
time disc 2 sinks ____
time disc 3 sinks ____
time disc 4 sinks ____

**10.** Record the time at which each disc sinks.

# Chapter 8: Bioassays with Fast Plants

**The students will observe the effects of detergent on the germination of Fast Plant seeds by using serial dilutions of liquid detergent with water as the control.** This can be a stand-alone observational exercise. The steps of each chapter are consistent with the boxed steps of the Science Exploration Flowchart. You can develop a complete scientific investigation using the questions your students ask as a result of this observational exercise. Some examples for complete scientific investigations are provided and identified by following specific icons; ●, ▲, ■ and ◆. If you don't have time to complete a full investigation, you might plan to continue with it later in the year.

## Background Information for the Teacher

Determining the effects of substances in the environment on living organisms can be accomplished using a *bioassay*. A substance found in the environment is tested at various concentrations with a living organism to determine what concentrations are beneficial or harmful to the organism. The pharmaceutical industry evaluates new medicines by measuring the quantity of a drug that results in a defined *effective dose*, or *ED*. One standard measurement of toxicity of a substance is the $LD_{50}$, the *lethal dosage* that causes the death of fifty percent of the organisms exposed.

The most common $LD_{50}$ is the *acute oral toxicity*, that is, the single internal dosage of a material necessary to kill half the test organisms. These $LD_{50}$ values are expressed in milligrams of chemical per kilogram of body weight. Therefore, the lower the $LD_{50}$ value for a substance, the greater the toxicity. The United States Environmental Protection Agency (EPA) has begun to test the toxic effects of materials in the environment on plants. A simple bioassay to set up with plants is to look at the effects of a substance on seed germination.

## Teaching Objectives

**Beginning Concept:** Specific substances in the environment can affect the germination of seeds.

**Advanced Concept:** Acceptable levels of potentially harmful substances can be determined by means of a bioassay.

**Preparation and Planning for Observational Exercise**

**Time required:** 1 hour preparation; 3-4 days observation and discussion, 15 minutes per day.

> **Materials needed per student/team:**
> - 14 Fast Plants seeds
> - 7 clear plastic 35 mm film cans
> - 1 one pound cottage cheese container with lid
> - 7 wicks made of strips of paper towel, 1.5 cm wide and 5 cm long
> - water
> - 10% liquid detergent solution (1 part detergent, 9 parts water)

**Tips and suggestions**

- Students will make dilutions of the 10% detergent solution. Seeds will most likely germinate only if the dilution is great enough so that few if any bubbles form in the diluted solution.
- A local film processing outlet or camera store is the source of the film cans. Ask them to save the film cans for you, since they are usually discarded.
- An alternative method of designating the dilutions or concentrations of the substance being assayed would be to have the students mark the full strength solution as 'x,' and successive dilutions — each reduced by 1/2 — as x/2, x/4, x/8, x/16 and x/32.

# Bioassays with Fast Plants Observational Exercise

1. Mark the 7 cans at the half-full line with a permanent marker. Label one film can "water." The "water" can is the control. Label the other 6 cans as shown.

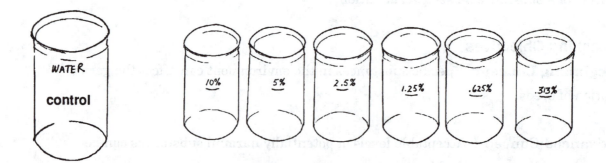

**2.** Fill the "water" can to the mark with water. Insert a wick by gently pushing the strip down the side of the can with the end of a pencil. The wick will stick to the sides of the can. Place two seeds at the top of the wick.

**3.** Make a mark on the other six film cans halfway between the first mark and the bottom of the can.

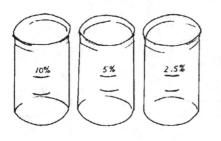

**4.** Fill the 10% can to the top mark (half-full) with the 10% liquid detergent solution. This is approximately 20 ml.

**10% detergent**

**5.** Pour half of the detergent from the 10% can into the 5% can. Add water to the 5% can to the half-full mark. The 5% can now contains a 5% detergent solution.

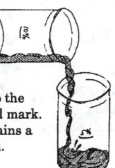

**6.** Making sure the liquid in the 5% can is completely mixed, pour half into the 2.5% can. Add water to the 2.5% can to the half-full mark, making a 2.5% solution.

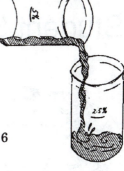

**7.** Repeat this procedure until all 6 cans are prepared.

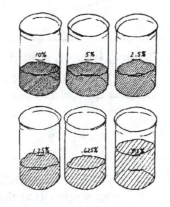

**9.** Place the 6 cans inside the cottage cheese container around the edge. Place the "water" can in the center.

**8.** Insert wicks in all 6 cans. When the wicks are moist at the top, place two seeds on each wick.

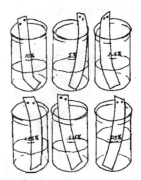

**10.** Secure the lid on the container and label your container with your name and the date.

**11.** Observe each day for the next 3-4 days and record observations.

# Student Science Exploration Flowchart

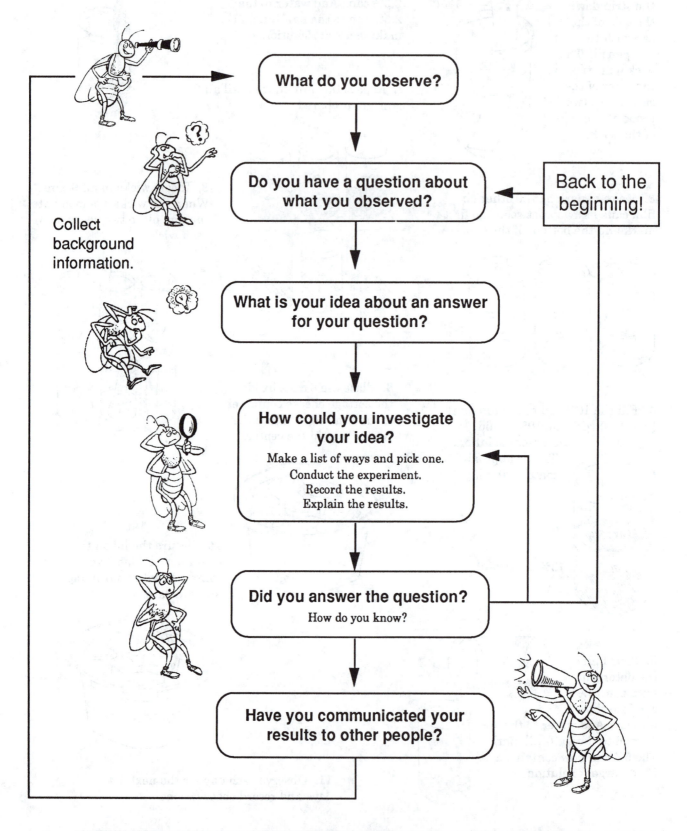

Collect background information.

What do you observe?

Do you have a question about what you observed?

Back to the beginning!

What is your idea about an answer for your question?

How could you investigate your idea?

Make a list of ways and pick one.
Conduct the experiment.
Record the results.
Explain the results.

Did you answer the question?
How do you know?

Have you communicated your results to other people?

## The Effects of Detergent on Seed Germination

> **Making observations**

**Some preliminary questions:** Begin your exploration by asking your students some questions and discussing ideas they might have about germination.

**As you conduct the observational exercise illustrated on pages 150-151**, your students will observe that germination is a continuing developmental process involving seed swelling, root and stem emergence and cotyledon spreading. Students will need to determine what stage of germination they will use to identify whether a seed has germinated. Many substances influence the rate of germination. Therefore, observations should be done at a particular, specified time during the experiment, at 48 hours, etc. See the Germination Observational Exercise (page 47).

> **Asking questions**

**What questions have your students raised from observing?** The students should be curious about some of the things they have observed. A class discussion should generate questions. Have your students make a list of questions. Prompt them with the words **"What if."**

**Example questions derived from observations:**
- ● What other liquids might affect seed germination? (Investigation #1)
- ▲ How does liquid plant food affect seed germination? (Investigation #2)

> **Forming a hypothesis**

**What are your students' ideas about answers for their questions?** Following the discussion of observations, students can turn their questions into statements and write them down as hypotheses.

**Example hypotheses derived from questions:**
- ● Orange juice is toxic to germinating seeds (other substances to assay: soft drinks, catsup, salt solutions, sugar solutions). (Investigation #1)
- ▲ Liquid plant food is not toxic to germinating seeds. (Investigation #2)

**Tips and suggestions:**

- If you use a volatile substance for the bioassay, such as vinegar or gasoline, each film can must be individually covered with clear plastic wrap and secured with a rubber band. If not covered, evaporation from one container may contaminate the others.

- Have the students check the Science Exploration Flowchart to see what the next steps need to be in their science problem solving.

| Testing the hypothesis |

**How could your students investigate their ideas?** Design an experiment. Devise ways to test the hypothesis, choose the best one and carry it out. Refer worksheet "Setting Up An Experiment" (pages 41-43) for help in designing the experiments.

**Control Experiments:** *A control* serves as a standard of comparison for verifying the results of an investigation. By controlling the variable factors of the experiment, the effects of changing one variable at a time are easily observed.

**Examples of ways to test hypotheses:**
- ● Use dilutions of orange juice in the film cans with water as the control. (Investigation #1)
- ▲ Use dilutions of plant food in the film cans with water as the control. (Investigation #2)

**Collect data:** See "Keeping Track of Things" (pages 23-26).

**Analyze the data:** Have the students explain the results. For example:
- ● Seeds do not germinate in full strength orange juice. Hint: Could citric acid be affecting germination? (Investigation #1)
- ▲ Plant food was probably toxic to the germinating seeds in all concentrations. Salts in the plant food are very toxic. Hint: Slow release fertilizer is used to grow Fast Plants to avoid the toxic salts. How much more dilute would the fertilizer have to be to avoid toxic effects on seed germination? Is there a dilution where the fertilizer would actually be beneficial to germination? (Investigation #2)

## Evaluating the hypothesis

**Was the hypothesis verified?** How do your students know that they know? For example: Was the test fair? Did they answer the question? Are they sure?

## Communicating the results

**Have your students communicated their results to others?** *No science investigation is complete until it is communicated in writing.* In addition, it can be communicated orally. Students can write their conclusions very simply, but the report should be understandable to anyone reading it, peers and teacher.

## References

### Books

Cochrane, J. 1987. *Plant Ecology*. New York: Bookwright Press. One of a series of books on ecology. Examines plants and how they are affected by other factors in the world: the sun, water, bacteria. Looks at the place of plants in the ecological scene and their future.

Williams, P. H. 1993. *Bottle Biology*. Dubuque, IA: Kendall/Hunt Publishing Co. An idea book full of ways to use recyclable materials to teach about science and the environment.

# Chapter 9: Tropisms

**The students will germinate seedlings and observe the effects of gravity and light on the orientation of plant parts.** This can be a stand-alone observational exercise. The steps of each chapter are consistent with the boxed steps of the Science Exploration Flowchart. You can develop a complete scientific investigation using the questions your students ask as a result of this observational exercise. Some examples for complete scientific investigations are provided and identified by following specific icons; ●, ▲, ■ and ◆. If you don't have time to complete a full investigation, you might plan to continue with it later in the year.

## Background Information for the Teacher

Plant growth involves cell division and cell enlargement. These processes are regulated by growth promoting hormones and growth inhibitor chemicals. As the plant grows, the balance between hormones and inhibitors is continually changing. The plant's response to gravity is known as *gravitropism* (the old term was geotropism). The response of the growing shoot to grow away from gravity is called *negative gravitropism*. The response of the root, to grow toward gravity, is called *positive gravitropism*. Downward growth of roots and upward growth of the shoot make sense for a plant to survive. How plants do this is just beginning to be understood.

The gravitropic response in plants is largely controlled by a group of growth promoting hormones called *auxins* and by inhibitors of auxins. This effect can be seen by turning a plant on its side. Auxins stimulate cell elongation in the cells on the lower side of the shoot causing it to bend up (away from gravity), but in the roots, cells on the upper side elongate causing the roots to grow down (toward gravity).

A similar response causes the shoot of the plant to bend toward light. This response is called *phototropism*. An unequal distribution of auxins and inhibitors on the side of the plant away from the light stimulates cell enlargement on the "dark" side of the plant, resulting in the plant bending toward the light. The growth of a plant toward light (sun) is an advantageous response in a photosynthetic organism.

## Teaching Objectives

**Beginning Objectives:**

- Plants of all ages respond to gravity and light.
- The growing shoot of a plant has a negative response to gravity.
- Root tips have a positive response to gravity.
- The growing shoot of a plant has a positive response to light.

## Preparation and Planning for Observational Exercise

**Time required:** 4 to 5 days.

### Tips and suggestions

- Set up the experiment on a Monday morning. Make observations on Thursday or Friday.
- As an alternative, do this experiment subsequent to the Germination Observational Exercise (page 47). Use the young seedlings in the petri dishes from the germination experiment and begin at step 8 of the Tropisms Observational Exercise (page 159).
- Use the circle grid as described on page 52 as a tool for gauging seedling response to gravity.
- Forceps for placing seed can be made from a plastic milk container. Placing black vinyl electrical tape on the inside of one tip of the forceps prevents seeds from slipping, or, instead of using the tape, the forceps tips can be dipped in water before picking up seed.

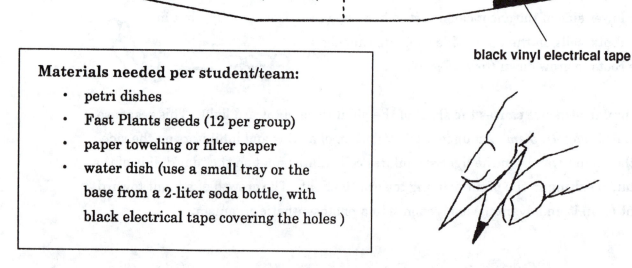

(actual size)

black vinyl electrical tape

**Materials needed per student/team:**

- petri dishes
- Fast Plants seeds (12 per group)
- paper toweling or filter paper
- water dish (use a small tray or the base from a 2-liter soda bottle, with black electrical tape covering the holes )

# Tropisms Observational Exercise

**1. Cut two layers of paper towels to fit in the cover (larger half) of a petri dish.**

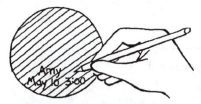

**2. With a pencil, label the bottom of the paper towel with your name, the date and the time.**

**3. On a Monday or a Tuesday morning, moisten the towels in the petri dish with an eye dropper.**

**4. Place two rows of six Fast Plants seeds (12) on the top half of the towel and cover with the bottom (smaller half) of the petri dish.**

water level

**5. Place petri dish at an angle in shallow water in the base of a two-liter soda bottle or in a tray so that the bottom 2 cm of the towel is below the water's surface.**

**6. Set experiment in a warm location (optimum temperature: 65-80°F). Record the day and time of setting up the experiment.**

**7. Over the next 3-4 days *check the water level to be sure the paper toweling stays wet.***

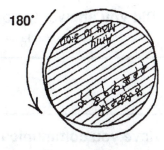

180°

**8. After initial observations on Day 4 or 5, rotate the dish 180°. Place back in tray as shown above. Water should not be touching the plants.**

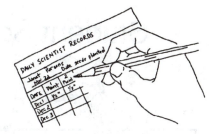

**9. Record observations after one hour.**

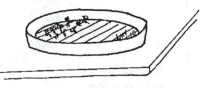

**10. Keeping the lid on the petri dish, place the dish flat on a table. After one hour, record observations.**

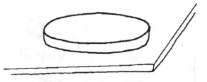

**11. Finally, turn the dish upside down on the flat surface. After one hour, record observations.**

**12. What other arrangements of the dish could you try?**

# Student Science Exploration Flowchart

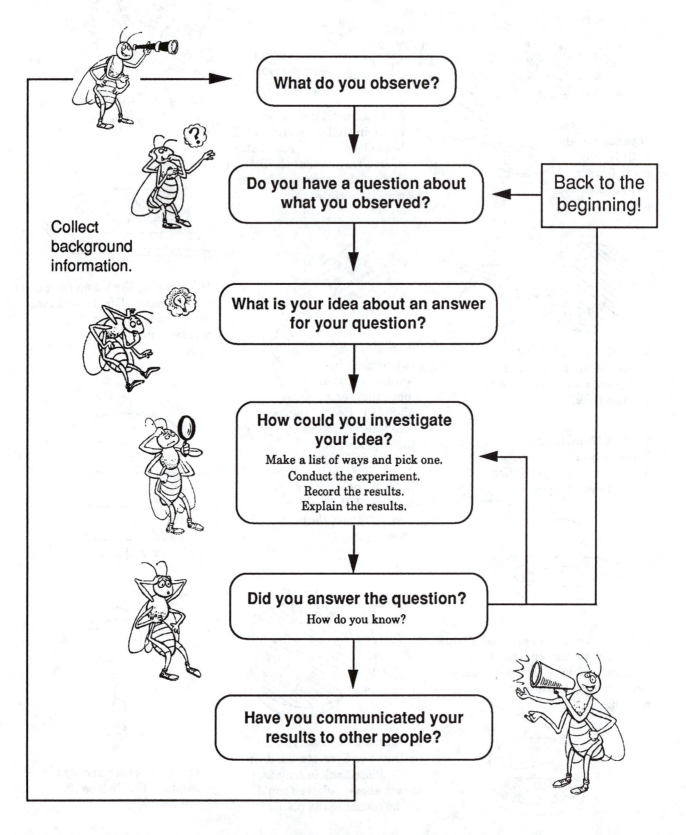

What do you observe?

Do you have a question about what you observed?

Back to the beginning!

Collect background information.

What is your idea about an answer for your question?

How could you investigate your idea?

Make a list of ways and pick one.
Conduct the experiment.
Record the results.
Explain the results.

Did you answer the question?
How do you know?

Have you communicated your results to other people?

- **Alternative Procedural Method:** Use a deep peanut butter jar lid or something smaller instead of a petri dish. After "planting," cover the lid with clear plastic wrap and secure with a rubber band. Punch one or two small holes at bottom of plastic wrap to let in water.

## When Plants Grow Up

**Making observations**

**Some preliminary questions:** Begin your exploration by asking your students some questions and discussing ideas they might have about plants and why they grow up.

**As you conduct the observational exercise illustrated on page 159,** your students will observe seed germination and swelling; seed coat splitting; root emergence and downward orientation; growth of root hairs, shoot emergence and upward orientation, cotyledon emergence and turning green. Students will also observe roots and shoots bending when they are reoriented with respect to gravity.

**Asking questions**

**What questions have your students raised from observing?** The students should be curious about some of the things they have observed. A class discussion should generate questions. Have your students make a list of questions. Prompt them with the words **"What if."**

**Example questions derived from the observation:**
- ● Without light, would plants grow up? (Investigation #1)
- ▲ Do plants respond to light and to gravity? (Investigation #2)
- ■ Do roots grow down because of gravity? (Investigation #3)
- ◆ Do plants prefer certain colors of light? (Investigation #4)

**Forming a hypothesis**

**What are your students' ideas about answers for their questions?** Following the discussion of observations, students can turn their questions into statements and write them down as hypotheses.

**Example hypotheses derived from questions:**

● Plants will grow in different directions without light. (Investigation #1)

▲ The growing shoot responds to light, but not to gravity. (Investigation #2)

■ Roots always grow towards the source of gravity. (Investigation #3)

◆ Plants grow toward green light. (Investigation #4)

**Tips and suggestions:** Ask students to check the Science Exploration Flowchart to see what the next steps need to be in their science investigation.

| Testing the hypothesis |
|---|

**How could your students investigate their ideas?** Devise ways to test the hypothesis, choose the best one and carry it out. Refer to worksheet "Setting Up An Experiment" (pages 41-43) for help in designing the experiments.

**Control Experiments:** A *control* serves as a standard of comparison for verifying the results of an investigation. By controlling the variable factors of the experiment, the effects of changing one variable at a time are easily observed. Discuss with your students what would be a suitable control for each of the following investigations.

**Examples of ways to test hypotheses:**

**Figure 1**

**Figure 2**

● Germinate Fast Plants seeds in the absence of light. Use a black 35 mm film can and paper toweling to make a "tropism chamber." Place two strips of paper toweling, approximately 1 cm wide, on the sides of the film can. Overlap the strips onto the bottom of the canister. Moisten both strips of paper toweling well, leaving enough water to cover the bottom of the film canister (Figure 1). Place seeds on the paper toweling strips. The seeds will stick. Snap canister lid on tightly and set in upright position (Figure 2). Observe after two to three days.

**Alternative method:** Set up petri dishes as shown in the Tropisms Observational Exercise (page 159). Wrap them in aluminum foil or place them in the dark. (Investigation #1)

**Management Strategy:** After 24 hours, make observations several times over the next 48 hours. The seeds can be knocked off the paper toweling by sharp taps to the can or rough handling. Try not to disturb the can when removing the lid for observations. Seedling tips should grow upward, away from gravity.

▲ Germinate Fast Plants seeds in a dark chamber. See Figures 3 and 4 for how to prepare the film can chamber. To set up the chamber, place two strips (approximately 1 cm wide) of paper towel on the sides of the film can, overlapping the strips onto the bottom of the canister. Moisten both strips of paper toweling well, leaving enough water to cover the bottom of the film canister. Place seeds on the paper toweling strips; the seeds will stick. Snap canister lid on tightly and set in upright

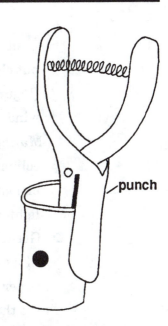

Figure 3: Punch one hole near top of black film canister.

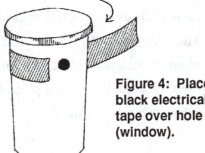

Figure 4: Place black electrical tape over hole (window).

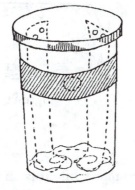

Figure 5: Chamber with black tape.

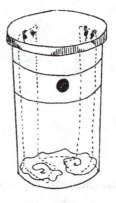

Figure 6: Chamber with clear cellophane tape.

position (Figure 5). After three days, remove black tape from the window, put clear cellophane tape over the window and place the seedlings in light (Figure 6). Twenty-four hours later, observe results. Replace black tape over window and observe again 24 hours later. (Investigation #2)

**Management Strategy:** Imagine the growing shoot as made up of two columns of cells, one on the dark side and one on the light side. As the cells elongated on the dark side more than the light side, the tip bends toward the lighted side. Allow about 5 days for this investigation.

■ Germinate seeds in a dark chamber with the lid on top. Use a black 35 mm film can and paper toweling to make a "tropism chamber." Place two strips of paper toweling, approximately 1 cm wide, on the sides of the film can. Overlap the strips onto the bottom of the canister. Moisten both strips of paper toweling well, leaving enough water to cover the bottom of the film canister (Figure 7). Place seeds on the paper toweling strips. The seeds will stick. Snap canister lid on tightly and set in upright position (Figure 8). Observe 24 hours later. After three days, pour out excess water. Then turn chamber on its side as shown in Figure 9. Stabilize the chamber so it won't roll over. Mark the top with tape or marker so that it will always be repositioned in the same orientation. After 24 hours with the chamber on its side, observe by removing the lid. Use a pipet to add some water to the toweling to keep it moist. (Investigation #3)

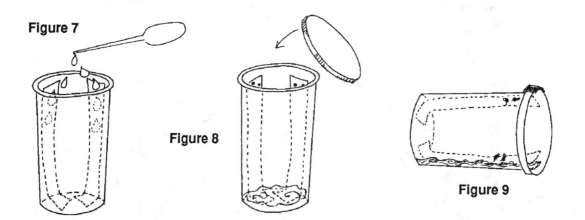

**Figure 7**

**Figure 8**

**Figure 9**

**Management Strategy:** To stabilize the chamber while it is on its side, place double-stick tape on the outside of the can at the location of one of the towel strips. The tape will stick to the table top.

◆ Punch three windows near top of black film canister at approximately 120°

intervals (Figure 10). With clear scotch tape, tape different colors of transparent film (such as the colored mylar
filters used in theater lighting) over each window of the
tropism chamber (Figure 11). Put seed on three wet
strips of paper toweling placed between the windows. Be
sure that there is a thin film of water on bottom of canister. Snap canister lid on tightly and place in an upright
position. Observe which window plants bend toward.
Hint: Use red, green and blue. (Investigation #4)
**Management Strategy:** Place the can under the light
bank so that light diffuses from above to all the windows
equally. Four days are needed for this investigation.

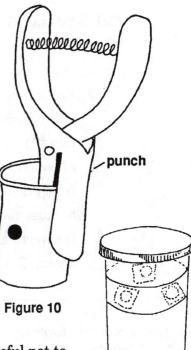

**Figure 10**

**Figure 11**

**Tips and suggestions for tropism chambers:**

- Check and maintain moisture on the wicks daily but be careful not to
  disturb your seedlings.
- Cut strips of overhead transparency sheets slightly smaller than the
  paper toweling wick strips. Wet transparency sheet strips will adhere to the
  wick strips on one side and to the inside of the film can on the other, providing a middle layer of "backbone" for the otherwise floppy wet wick strips.
  This will make it easier to place the seed on the wet wick strips and to guide
  them down into the film can and, later, to check the germinating seed and/or
  seedlings.

**Suggestions for additional investigations:**

- Set up a tropism chamber as described in Investigation #1. Empty excess
  water out of chamber and snap lid on tight. Using sticky-backed velcro,
  attach the side of the tropism chamber to the minute hand of a large wall
  clock, lining up the paper towel strip so that it's parallel to the minute hand.
  Observe after 72 hours. Sketch the roots' growth patterns.
- Use quads of plants and place them on their side in both light and dark. Try
  this with various ages of plants and record the time to respond.
- Construct a chamber with only one window. Place the chamber window-side
  down. Allow some light to enter the window.
- Make a "Hypocotyl Hypothesis" and set up tropism chambers with cut seedlings (pages 168-169).

**Collect data:** See "Keeping Track of Things" (pages 23-26).

**Analyze the data:** Have the students explain the results. For example:

● Fast Plants grew up in the dark, just as if they were under the light. Hint: Growing tip of plant has grown up, away from gravity. (Investigation #1)

▲ Shoots respond to both gravity and light. Hint: Plants grow up away from gravity in the dark. With light, they appear to bend toward the window because the cells elongate on the darker side of the plant. When the window is covered again and the light factor eliminated, plants will grow straight up again. (Investigation #2)

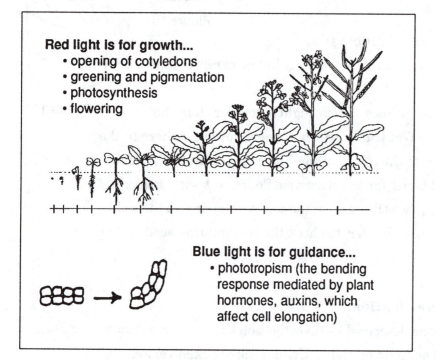

**Red light is for growth...**
• opening of cotyledons
• greening and pigmentation
• photosynthesis
• flowering

**Blue light is for guidance...**
• phototropism (the bending response mediated by plant hormones, auxins, which affect cell elongation)

■ Roots bend toward gravity. (Investigation #3)

◆ Fast Plants bend toward blue light in preference to red or green light, and prefer green over red. Hint: A yellow pigment of plants [not chlorophyll] absorbs mainly blue light. This activates bending toward the light source through the action of auxin, a plant hormone. (Investigation #4)

**Evaluating the hypothesis**

**Was the hypothesis verified?** How do your students know that they know? For example: Was the test fair? Did they answer the question? Are they sure?

## Communicating the results

**Have your students communicated their results to others?** *No science investigation is complete until it is communicated in writing.* In addition, it also can be communicated orally. Students can write their conclusions very simply, but the report should be understandable to anyone reading it, peers and teacher.

## References

### Books

Hunken, J. and the New England Wild Flower Society. 1989. *Botany for All Ages*. Chester, CT: Globe Pequot Press. Activity-oriented botany for inquisitive children and adults, approached from the principles of observation and experimentation.

National Council for Agricultural Education. 1994. *Using Fast Plants and Bottle Biology in the Classroom*. Reston, VA: National Association of Biology Teachers. A teacher manual including background information and 12 detailed lessons incorporating agricultural and biological science.

Stockley, C. 1986. *Dictionary of Biology (Usborne Illustrated)*. London: Usborne Publishing, Ltd. A densely illustrated, clear guide to key terms and subject areas of plants and animals.

Suzuki, D. and B. Hehner. 1985. *Looking at Plants*. Toronto, Canada: Stoddart Publishing Co., Ltd. A tour through the plant world in clear and interesting language for students, plus short and long term projects.

Williams, P. H. 1993. *Bottle Biology*. Dubuque, IA: Kendall/Hunt Publishing Co. An idea book for exploring the world through plastic bottles and other recyclable materials.

Wisconsin Fast Plants. 1995. *Plants Know the Way to Grow*. An information document, available from Wisconsin Fast Plants, UW-Madison, Dept. of Plant Pathology, 1630 Linden Drive, Madison, WI 53706.

Wisconsin Fast Plants. 1988. *Do Fast Plants Prefer the Blues?* An information document, available from Wisconsin Fast Plants, UW-Madison, Dept. of Plant Pathology, 1630 Linden Drive, Madison, WI 53706.

### Films and videos

*Growth of Plants*. 1962. Encyclopedia Britannica. Film - 21 minutes. An older but excellent film on the dynamics of plant growth, cell division, elongation, differentiation and the effects of various stimuli and hormones on plant growth. Appropriate for intermediate students.

# The Hypocotyl Hypothesis

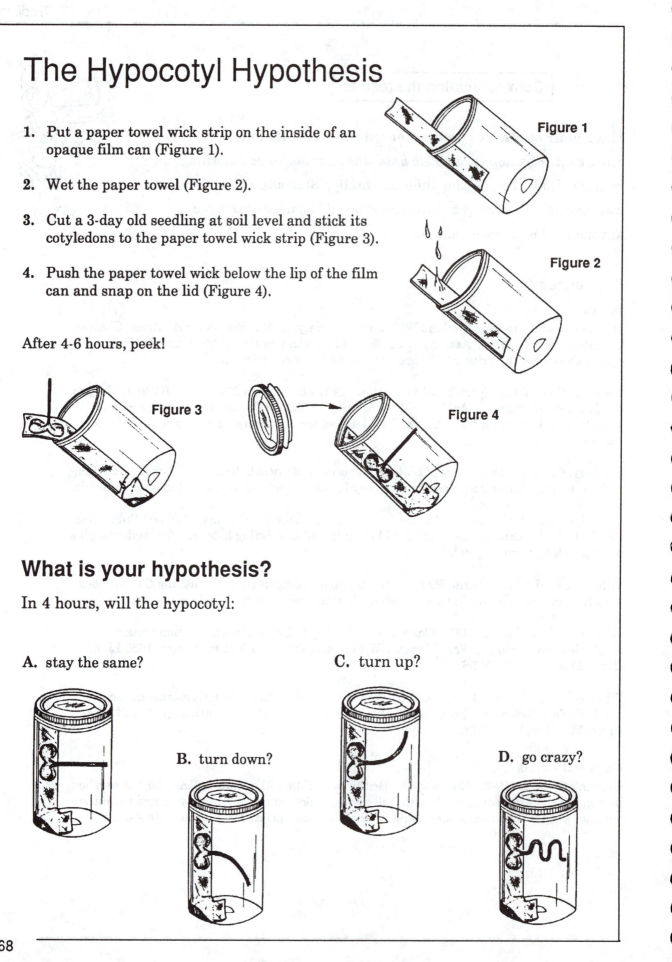

1. Put a paper towel wick strip on the inside of an opaque film can (Figure 1).

2. Wet the paper towel (Figure 2).

3. Cut a 3-day old seedling at soil level and stick its cotyledons to the paper towel wick strip (Figure 3).

4. Push the paper towel wick below the lip of the film can and snap on the lid (Figure 4).

After 4-6 hours, peek!

**Figure 1**

**Figure 2**

**Figure 3**

**Figure 4**

## What is your hypothesis?

In 4 hours, will the hypocotyl:

**A.** stay the same?

**C.** turn up?

**B.** turn down?

**D.** go crazy?

# The Crucifer Cross
## Gravitropism Revisited

Despite ongoing research efforts by plant physiologists there is still much to learn and study in the area of plant responses to gravity, or *gravitropism*. For this very reason we feel that this is an excellent topic for students to explore.

This activity utilizes both the rapid response time of Wisconsin Fast Plants to changes in the environment and the microtechnology of Bottle Biology in film cans. Two to three hours after setting up your film can gravitropism chamber you should be able to observe results which will keep you wondering!

## Materials

- 35 mm opaque film can with lid
- extra film can lid
- double-stick foam tape (poster mounting tape)
- eye dropper or small pipette
- paper toweling (ScotTowels™ work well)
- 3-day old Fast Plants seedlings

## Chamber Construction and Tips

1. Tape a film can lid to the side of a film can using the double stick foam tape. This lid acts as a pedestal for the can, allowing it to sit on its side without rolling around.

2. Fold and cut a piece of paper towel to produce small wick strips which are approximately 4.5 cm long and 1 cm wide.

3. Pre-moisten four wicks with several drops of water and place them along the inner sides of the film can so that there is one wick each on the top, bottom and both sides of the can when

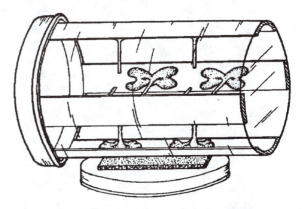

**Figure 1:** Film can gravitropism chamber

it is placed on its pedestal. Each wick can be slid in and out of the can by gently pushing or pulling it with the sharp tip of a pen or pencil.

4. Cut eight 3-day old Fast Plants seedlings at soil level leaving the small stem *(hypocotyl)* and seed leaves *(cotyledons)* intact. Stick two of these seedlings onto each wick by placing the cotyledons against the wick. The water on the wick should hold the seedling in place. If the plant is reluctant to stick, you may need to add an additional drop of water on the wick.

5. Add a couple of drops of water to the bottom of the film can when all of the plants are in place and put a lid on the can. Make sure the ends of the wicks don't protrude out of the can. The extra drops of water in the can should keep the air in the can moist. This will prevent the wicks from drying out.

6. Place the chamber in a warm (but not hot) location, a Fast Plants light bank works well. After 2 to 4 hours, gently remove the lid and observe the orientation of the hypocotyls. Continue your observations for the next five to seven days. Keep your eye out for new growth of your seedlings!

Note: This construction is called "The Crucifer Cross" because Fast Plants belong to the botanical family of crucifers and the seedlings in your film can form a four-way cross.

**Figure 2:** Cross-section view of chamber

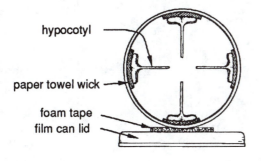

hypocotyl

paper towel wick

foam tape
film can lid

# Chapter 10: Modifying the Atmosphere

**Students will explore the effects of repeated exposure of Fast Plants to cigarette smoke.** Further investigations examine the effects of other chemicals introduced into the plant's atmosphere. This can be a stand-alone observational exercise. The steps of each chapter are consistent with the boxed steps of the Science Exploration Flowchart. You can develop a complete scientific investigation using the questions your students ask as a result of this observational exercise. Some examples for complete scientific investigations are provided and identified by following specific icons; ●, ▲, ■ and ◆. If you don't have time to complete a full investigation, you might plan to continue with it later in the year.

## Background Information for the Teacher

With the explosion of human populations on Earth, industrialization and urbanization, human activity has resulted in major modifications in the global atmosphere. Evidence of these modifications is apparent in the health of plants in many parts of the globe. Investigations of the effect of modifying the Fast Plants environment using smoke from burning tobacco, or some other atmospheric pollutant, provides an opportunity for investigating the influence of environmental pollution.

What might be the effect of daily exposure of the plants to tobacco smoke? The plants may be affected differently, depending on their age, e.g., young plants (3-7 days old) demonstrate the greatest effect by wilting, leaves yellowing and eventual death while older plants (14-20 days old) will slow down in their growth cycles and some leaves will turn yellow.

## Teaching Objectives

**Beginning Concept:** Chemicals introduced into the environment of a plant may modify the growth of a plant.

## Preparation and Planning for Observational Exercise

**Time required:** 7 days prior, advance preparation of plants by teacher; 15 minutes a day for 5 consecutive days.

**Materials needed per student/team:**
- 2 environmental chambers made from two-liter clear soda bottles
- 2 quads of 7-day old Fast Plants
- 2 noncombustible saucers or plates
- masking tape
- marking pen
- chart for recording observations

**Tips and suggestions:**
- Cigarettes should not be a low tar, filtered cigarette.
- The cigarette inside the smoke chamber may go out before the five minute "treatment" is up. The smoke that is already in the chamber should be sufficient.
- An alternative to using the paper clip holder is to prop up the burning cigarette on a small lump of modeling clay.

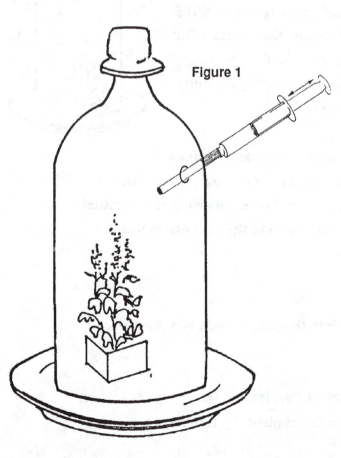

Figure 1

- An alternative method of introducing cigarette smoke into the bottle would be to first melt a small, round hole in the side or bottom edge of the bottle. Then push a cigarette onto the end of a 5cc syringe and light the cigarette (Figure 1). Put the burning tip into the hole. Pumping the plunger of the syringe back and forth will force the cigarette smoke into the chamber. Note: Syringes without needles can be purchased at a drug store.

# Modifying the Atmosphere Observational Exercise

**1.** Fill the bottle with hot water and replace cap. The heat will melt the glue and allow you to peel off the label and twist off the base. Remove cap; pour out water.

**2.** Replace the cap on the bottle. Turn the bottle on its side against a solid object, such as the side of a drawer. Mark a ring on the bottle just below the flared area at the bottom of the bottle.

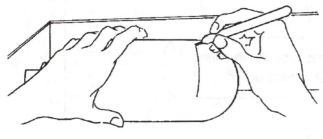

**3.** Using a razor blade or sharp knife, poke a hole along the ring mark and cut along the mark one or two inches. Insert scissors in the hole and cut along the mark to remove the bottom of the bottle. Place the chamber on a noncombustible plate.

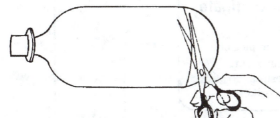

**4.** Construct a second environmental chamber. Place a quad of 7-day old plants in each.

**5.** Make a cigarette holder from a large (2 inch) paper clip. Bend the outside end of the paper clip upwards at a 45° angle as shown. Push cigarette onto the end of the paper clip.

**6.** Make sure the cigarette/clip balances. If it tends to fall over, adjust the angle of the paper clip. Light the cigarette.

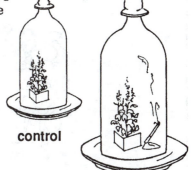

**7.** Place the burning cigarette/clip on the saucer inside one of the chambers. The chamber without the cigarette is the control. Leave the plants in their chambers for 5 minutes.

**control**

**experimental**

**8.** Remove plants from chambers and record your observations. Repeat this procedure for 5 days. Record observations each day.

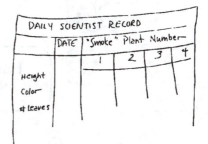

DAILY SCIENTIST RECORD

| | DATE | "Smoke" Plant Number | | | |
|---|---|---|---|---|---|
| | | 1 | 2 | 3 | 4 |
| Height | | | | | |
| Color | | | | | |
| # leaves | | | | | |

# Student Science Exploration Flowchart

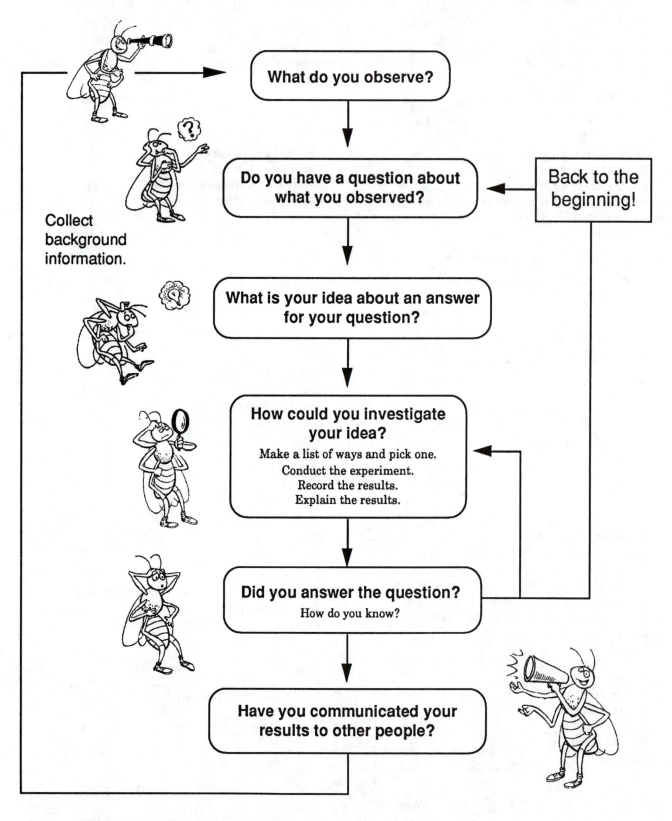

Collect
background
information.

What do you observe?

Do you have a question about
what you observed?

Back to the
beginning!

What is your idea about an answer
for your question?

How could you investigate
your idea?

Make a list of ways and pick one.
Conduct the experiment.
Record the results.
Explain the results.

Did you answer the question?

How do you know?

Have you communicated your
results to other people?

## Effects of Tobacco Smoke on Fast Plants

### Making observations

**Some preliminary questions:** Begin your exploration by asking your
students some questions and discussing ideas they might have about seeds
and germination.

**As you conduct the observational exercise illustrated on page 173,** your students will observe the effects that cigarette smoke has on their developing plants.
Watch for differences in leaf color and in the stages of maturity of developing flowers,
as compared with the control plants.

### Asking questions

**What questions have your students raised from observing?** The
students should be curious about some of the things they have observed. A
class discussion should generate questions. Have your students make a list of
questions. Prompt them with the words **"What if."**

**Example questions derived from observations:**
- What other burning materials might affect a plant's growth?
  (Investigation #1)
- ▲ What chemicals might affect a plant's growth? (Investigation #2)
- ◆ What would happen to the plants if, instead of subjecting them to cigarette
  smoke, chewing tobacco were added to the soil? (Investigation #3)

### Forming a hypothesis

**What are your students' ideas about answers for their questions?**
Following the discussion of observations, students can turn their questions
into statements and write them down as hypotheses.

**Example hypotheses derived from questions:**
- Burning charcoal or dry leaves or wood next to Fast Plants will make
  the plants grow better. (Investigation #1)

▲ Perfume or hair spray will slow down growth of Fast Plants.
(Investigation #2)

◆ Adding chewing tobacco to the soil will stunt the plants' growth.
(Investigation #3)

**Other possible chemicals to test in the classroom:**

· Incense, ammonia (diluted), bleach (diluted), ditto fluid, plastic cement, peppermint oil, dry ice.

· **Alternative Procedural Method:** Take the constructed bottle chamber setup and melt a hole in the side near the top (see Figure 1, page 172). Use a Pyrex® test tube that has been heated in a flame to melt a hole in the plastic. Chemicals can be introduced through this opening. More elaborate chambers can be created. You may wish to burn some material in one chamber and blow the fumes through a tube into a second chamber which contains the plants. *Caution: Melting holes in the plastic bottles produces fumes and should be done under a fume hood or in a well-ventilated area.*

**Tips and suggestions:** Students may check the Science Exploration Flowchart to see the next steps necessary in their scientific problem solving.

| Testing the hypothesis |

**How could your students investigate their ideas?** Devise ways to test the hypothesis, choose the best one and carry it out. Refer to worksheet "Setting Up An Experiment" (pages 41-43) for help in designing the experiments.

**Control Experiments:** A *control* serves as a standard of comparison for verifying the results of an investigation. By controlling the variable factors of the experiment, the effects of changing one variable at a time are easily observed.

**Examples of ways to test hypotheses:**

● Introduce the burning material into the chamber each day. Observe the effects when compared to a control chamber with only air in the chamber. (Investigation #1)

**Management Strategy:**  Burn charcoal, dry leaves or wood shavings in a metal can <u>slowly</u> to generate smoke, but control the amount of heat given off at any one time.  Use small amounts so that the heat released does not melt the plastic bottle.  Keep the control chamber *far away* from the experimental chamber receiving the chemical treatment!

▲ Introduce volatile chemicals in the chamber by placing samples of the chemical in a film can next to the quad in the chamber.  Observe the effects compared to a control chamber with just air.  (Investigation #2)

◆ Mix increasing amount of tobacco (double the amount each time) into several equal containers of soil.  Keep one container of soil with no tobacco added as the control.  (Investigation #3)

**Collect data:**  See "Keeping Track of Things" (pages 23-26).

**Analyze the data:**  Have the students explain the results. For example:

● Fast Plants grew slower than normal with charcoal, wood or dry leaves.  Hint:  Combustion produces carbon dioxide which is needed for photosynthesis and plant growth, but other chemicals in the smoke have a negative affect on growth.  (Investigation #1)

▲ Perfume/hair spray affects the appearance of Fast Plants.  Hint:  Some chemicals in these products disturb the plant's growth and cause the plant to die after repeated treatments.  (Investigation #2)

◆ The health of the plants is noticeably affected with each increased amount of tobacco in the soil.  Hint:  Essentially you have run a bioassay for chewing tobacco.  See Bioassays with Fast Plants (pages 149-156).  (Investigation #3)

---

### Evaluating the hypothesis

**Was the hypothesis verified?**  How do your students know that they know?  For example:  Was the test fair?  Did they answer the question?  Are they sure?

## Communicating the results

**Have your students communicated their results to others?**
*No science investigation is complete until it is communicated in writing.* In addition, it can be communicated orally. Students can write their conclusions very simply, but the report should be understandable to anyone reading it, peers and teacher.

## References

### Books

Beller, J. 1985. *Experimenting with Plants.* New York: Prentice Hall Press. Over 70 experiments with a step-by-step guide to choosing, designing and reporting projects. Suggests the kinds of questions to ask in order to invent your own experiments, with a focus toward competitions.

Cochrane, J. 1987. *Plant Ecology.* New York: Bookwright Press. One of a series of books on ecology. Examines plants and how they are affected by other factors in the world: the sun, water, bacteria. Looks at the place of plants in the ecological scene and their future.

Wisconsin Fast Plants. 1988. *The Great School Smoke Out.* An information document, available from Wisconsin Fast Plants, UW-Madison, Dept. of Plant Pathology, 1630 Linden Drive, Madison, WI 53706.

# Chapter 11: Salt Effects on Plants

**Students will look at the effects of salt on seed germination.** The salt source can be melted snow from salted roadsides, fertilizer pellets, sea water or table salt. Further investigations explore the effect of salts on Fast Plants and the concentration of salt that plants can tolerate. This can be a stand-alone observational exercise. The steps of each chapter are consistent with the boxed steps of the Science Exploration Flowchart. You can develop a complete scientific investigation using the questions your students ask as a result of this observational exercise. Some examples for complete scientific investigations are provided and identified by following specific icons; ●, ▲, ■ and ◆. If you don't have time to complete a full investigation, you might plan to continue with it later in the year.

## Background Information for the Teacher

This exploration looks at damage to plants due to salts. The source of these salts may be road salts, or sea water. Sodium chloride and/or calcium chloride is used as "road salt" for deicing roads and walkways in winter. As the ice melts, the salt mixes with the water. This solution may be sprayed on plants by vehicles or it may be absorbed by the soil. Examples of concentrations that have been measured along highways[1] are:

> 10-800 ppm — edge of highway*
>
> 20-700 ppm — 10 meters from highway*
>
> 20-400 ppm — 20 meters from highway*
>
> *10,000 ppm (parts per million) equals a 1% solution

[1] Hutchinson, F. E. and B. E. Olson. 1967. The relationship of road salt applications to sodium chloride levels in the soil bordering major highways. Highway Research Record 193:1-7.

Langilla, A. R. 1976. One season's salt accumulation in soil and trees adjacent to a highway. Hort. Science 11:575-576.

Lumis, G. P., G. Hofstra and R. Hall. Salt damage to roadside plants. Journal of Arboriculture 1:14-16.

Excess fertilizer may also result in salt damage. This often occurs in areas where crops are successively grown year-round and commercial fertilizers are heavily used. Salts in irrigation or ground waters are concentrated through evaporation. Moderate damage results in "burning" of the leaf edges on the plants. Severe damage is demonstrated by death of the plants before or just after emergence from the soil.

Sea water may produce effects similar to those of road salt or excess fertilizer. Sea water may be sprayed on plants during storms. Sea water normally has salt at the concentration of 3.5% or 35,500 parts per million. Salt in body fluids— for example, serum or physiological saline— is at 0.9% or 9,000 parts per million.

## Teaching Objectives

**Beginning Concept:** Pollutants are chemicals in our environment that produce harmful effects on living things.

**Advanced Concept:** A pollutant's effect on organisms (plants) may be observed long after the pollutant is introduced into the environment.

## Preparation and Planning for Observational Exercise

**Time required:** on 3 consecutive days; Day 1: 30 minutes for setup; Day 2: observe; Day 3: observe

---

**Materials needed per student/team:**
- petri dishes or transparency film. See Tips and suggestions (page 183).
- Fast Plants seeds
- paper toweling or filter paper
- table salt (NaCl) or snow collected from intersections near salted roads or fertilizer pellets or sea water
- tap water
- eyedroppers
- hand lenses
- shallow trays for water and salt solutions (bottom portion of a 2-liter soda bottle works well)

---

# Salt Effects on Plants Observational Exercise

**1.** Cut two layers of paper towels to fit in the cover (larger half) of each of two petri dishes.

**2.** With a pencil, label the bottom of each paper towel with your name, the date and the time. Label one dish "experimental" and the other "control."

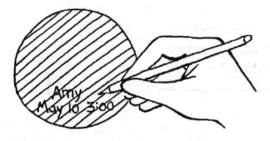

**3.** Moisten the towels in the control dish with water.

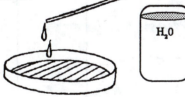

**4.** Moisten the towel in the experimental dish with salt solution (either melted snow, sea water, fertilizer solution or NaCl solution).

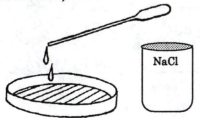

**5.** Place five Fast Plants seeds on the top half of each towel and cover each with the bottom (smaller half) of the petri dish.

**6.** Place each petri dish at an angle in the base of a two-liter soda bottle or tray. Add solution (water = control, salt = experimental) until the bottom 2 cm of the towel is below the liquid's surface.

**control**

**experimental**

**7.** Place the experimental and control trays in plastic bags to prevent evaporation.

**8.** Set both trays in a warm location (optimum temperature: 65-80°F). Record the day and time of setting up the experiment.

**9.** Over the next 3 days use a hand lens or magnifying glass to observe the stages of the germinating seeds and young plants. *Each day check the liquid level to be sure the paper towel stays wet.*

**10.** Record observations.

# Student Science Exploration Flowchart

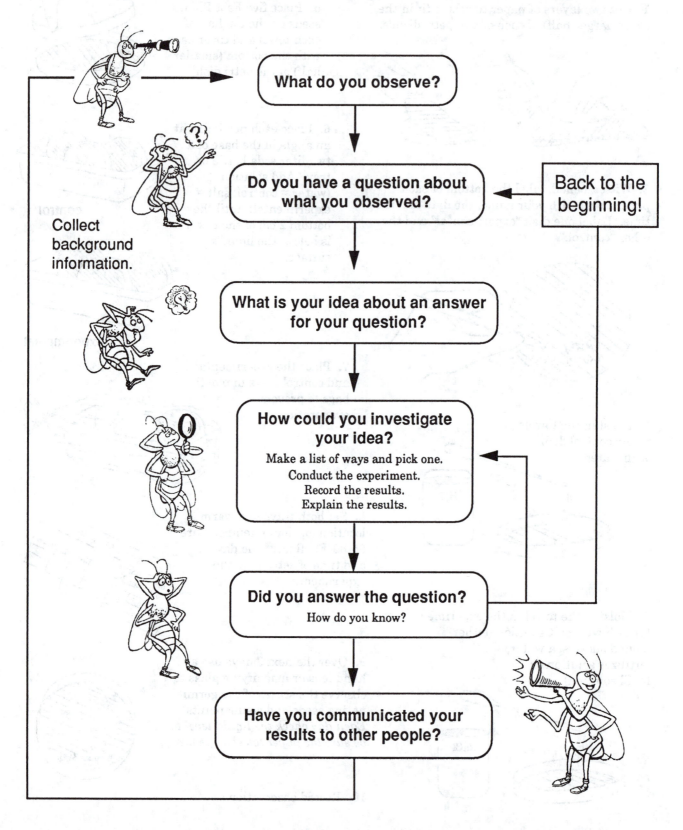

Collect
background
information.

What do you observe?

Do you have a question about
what you observed?

Back to the
beginning!

What is your idea about an answer
for your question?

How could you investigate
your idea?

Make a list of ways and pick one.
Conduct the experiment.
Record the results.
Explain the results.

Did you answer the question?
How do you know?

Have you communicated your
results to other people?

**Tips and suggestions:**

- Set up the exploration on a Monday morning so students can observe seeds again before leaving school on Monday.
- If petri dishes are not available, place wet paper towel between two sheets of transparency film, attach seeds and staple the "sandwich" together in several places. Cut an $8\frac{1}{2}$ x 11 inch film sheet into four equal-sized pieces to make a convenient-sized germination "sandwich."
- Complete the Germination Observational Exercise (page 47) before beginning this exploration.
- If using table salt, a 2% solution can be made up by dissolving 2.0 grams (approximately $\frac{1}{8}$ teaspoon) NaCl in 100 ml of water.
- Melted snow from heavily salted urban intersections yields graphic results.

## How Salt Affects Germination

**Making observations**

**Some preliminary questions:** Begin your exploration by asking your students some questions and discussing ideas they might have about road salt, commercial fertilizers and seed germination.

**As you conduct the observational exercise illustrated on page 181,** your students will observe the normal processes of germination (see Germination Observational Exercise, page 47) in a water control and note the difference in that process (seed swelling, seed coat splitting, root emergence, root hair growth, hypocotyl extension and cotyledon expansion) from the one in which seeds are placed in an experimental salt solution.

**Asking questions**

**What questions have your students raised from observing?** The students should be curious about some of the things they have observed. A class discussion should generate questions. Have your students make a list of questions. Prompt them with the words "**What if.**"

**Example questions derived from observations:**
- ● How much salt is needed to affect germination?  (Investigation #1)
- ▲ If seeds are affected by salts, would plants also be affected?  (Investigation #2)
- ■ If plants are affected by salts, what amount of salts can plants tolerate and still complete their life cycle?  (Investigation #3)

## Forming a hypothesis

**What are your student's ideas about answers for their questions?**
Following the discussion of observations, students can turn their questions into statements and write them down as hypotheses.

**Example hypotheses derived from questions:**
- ● More salt interferes more with germination.  (Investigation #1)
- ▲ Salt interferes with germination but will not affect older plants.  (Investigation #2)
- ■ At X levels of salt concentration plants will show no differences when compared to plants with plain water.  (Investigation #3)

**Tips and suggestions:**  Have the students check the Science Exploration Flowchart to see what the next steps need to be in their science problem solving.

## Testing the hypothesis

**How could your students investigate their ideas?**  Design an experiment. Devise ways to test the hypothesis, choose the best one and carry it out.  Refer to worksheet "Setting Up An Experiment" (pages 41-43) for help in designing the experiments.

**Control Experiments:**  A *control* serves as a standard of comparison for verifying the results of an investigation.  By controlling the variable factors of the experiment, the effects of changing one variable at a time are easily observed.

**Examples of ways to test hypotheses:**

● Vary the concentration of salt in the germination experiment. Take a 2% solution and dilute it in half, then half again, etc. Then also double the amount of salt to make a 4% solution, etc. Use water as the control. (Investigation #1)

▲ Use 5- to 9-day old Fast Plants. Treat some with salt by either adding the salt to the reservoir or dipping the plants in the salt solution daily. Use some plants with just water for the control. (Investigation #2)

■ Treat plants with various concentrations of salts from no salt to high concentrations (up to 5%). Compare the amount of seed harvested and the germination of the seed (progeny) as a measure of successful completion of the life cycle. (Investigation #3)

**Suggestions for additional investigations:** See Activity Ideas/Exploratory Questions (page 191) for ways in which environmental factors might change the shape of height frequency curves of Fast Plants.

**Collect data:** See "Keeping Track of Things" (pages 23-26).

**Analyze the data:** Have the students explain the results. For example:

● In general, germination will be affected by increasing concentrations of salt. Different aspects of germination (for example, seed swelling, root elongation, root hair development, etc.) may be affected differently by different salt concentrations. (Investigation #1)

▲ Plants as well as seeds are affected by salts. Hint: Excess salts somehow interfere with growth of a plant. (Investigation #2)

■ At concentrations of salt less than 0.1% (5 ml of 2%, add 95 ml of water), plants showed no negative effects in completing their life cycle. Hint: This is the salt tolerance level of Fast Plants. (Investigation #3)

**Evaluating the hypothesis**

**Was the hypothesis verified?** How do your students know that they know?
**For example:** Was the test fair? Did they answer the question? Are they sure?

## Communicating the results

**Have your students communicated their results to others?** No science investigation is complete until it is communicated in writing. In addition, it can be communicated orally. Students can write their conclusions very simply, but the report should be understandable to anyone reading it, peers and teacher.

## References

### Books

National Council for Agricultural Education. 1994. *Using Fast Plants and Bottle Biology in the Classroom.* Reston, VA: National Association of Biology Teachers. A teacher manual including background information and 12 detailed lessons incorporating agricultural and biological science.

Williams, P. H. 1989. *Wisconsin Fast Plants Manual.* Burlington, NC: Carolina Biological Supply Co. High school level manual containing background information, taxonomy of Fast Plants, growing instructions and procedures for exercises and activities.

Wisconsin Fast Plants. 1995. *From Above or Below: The Effect of Salt on Fast Plants.* An information document available from Wisconsin Fast Plants, UW-Madison, Dept. of Plant Pathology, 1630 Linden Drive, Madison, WI 53706.

# Variation, Heredity and Evolution

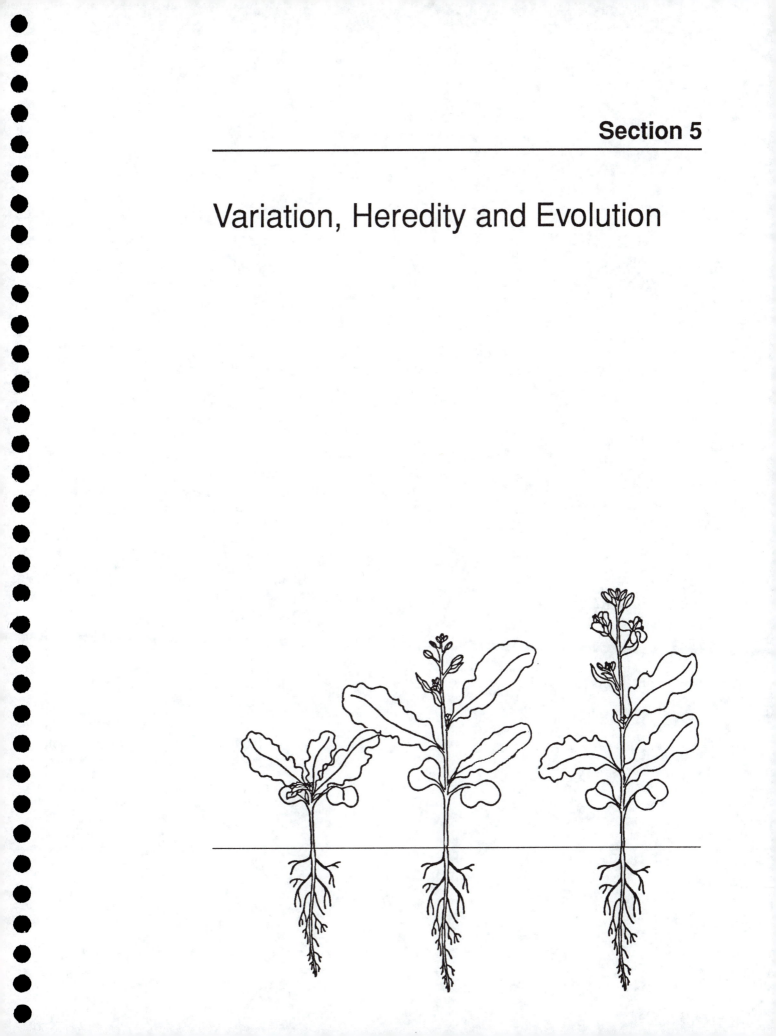

# Concepts: Variation, Heredity and Evolution

An important attribute of life is variation. Within a species or population, individuals vary in their measurable or observable characteristics known as phenotype. Phenotypic variation is affected both by the genetics (genotype) of the individual and by the environment in which the individual lives acting on the genotype. Variation is conditioned both by many genes of individually immeasurable effect and by single or few genes of measurable effect. Heredity is the genetic transmission of characteristics from parent to offspring. Adaptation in the evolutionary sense is some heritable feature of an individual's phenotype that improves its chances of survival and reproduction in the existing environment. The progressive adaptation through either natural selection or human-influenced artificial selection is responsible for evolutionary changes within species.

In order to understand the fundamental role of genetics as it influences variation among individuals in a population, it is important to grow individuals in as uniform an environment as possible so that the genetic component of the observed variation can be identified.

- *Of the variation observed in a population, what is contributed by the genetics of the individual and how is it inherited?*

## Investigating Populations and Individuals of Fast Plants

**Getting a Handle on Variation:** measuring and graphing height, etc.
**Fast Plants and Families:** inheritance of measured characteristics.
**Hairy's Inheritance:** quantifying [measuring] a trait, e.g., hairs.

## The Role of Inheritance on Variation in Plant Growth

**Plant Breeding:** articifial selection, domestication, human-guided evolution, a biological riddle.

# Chapter 12: Getting a Handle on Variation
## Quantifying differences in plant height

### Background Information for the Teacher

The system that guides generation after generation of species through the spiral of life has in its design the ability to generate sufficient variation to accommodate an ever-changing environment. Variation is a fundamental attribute of life; understanding its nature is important for all of us.

The following article is designed to help students and teachers think about the nature of various determinants underlying biological variation. Fast Plants, rapid-cycling *Brassica rapa* (Rbr), are ideally suited for getting a handle on variation.

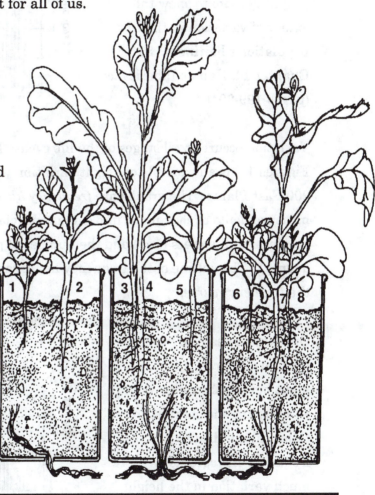

Variation between individuals of a particular visible trait (*phenotype*) is conditioned both by the genetic makeup (*genotype*) of the individuals and by their environment. To identify variation, a trait must be observed, described, and measured or quantified.

Some of these traits, such as plant height, cotyledon width, or the intensity of purple anthocyanin pigment in the stems, can vary from plant to plant of the same age. When, for example, the height of many plants of the same age is recorded and organized (graphed), the population expresses a variety of heights within a range from the shortest to the tallest.

Another way to view variation is to determine whether the trait is present or absent. For example, the purple color in the Rbr stem may be present or absent and, if present, the intensity of the purple may vary. Other traits vary in their numbers or degree of expression. Your students will notice in an Rbr population that the total number of hairs on the stems and leaves varies considerably from plant to plant and varies with respect to hair location. Just as with height, the number of hairs can be quantified by counting and graphing them to show the extent of variation in the Rbr population's hairiness. See Chapter 14, Hairy's Inheritance (pages 199-204).

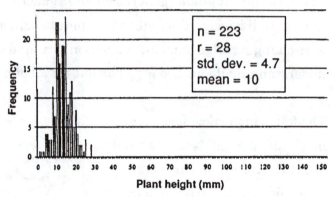

Figure 1: Day 5

n = 223
r = 28
std. dev. = 4.7
mean = 10

Variation occurs at all stages of the life cycle. The data collected and graphed in Figures 1-3 is an example of height variation within a population of approximately 200 Fast Plants. The graphs are *frequency histograms* which organize the height measurements of each plant into categories (classes or intervals) according to the height in millimeters (mm) and the number of plants in each height class (frequency). The outline of the frequency histogram roughly depicts a curve known as the *frequency curve*.

One way to describe variation is in terms of *range* (r). For plant height, the range would extend from the shortest to the tallest plant. Looking at the frequency histograms, is there much variation in the height range of 5 day old plants as compared to the range of 10 day old plants?

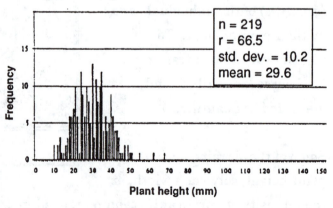

Figure 2: Day 10

n = 219
r = 66.5
std. dev. = 10.2
mean = 29.6

day old plants? By the time the plants are 14 days old and beginning to flower, has the range widened even further? What is the range from shortest to tallest plant by Day 14? *(The range on Day 5 is 27 mm (29-2); the range on Day 10 is 58 mm (68-10); the range on Day 14 is 176 mm (180-4).*

Another way to describe variation is in terms of *averages*. Continuing with our examples, the average (arithmetic mean) height of the plants increased from 13.4 mm on day 5 to 100 mm on day 14. The *mean* is the sum of the height of all plants divided by the number of plants (n).

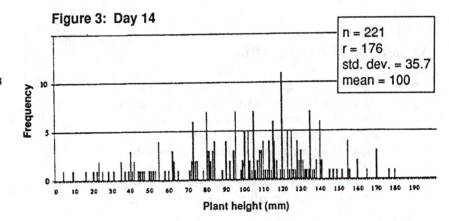

Figure 3: Day 14

n = 221
r = 176
std. dev. = 35.7
mean = 100

Did you notice that as the plant population ages, the shape of the frequency curve changes? This variation results from the environment and the genetic make-up of individual plants.

## Activity Ideas/Exploratory Questions

1. Could you change the shape of the population curves by altering environmental or genetic factors? For instance, if you grew the plants under stress — with low nutrients or in the presence of salt or other pollutants — would the shape of the frequency curve change when you measured the plants on days 5, 10, and 14?

2. Could you change the frequency curve by altering the genetic base of the population? For example, what if you selected the tallest 10% of the plants and crossed them, do you think the curves describing plant height of the progeny would differ from the curve of the parents? How could you investigate this?

## Additional Questions to Consider

- Are there other plant characteristics that can be quantified?
  - the number of true leaves on a plant?
  - the number of days it takes for the first flower to appear?
  - the number of pods a plant produces?
  - the length of the seed pods?
- Is the length of the pod related to the number of seeds it produces?
- Is the number of seeds produced related to the number of times you pollinate?

# Let your students try their hand at quantifying variation

### Activity 1:
### Observing and measuring

Learning how to measure plants is a basic plant
science skill, and one that can be challenging
for small fingers! This activity gives younger
children the opportunity to practice this skill
before they measure live plants in the lab.

Photocopy the drawing which appears on the first page of this activity
(page 189) and the ruler at the right of this column.

Students can practice measuring plant height with their drawing using the
ruler. Measure from soil level to tip of bud. Then, they can find
the range and average of the heights.

After your class gets the hang of plant measuring, students can color or
paint their Fast Plant pictures and you can have a Fast Plants
Gallery opening!

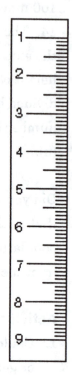

Metric ruler

### Activity 2:
### Analyzing and predicting

1. Pick a small — approx. 20% — random sample of students from your class. Measure
   each student and calculate the average height and range from tallest to shortest.

2. Now, make a prediction: do you think the variation as expressed in average and range of
   height for the sample will accurately predict the average and range for the full class?

3. If you wish, select another random sample of students. Is the average height and range of
   this sample different from the first group? If you combine the data from both
   samples, will your prediction of variation among the entire class improve?

4. Then, measure all of the students and calculate the class mean and range. How accurate
   were each of your samples? Was the combined data from both samples more accurate
   in predicting the variation of the total class than either sample used alone? Organize
   the class data into a frequency histogram.

5. Finally, do you think the variation in student height in your classroom is typical for all
   students in the same grade in your school? How confident are you of your prediction?
   (____ very  ____ somewhat  ____ not confident). How could you improve your
   prediction further?

# Chapter 13: Fast Plants and Families
## How is variation generated and maintained?

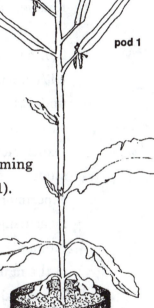

### Background Information for the Teacher

One of the essential attributes of living organisms is *varia-tion*. Understanding how variation is generated and maintained is central to an understanding of biology and is an important theme in the study of genetics. A "family approach" to investigating with rapid-cycling *Brassica rapa* (Rbr or Fast Plants) provides a rich introduction to the complexities underlying biological variation.

### Preparing the seed pods as "mother"

The time to establish Fast Plants families is just as one generation is coming to an end and the plants are drying (35-40 days after planting) (Figure 1).

Rather than harvesting and combining the seeds from all the dried fruits (pods), each dried pod can be gently removed from the plant and placed between folded clear adhesive tape (see Figure 2), being careful not to lose any seeds. In this way, you can preserve the seed containing the embryo of the new generation as well as the pod that is part of the maternal parent (mother) that produced the seed. Since each of the seeds are offspring of a common maternal parent, they are siblings within a single family.

**Figure 1**

Pods from each plant can be color coded with a marking pen to identify them as having the same "mother."

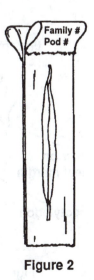

**Note:** If the students have a whole plant with mature seed pods, the plant itself would be viewed as the "mother," and all pods from the same plant have the same family number. Use the "Family Data Chart" (page 197). If they begin only with harvested seed pods, the pods themselves can be viewed as "mother." Use the "Pod Data Chart" (page 198).

**Figure 2**

## Activity ideas/Exploratory Questions

1.  Looking at the seed pod, protected between the layers of clear tape, various features of the maternal parent (such as pod, style and ovary length) can be observed, measured and recorded on the chart (Figure 3). A 5X magnifying lens is helpful in making observations and careful measurements. After recording characteristics of the "mother," the pod can be thoroughly crushed within the tape. As the tape is peeled open, the seeds will stick to the adhesive. The seeds should also be observed carefully with a magnifier and then counted and their number recorded on the chart.

2.  Sibling seeds can be sown in two minipots, with one pair of plants in one pot growing under the "standard" conditions in the classroom, and the other under "experimental" conditions, perhaps at the student's home. Be sure that the experimental conditions are recorded. By measuring each sibling plant in each environment, as indicated on the data charts and in the figures, a large amount of data on individuals will be obtained. These data can be used in many ways to examine variation within , between and among individuals, families and populations of Fast Plants.

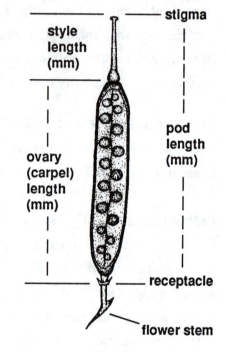

Figure 3

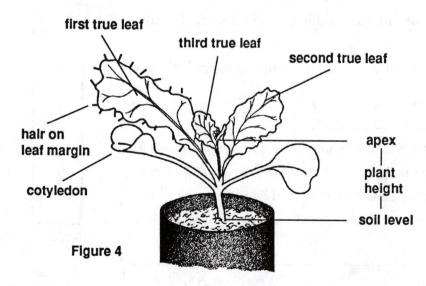

Figure 4

3. Mathematics and statistics can be applied to the data to help understand the variation. The data can be presented graphically in many ways. By observing variation among individuals of a population or family, students will be able to explore the influences of environment on the growth and form of plants.

4. By beginning the exploration with seeds from a common mother, many interesting ideas can be pursued. Important questions relating to origins of the parents and the make-up or structure of the family can be investigated, e.g., do all siblings have a common father as in a nuclear family? Characteristics that vary among individuals in the population such as plant height, number of hairs on the plant, and color of parts will be observed. By crossing individuals within or between families (controlling the pollinations), heredity of such characteristics can be investigated experimentally.

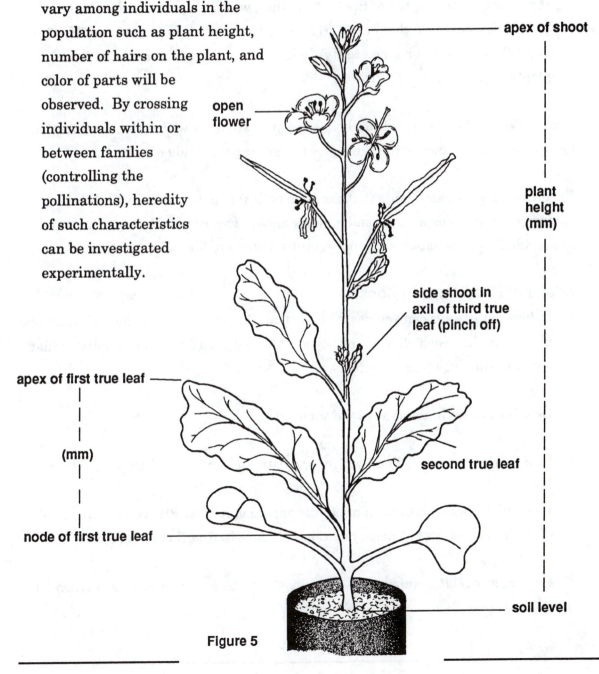

apex of shoot

open flower

plant height (mm)

side shoot in axil of third true leaf (pinch off)

apex of first true leaf

(mm)

second true leaf

node of first true leaf

soil level

**Figure 5**

5. Pods from each plant could be color coded with a marking pen to identify them as having the same "mother." The progeny (seeds) from two maternal plants (e.g., red and blue) could be planted and grown in two separate populations. Characteristics of the two families could be measured and compared. For example, the length of the style (see Figure 3) of the seed pods in each family could be compared. Is the style length of all the pods on each maternal plant similar?

If you intermate progeny of the "red" mother, will the style lengths of these progeny be similar to that of the original red mother? What about the "blue" family? What would happen to style length if you crossed a "red" and "blue" plant?

Such experiments will provide both you and your students with a rich introduction for understanding some of the principles underlying the study of genetics.

Experiments with Fast Plants that examine both the role of heredity and the environment in the expression and maintenance of variation will deepen a student's understanding of variation as an important attribute of life.

## Additional Questions to Consider

- In how many ways can you describe the pod (the mother)? Are the pods from one plant more like each other than they are like the pods from other plants? What about the siblings from a single pod?

- Do all the seeds in a pod have the same father?

- How much variation is there within and between families of Fast Plants?

- How much does environment affect the variation in Fast Plants, e.g., the number of seeds per pod, style length, plant height, days to first flowering, etc.

- Is there any relationship between the length of the seed pod and its position on the maternal plant?

# Family Data Chart *

**Family #** _____

| | |
|---|---|
| Student name _____ | Pod # _____ |
| Student name _____ | Pod # _____ |
| Student name _____ | Pod # _____ |

**Environment**

| | |
|---|---|
| Temperature _____ | Soil moisture _____ |
| Irradiance _____ | Atmosphere _____ |
| Soil (substrate) _____ | Gravity vector _____ |
| Nutrients _____ | Biota _____ |

## plant and pod measurements

| date | das | character/activity | | family # ___ pod # ___ | | | | family # ___ pod # ___ | | | | family # ___ pod # ___ | | | | family # ___ pod # ___ | | | | n | r | $\bar{x}$ | σ |
|---|---|---|---|---|---|---|---|---|---|---|---|---|---|---|---|---|---|---|---|---|---|---|---|
| | | family and pod numbers | | | | | | | | | | | | | | | | | | | | | |
| | 0 | pod length | (mm) | 1 | 2 | 3 | 4 | 1 | 2 | 3 | 4 | 1 | 2 | 3 | 4 | 1 | 2 | 3 | 4 | | | | |
| | 0 | style length | (mm) | | | | | | | | | | | | | | | | | | | | |
| | 0 | # seeds per pod | (#) | | | | | | | | | | | | | | | | | | | | |
| | 0 | # seeds sown | (#) | | | | | | | | | | | | | | | | | | | | |
| | 3 | # seeds germinated (# seedlings) | (#) | | | | | | | | | | | | | | | | | | | | |
| | 4 | thin to 4 plants | | | | | | | | | | | | | | | | | | | | | |
| | | plant number | | 1 | 2 | 3 | 4 | 1 | 2 | 3 | 4 | 1 | 2 | 3 | 4 | 1 | 2 | 3 | 4 | | | | |
| | 7 | largest cotyledon width | (mm) | | | | | | | | | | | | | | | | | | | | |
| | 7 | plant height (soil to apex) | (mm) | | | | | | | | | | | | | | | | | | | | |
| | 14 | plant height (soil to apex) | (mm) | | | | | | | | | | | | | | | | | | | | |
| | 14 | leaves on main stem including cotyledons | (#) | | | | | | | | | | | | | | | | | | | | |
| | 14 | # hairs on margin of first true leaf | (#) | | | | | | | | | | | | | | | | | | | | |
| | 17 | pollinate and terminalize plants | | | | | | | | | | | | | | | | | | | | | |
| | 17 | plant height (soil to apex) | (mm) | | | | | | | | | | | | | | | | | | | | |
| | 17 | # flowers pollinated | (#) | | | | | | | | | | | | | | | | | | | | |
| | 42 | # pods | (#) | | | | | | | | | | | | | | | | | | | | |

das = days after sowing, n = number of measurements, r = range (maximum - minimum), $\bar{x}$ = mean (average), σ = standard deviation

* this chart should be used starting with a mature plant as "mother." The plant number is the family number. Students should work in groups of three, with each student in the group getting a pod from the same mother plant. Therefore each pod will have the same family number, but will be assigned its own pod number (see page 193). Each student should raise 4 plants to maturity, using this chart to follow and compare growth and development of seeds from sibling pods.

Name _____

# Pod Data Chart

**Environment**

Temperature: _____     Soil Moisture: _____     Irradiance: _____

Atmosphere: _____     Soil (substrate): _____     Gravity Vector: _____

Nutrients: _____     Biota: _____

| Day | Date | Stage | Measure/Activity | Record | Record |
|-----|------|-------|------------------|--------|--------|
| 0 | _____ | seed pod | • pod length | _____ mm | |
| | | | • style length | _____ mm | |
| 0 | | seed | • # seeds in pod | # _____ | |
| | | | • # seeds sown | # _____ | |
| 3 | _____ | germination | • # seedlings | # _____ | |
| 5 | _____ | seedling | • thin to 2 seedlings | | |
| | | | • number each plant | # _____ | # _____ |
| | | | • height (soil to apex) | _____ mm | _____ mm |
| 7 | _____ | vegetative | • height (soil to apex) | _____ mm | _____ mm |
| 10 | _____ | vegetative/prefloral | • height (soil to apex) | _____ mm | _____ mm |
| 12 | _____ | prefloral | • # leaves (include cotyledons) | # _____ | # _____ |
| | | | • height (soil to apex) | _____ mm | _____ mm |
| | | | • # hairs on margin of first true leaf | # _____ | # _____ |
| 14 | _____ | flowering/pollination | • height (soil to apex) | _____ mm | _____ mm |
| | | | • cross, X, or self, ⊗ record X or ⊗ | _____ | _____ |
| 17 | _____ | flowering/pollination | • height (soil to apex) | _____ mm | _____ mm |
| | | | • # flowers | # _____ | # _____ |
| | | | • pollinate | | |
| | | | • remove shoot apex and all side shoots and buds | | |
| 40 | _____ | seed pods | • height (soil to apex) | _____ mm | _____ mm |
| | | | • # pods | # _____ | # _____ |
| | | | • mean pod length | X̄ _____ mm | X̄ _____ mm |
| | | | • total # seeds per plant | # _____ | # _____ |
| | | | • mean # seeds per pod | X̄# _____ | X̄# _____ |

# Chapter 14: Hairy's Inheritance
## Getting a handle on variation

### Background Information for the Teacher

Within the population of Fast Plants (Rbr) there is an observable trait *(phenotype)* that might escape some students' notice, but which lends itself easily to investigating variation and inheritance. Varying numbers of hairs can be seen along the stem, on the upper and lower surfaces of the leaves, on leaf edges and even on the buds of plants.

The hairs found on the basic *Brassica rapa* plants constitute a trait that is variable, quantifiable and heritable. Scientists are not sure why plants have hairs although they have some ideas. Furthermore, very little is known about the genetics and inheritance of hairiness.

The number of different genes that control the number and location of hairs is also unknown. Observing and counting the hairs on Fast Plants will challenge and sharpen students' observational skills and provide them with the opportunity to ask many questions.

Students often measure the height of Fast Plants with a ruler and estimate the actual height in units such as millimeters. Determining the number of hairs is different than estimating height in that each hair is a *discreet unit* that can be counted directly.

Each plant or plant part has a certain number of hairs, but the number of hairs will vary from plant to plant. The number of hairs counted on each plant can be recorded in a table as a class data set and graphed as a frequency histogram.

Figure 1 (page 200) depicts a frequency histogram of the number of hairs counted on the right margin of the first true leaf in a population of 295 Fast Plants. Notice that the outline of the frequency histogram in Figure 1 roughly depicts a curve known as a *frequency curve*. Do the majority of plants in Figure 1 have few or many hairs?

## Activity Ideas/Exploratory Questions

1. Students first need to decide how and where to count the hairs on their plants. They can look over the plants and identify where hairs appear. Students could describe and map with sketches where the hairs are located.

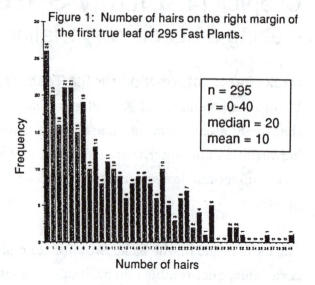

Figure 1: Number of hairs on the right margin of the first true leaf of 295 Fast Plants.

n = 295
r = 0-40
median = 20
mean = 10

Next, they need to decide where on the plant they could accurately count the hairs. Younger students may have difficulty counting, for instance, the hairs all around one portion of the stem.

It may be easiest to count the hairs on the edge of the first true leaf. This can be done as early as Day 8 or 9 in the life cycle when this leaf is well developed. Students will need a good light coming over their shoulder and a hand lens.

By observing the plant against a dark, contrasting background (construction paper, a classmate's sweater, etc.) they could count all the hairs on the edge of the leaf. Each student can record the number of hairs at the particular agreed upon location on their plant, and then all the data from the class could be incorporated into a frequency histogram as suggested in Figure 1. From observing the graph, students will be able to identify characteristics of the population with respect to the hairy phenotype.

2. After looking at their graphed data and statistics, students will "brainstorm" ideas and develop questions relating to hairiness and inheritance. Questions may include: Is hairiness inherited? How is hairiness inherited? Could hairless or super hairy populations be produced?

By choosing the top ten percent of the hairiest plants in the class population as an experimental group and intermating (pollinating) only those plants, students would be applying what Charles Darwin called *artificial* or *directed selection* on the population.

If hairiness were inherited through the combined effects of many different genes *(polygenically)*, one would expect that by repeatedly selecting the hairiest parents for subsequent generations the number of genes for hairiness in the population would be increased. Would this directed selection increase the population mean (average) for hairiness?

To investigate this question, students would first want to record the data of numbers of hairs for the experimental group of parent plants, so that they can compare the initial data with the numbers of hairs that occur on the next generation (the *progeny* or offspring).

Will the offspring of the first intermating have more hairs on average than the parents? Through how many generations would the students have to repeat the directed selection experiment before producing a super hairy plant?

## Additional Questions to Consider

Older students, who ponder these questions and who are trying to understand the inheritance of the hairy trait, will continue to ask more questions.

- If all the plants from the first (parental) generation are intermated, will all the offspring have hairs? Will the hairs show up in the same places on the offspring?

- Will the progeny of a hairless and a hairy plant have hairs? Will all the offspring in the $F_1$ (first filial generation) have hairs? If many genes are functioning to produce hairiness, can you keep increasing hairiness?

- Is there a limit to the number of hairs that a plant can have? Conversely, how quickly might students develop a population of hairless plants? Can they change the shape of the frequency curve by altering the genetic base?

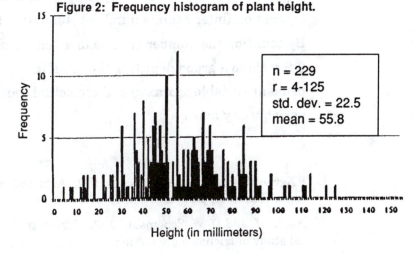

**Figure 2: Frequency histogram of plant height.**

n = 229
r = 4-125
std. dev. = 22.5
mean = 55.8

Height (in millimeters)

## The environment and phenotype

Environment is ever present in the expression of the phenotype. See "Concepts" (page 187) and "Observing the Phenotype" (page 204). The degree to which components of the environment, such as light, temperature and nutrition, contribute to the expression of phenotypes is an important part of genetics. Little is known about the influence of environmental factors on the inheritance of hairiness. Investigation by students might provide insight into the influence of these and other environmental factors on the expression of the hairy phenotype.

## Environmental applications

Students may ask why plants have hairs at all. Does there have to be a purpose for any given trait on a plant? What are their hypotheses? A few scientists have asked the similar questions.[1]

## Extensions

**Extension 1:** Ponder the shape of the frequency histogram.

Geneticists know that normally distributed *continuous variation* is usually produced by the combined effects of many genes. Such traits are said to be under *polygenic* control ("poly" = Greek for many). Figure 2 (page 201) is a frequency histogram showing a normal distribution curve. What questions about the inheritance of hairs does the frequency distribution in Figure 1 raise?

**Extension 2:** Develop a scale for hairiness (Hir).

Since hairiness is a phenotype that shows wide variation in its expression, use a scale from 0-9 to define roughly the range in expression of hairiness, where 0 = no expression (no hair), 1-2 = very low expression (very few hairs), 4-6 = intermediate expression (intermediate numbers of hairs) to 9 = very high expression (very hairy). By counting the number of hairs in a defined area on the plant, you can convert the 0-9 scale to a graph depicting the relationship of the scaling numbers 0-9 (the independent variable or x axis) and the actual count of number of hairs (the dependent variable or y axis.)

[1] Agren, J. and D. W. Schemske. 1992. Artificial selection on trichome number in *Brassica rapa*. Theor. Appl. Genet. 83:673-678.

Agren, J. and D. W. Schemske. 1993. The cost of defense against herbivores: an experimental study of trichome production in *Brassica rapa*. Amer. Naturalist 141-338.

Name _____

# How hairy is hairy?

Directions:
1. Find the first true leaf on each plant and color it green.
2. How many hairs can you find on the top of the first true leaf?
3. How many hairs can you find around the edge (margin) of the first true leaf?
4. Do you see hairs anywhere else on the plant?
5. Circle the places where you find hairs.

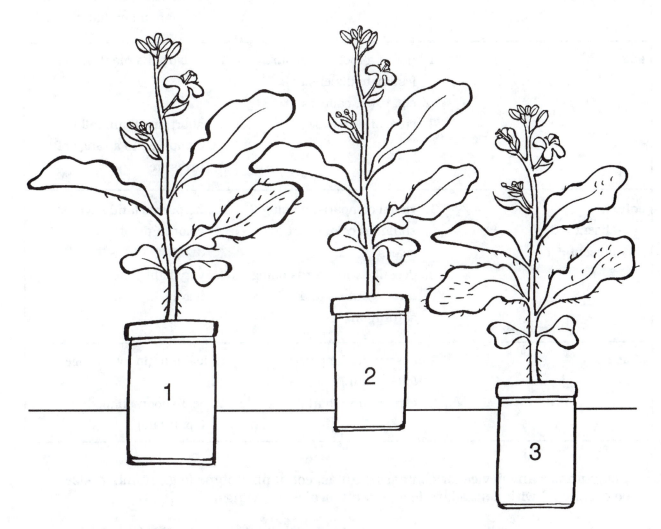

Answers: Question 2; plant 1 = 7, plant 2 = 0, plant 3 = 9. Question 3; plant 1 = 11, plant 2 = 3, plant 3 = 11, do not count the hairs on the stem (petiole) of the leaf.

# Observing the Phenotype
## Plant Growth and Development

Characteristics of the plant that are observed constitute the *phenotype*. Phenotype is the genetically and environmentally determined appearance of an organism. Specific characteristics can be described using various *descriptors*.

| Example of descriptors | Method of description | Examples |
| --- | --- | --- |
| **number**<br><br>-absent = 0<br><br>-present = 1 to n | 1. direct count<br>2. comparator scale | 1. hair on margin of first leaf<br>2. very hairy = Hir (8-9) on a scale of 0 = no hair to 9 = very many hairs |
| **size** | 1. use of a tool to measure (estimate dimension), e.g. ruler, calipers<br><br>2. comparator scale | 1. height of a plant in mm<br><br><br>2. short, medium, tall compared to a range of measure |
| **color**<br><br>-absent = 0<br><br>-present = 1 | 1. visual comparison using standard color chart or scales<br>2. describe with words using hue, lightness and saturation | 1. no purple (anthocyanin) color in plant<br><br>2. very light yellow-green leaves |
| **shape** | 1. descriptive language (often Latin)<br>2. comparator charts | 1. leaf margin lobed edge<br><br>2. leaf spoon-shaped (spatulate) |

• *Comparator:* any device for comparing an aspect of phenotype (e.g., number, size, color, shape) with a standard (e.g., charts, scales, drawings).

• *Accuracy:* done with care, deviating within certain limits of a standard.

• *Precision:* an action (measurement) repeated within closely specified limits.

# Chapter 15: Plant Breeding

## Background Information for the Teacher

A trip to the produce section of any supermarket illustrates the great diversity that exists among plants. The mature vegetative stages of the various forms of *Brassica rapa* appear to have little in common.

If you examine turnip, Chinese cabbage, pak choi, rapini, turnip greens (with the roots on) and Fast Plants (Rbr), you see noticeable differences in shape, size and form (see illustrations below). Yet all belong to the same *species* as defined as a population of organisms having many characteristics in common and which produce fertile offspring through the exchange of genetic information. This definition can be tested experimentally by cross-pollinating one of these vegetables with Fast Plants. The most likely candidates are the turnip and Chinese cabbage, commonly found in the produce department of the grocery store. To convert the turnip or Chinese cabbage to the flowering stage, a cold treatment of four to six weeks is necessary to simulate overwintering. This is called *vernalization*.

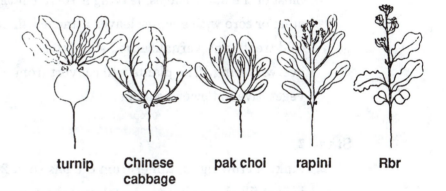

turnip    Chinese cabbage    pak choi    rapini    Rbr

## Teaching Objectives

**Beginning concept:** Plants within the same species can look quite different.

**Advanced concept:** Plants within the same species can interbreed and produce fertile offspring.

**Time required for exercise:** Stage 1: 4-6 weeks (vernalization period in refrigerator); Stage 2: 3-4 weeks (flowering stage); Stage 3: approximately 20 days (seed pod production on Rbr).

---

**Materials needed per student/team:**

- turnip or Chinese cabbage
- Wisconsin Fast Plants seeds
- rooting powder (for example, Rootone®)
- plastic bag, refrigerator
- potting mix with peat moss
- 2-liter soda bottles

---

### Exploratory questions:

- What does it mean to be the same species?
- How can you prove that two plants are the same species?
- If you cross a Fast Plant with a turnip or Chinese cabbage, what will the offspring look like?

### Exploration

### Stage 1

1. Place a turnip or Chinese cabbage core in a plastic bag in the refrigerator for four to six weeks (Figure 1). Before refrigerating the Chinese cabbage, cut off most of the outer leaves, leaving a 10-15 cm thick stem or core with smaller leaves attached. The cold treatment, vernalization, simulates overwintering. The plants will convert from vegetative to flowering stage.

**Figure 1**

### Stage 2

2. Make a growing container from the base of a 2-liter soda bottle. If the bottle is first filled with hot tap water and the cap replaced, the bottom of the bottle will twist off easily. Fill the base with a potting mix that contains some peat moss.

3. After the vernalization period, remove the turnip or Chinese cabbage from the refrigerator. At this time, leaves may already be forming at the top of the turnip and floral buds may be forming down inside the cabbage core. Sprinkle rooting powder (available from a garden store) on the root-end of the turnip, or on the already cut "stem" surface of the Chinese cabbage. This will stimulate root formation.

4. Place the turnip or Chinese cabbage on the potting mix in the growth container. Keep the potting mix moist at all times. Place your vegetable in good light, but keep it cool and partly covered to prevent excess wilting. The top portion of a 2-liter soda bottle, cut to be approximately 20 cm high, can be used for the cover (Figure 2). Keep soil moist.

**Figure 2**

5. Within two to three weeks, the plants should produce flower buds (Figure 3). When the first buds appear, plant several quads of Fast Plants. In two more weeks, both the turnip or Chinese cabbage and the Fast Plants should both be in flower.

## Stage 3

6. Construct beesticks according to the "Illustrated Growing Instructions" (page 32).

**Figure 3**

7. Collect lots of pollen from the turnip or Chinese cabbage and pollinate the Fast Plants, as detailed in Figure 4. If you need to collect more pollen from the turnip or Chinese cabbage flowers, use a fresh beestick.

8. After pollinating, pinch the remaining flower buds off the Fast Plants. Seed pods should mature on the Fast Plants after 20 days.

9. Harvest seed from the Fast Plants and plant some in quads and some in growing containers made from the bottom of 2-liter soda bottles. What will this $F_1$ (first) generation look like? Can you grow these plants and cross them? If so, what will the $F_2$ (second) generation look like? When you get this far, you are becoming a plant breeder!

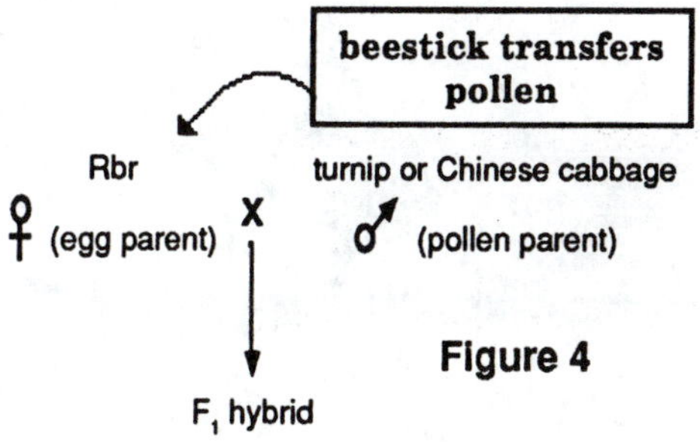

> beestick transfers pollen

Rbr  $\times$  turnip or Chinese cabbage
♀ (egg parent)   ♂ (pollen parent)

$F_1$ hybrid

**Figure 4**

## Additional Activities

- $F_1$ generation investigation:

  Plant the seeds that you harvested from the preceding experiment in as many quads as you want. For comparison, plant one quad of the original parent Fast Plants seed and one quad of packaged turnip seed. Compare the seedling traits of the parents and their $F_1$ offspring. As an additional comparison, start two turnip plants eight or nine weeks before planting the seed of the $F_1$ generation, using the same procedure as in the preceding experiment. The turnips should come into flower at the same time as the Fast Plants parents. Does the $F_1$ generation flower at the same time as the Fast Plants parents? Compare the $F_1$ plants with both kinds of parents for height. Can you produce seed when you interpollinate the $F_1$ plants?

- $F_2$ generation investigation:

  Plant the $F_2$ seeds in large containers. Grow the plants to full maturity. What do these plants look like? Did they produce anything that looks like a vegetable (above or below the soil)?

## References

### Books

Rupp, R. 1987. *Blue Corn and Square Tomatoes.* Pownal, VT: Storey Communications, Inc. Fascinating reading containing unusual facts about common garden vegetables — origins, reputations, connections with human history, etc.

Wisconsin Fast Plants. 1989. *A Biological Riddle: How Can Things That Look So Different Be the Same?* An information document available from Wisconsin Fast Plants, UW-Madison Dept. of Plant Pathology, 1630 Linden Drive, Madison, WI 53706.

# Energy and Nutrient Recycling

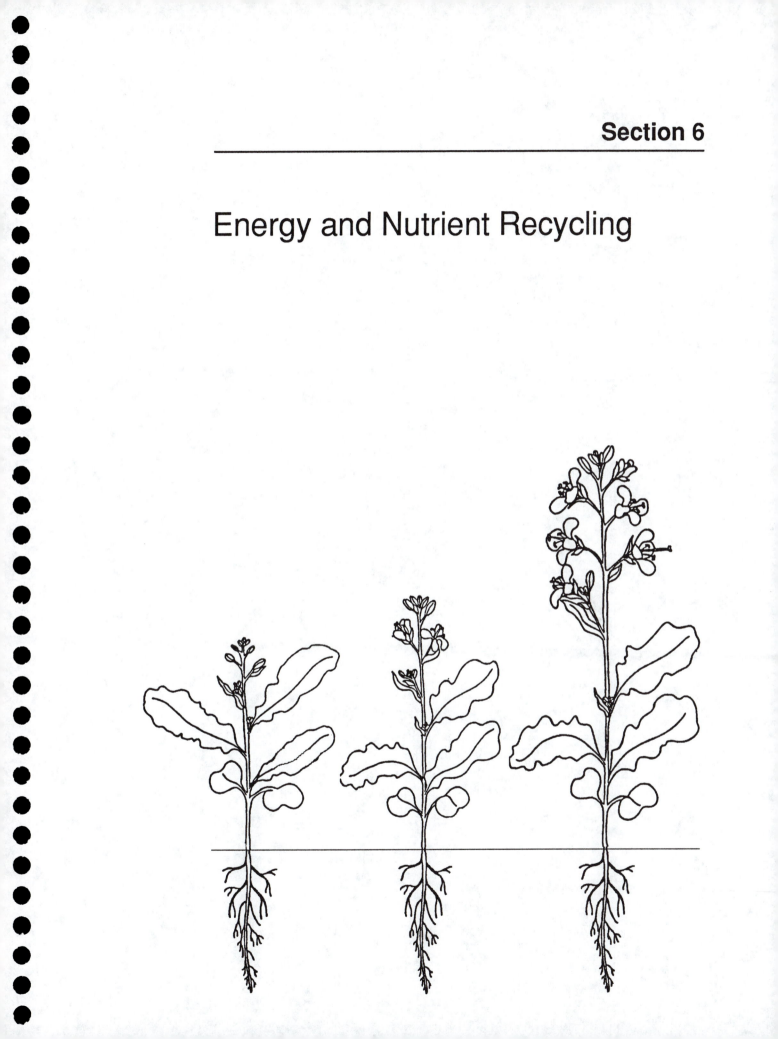

# Concepts: Energy and Nutrient Recycling

## Biocolumn Composting

Decomposition is the process of returning elements and molecules to the soil, water and atmosphere. Decomposition involves many kinds of organisms (insects, earthworms, fungi and other microbes) interrelated in complex food/energy webs. Upon death, the highly coordinated state of energy in the living plant or plant parts is lost. Through complex microbial food webs involved in decomposition this energy is reallocated to become available again to new generations of plants as carbon dioxide, minerals and complex molecules.

- *What is the process of decomposition?*

## Fermentation

Fermentation is a form of microbial decomposition which occurs in the absence of oxygen. This anaerobic decomposition stops at a certain stage because acidity prevents further microbial growth and activity.

- *What is the process of fermentation?*

# Chapter 16: Biocolumn Composting

## Background Information for the Teacher

As your students grow Fast Plants, they will explore a plant's life cycle from germination, through growth and development, pollination and fertilization, to embryo and seed development. Each major stage allows students to observe the plant's ability to use nutrients from the soil, carbon dioxide from the air, and light energy from the sun to complete its cycle and produce seeds for the next generation. After your students have harvested seeds from the dried plants for storage and future planting, one more stage remains to fully understand the natural cycle.

In nature, the recycling of matter produced by living organisms is accomplished by decay organisms, largely bacteria and fungi. A succession of organisms, each group breaking down biodegradable materials into simpler and more usable material, is at the heart of the process. The end product is *humus*, a dark, crumbly material that then becomes part of the soil.

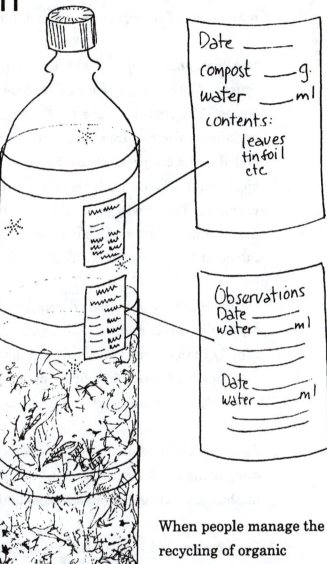

When people manage the recycling of organic matter, the process is called *composting*. Often this activity involves putting organic refuse (such as leaves, lawn clippings and garbage) into a compost pile, where the materials decompose. The resulting *compost* (humus) can be used as a soil conditioner, and as a source of plant nutrients. Almost any plant or animal material (leaves, grass clippings, straw, newspapers, food scraps or sawdust, for example) can be composted.

Decay organisms use some of the nutrients left in these materials as their food source. As these organisms decompose plant and animal material, energy is released. The organisms use some of this energy, but some is lost as heat. Decay organisms also require a moist environment to grow, so water (or rain) must be added to the compost. *Decomposition* occurs faster in the presence of oxygen (aerobic) than in its absence (anaerobic conditions). Therefore, good aeration must be provided. This is why gardeners will "turn" a compost pile. Composting will occur most rapidly when organic matter is lightly moistened, loosely packed and maintained at temperatures favorable for decay organisms to grow and reproduce.

Different organic materials decompose at different rates. Succulent materials containing water and nutrients, such as fruits and vegetables, decompose more rapidly than fibrous and woody cellulose-containing items. Lignin, the structural material coating cellulose fibers in wood, is very resistant to decay. Only a few microorganisms are capable of decomposing lignin.

As municipal landfill sites become filled with refuse from our throw-away society, composting of all organic wastes becomes increasingly important. Composting is a method of returning organic wastes to the earth in an easily reusable form.

Composting Fast Plants after the seed has been harvested helps reinforce the idea of the completion of the life cycle of an individual organism, of returning elements to the soil, water and atmosphere to again support life, and thus connects the life spiral with energy and nutrient cycles.

## Teaching Objectives
### Beginning concepts:
- Living organisms produce organic matter.
- Compost consists of decayed organic matter.
- Just as there is a cycle of life, there is a cycle of decomposition in which once-living materials break down and release their nutrients to again support life.
- Many synthetic materials created by humans do not decompose.

**Advanced concepts:**
- Humus is a dark, crumbly material resulting from the decomposition of organisms and parts of organisms, and becomes part of the soil.
- As decomposition occurs in a compost pile, heat is generated.
- Composting is the management of the biodecay of organic matter into a humus-like material by other living organisms.

**Time required for exercise:** Construct the bottle columns: 2 to 3 hours; fill the compost columns: 1 hour; composting: observation over several months.

---

**Materials needed:**
- dried Fast Plants and their potting mix
- several 2-liter soda bottles
- scissors and razor blade or knife
- thermometer (optional)
- sharp needles and a candle, or a small, fine-tipped soldering iron
- other plant and animal matter for composting along with the Fast Plants
- marking pen
- water
- pH paper (optional)

---

**Exploratory questions:** Ask your students questions and discuss ideas they might have, such as:
- What would happen if plants and animals (organisms) that die did not decay?
- How are organisms broken down?
- How long does it take for plant and animal matter to decay into humus?

## Exploration

1. **Construct a compost column from 2-liter soda bottles.**
   a. Fill a two-liter bottle with hot water and replace the cap. The heat will melt the glue and allow you to peel off the label and twist off the bottom easily (Figure 1).
   b. Use Figures 2 through 5 (page 214) to determine where to cut the bottles for a two or three bottle compost column.

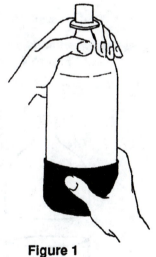

**Figure 1**

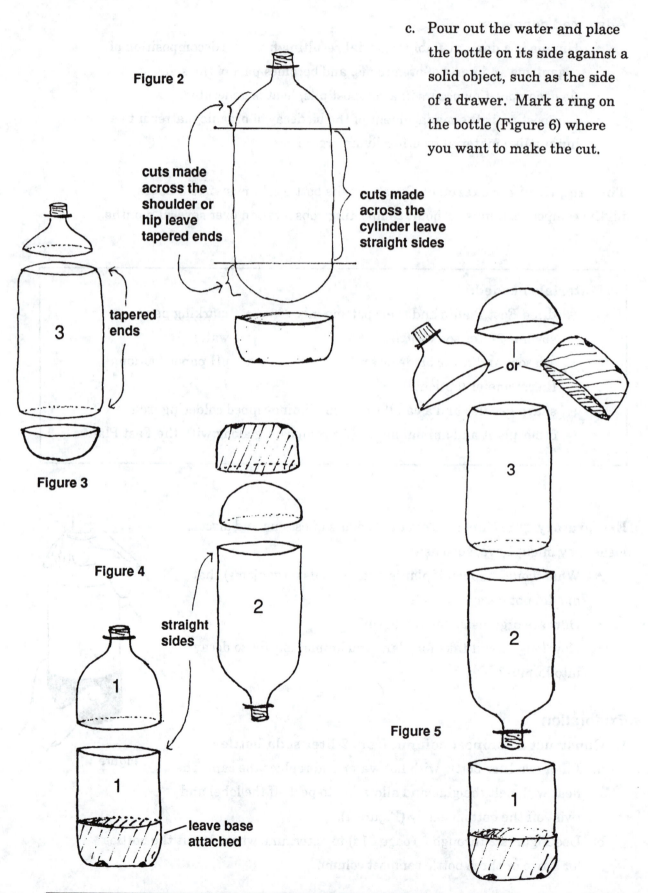

Figure 2

cuts made across the shoulder or hip leave tapered ends

cuts made across the cylinder leave straight sides

c. Pour out the water and place the bottle on its side against a solid object, such as the side of a drawer. Mark a ring on the bottle (Figure 6) where you want to make the cut.

tapered ends

3

Figure 3

Figure 4

straight sides

2

1

1

leave base attached

or

3

2

Figure 5

1

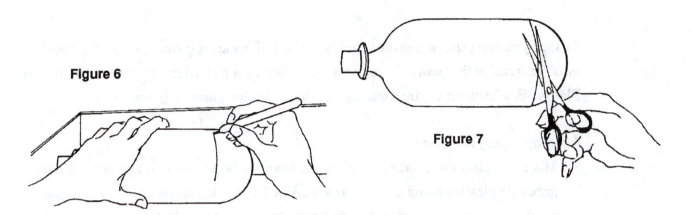

**Figure 6**

**Figure 7**

d. Use a razor blade or knife to start a cut after marking the bottles, and then finish the cut with a scissors (Figure 7). Note in Figure 5 that bottle #3 is cut with tapered ends (shoulder and hip) so that it fits into bottle #2.

e. Provide air and testing holes by poking holes in the sides of the bottle with a hot needle (heated in a candle or a Bunsen burner flame) or soldering iron.

f. Put a piece of netting or nylon stocking over the spout of bottle #2, securing it with a rubber band.

g. Put the pieces of the column together (Figure 8).

2. **Fill the compost column.**

a. Place the dried Fast Plants and potting mix in the compost column along with grass clippings, newspaper, food waste, etc. Ask students to bring in whatever they like.

b. Add just enough water to lightly moisten the materials in the column. No additional water should drain from the column at the onset.

3. **Observe periodically and record observations.**

a. Observe the odor of the column.

b. Recycle the liquid which drains into the bottom of the bottle column. Check the pH of the liquid as composting proceeds.

c. Look for evidence of the chain of decay organisms which will cycle through the composting process.

d. The temperature in the column can be checked by melting a small hole in the sides of the column with a large, hot nail or soldering iron and putting a meat thermometer into the decaying matter.

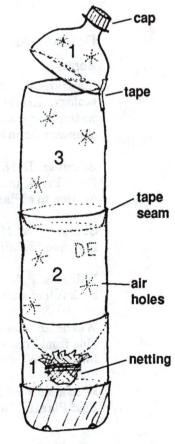

**Figure 8**

**Tip:** If you start the compost column/s in the fall, by spring you can use the "humus" to fertilize the plants in your school, or set up a nutrition experiment with Fast Plants. See "Accompanying Activity" in the Nutrition chapter (page 145).

### Accompanying Activities

•   Mix some pieces of plastic, metal, bone, bean seeds, styrofoam, and some biodegradable plastics along with organic matter (sticks, leaves, etc.) in the compost column. After several months, students can observe that the synthetic material did not decay. What is the position of the synthetic materials within the column now?

•   Make a second column, identical to the first. Add earthworms or something you want to test and observe the difference between the two (see the reference for "Composting with a Wiggle," below).

•   Measure the total mass (amount) of material added to the column, including liquid. How does the amount of the mass change over a period of time? Does the amount of liquid change?

### References

#### Books

Cochrane, J. 1987. *Plant Ecology*. New York: Bookwright Press. One of a series of books on ecology. Examines plants and how they are affected by other factors in the world: the sun, water, bacteria. Looks at the place of plants in the ecological scene and their future. See chapters 5 and 6.

Schuman, D. N. 1980. *Living with Plants, A Guide to Practical Botany*. Eureka, CA: Mad River Press, Inc. Excellent introductory chapter for background information entitled, "Introduction to a Plant," as well as other topics such as nutrients, soils and plant hormones.

Spurgeon, R. 1988. *Ecology (Usborne Science and Experiments)*. Tulsa, OK: EDC Publishing. See "Building a Compost Heap," page 38.

Williams, P. H. 1993. *Bottle Biology*. Dubuque, IA: Kendall/Hunt Publishing Co. An idea book full of ways to use recyclable materials to teach about science and the environment.

Wisconsin Fast Plants. 1992. *Composting with a Wiggle*. An information document available from Wisconsin Fast Plants, UW-Madison, Dept. of Plant Pathology, 1630 Linden Drive, Madison, WI 53706.

Wisconsin Fast Plants. Spiral of Life. Laminated 11" x 19" poster available from Wisconsin Fast Plants, UW-Madison, Dept. of Plant Pathology, 1630 Linden Drive, Madison, WI 53706.

# Chapter 17: Fermentation
## Making Kimchee in Soda Bottles

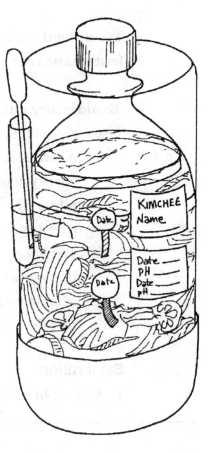

### Background Information for the Teacher

Pickling is one of the most ancient forms of preserving food. It involves the microbial conversion of sugars into lactic acid through the growth and activity of acid-forming bacteria known as *lactobacilli*. As lactobacilli grow, they convert the natural sugars in plant juices into lactic acid. Under the high acidity ( = low pH ) created by the lactobacilli other food spoiling organisms cannot grow. Lactobacilli are found almost everywhere in our environment and are known as *anaerobes*, because they grow under conditions in which oxygen is lacking.

Many foods can be preserved through natural pickling. Some common ones are sauerkraut, yogurt, dill pickles, and silage for cattle. The ancient Chinese and other cultures learned the value of pickling thousands of years ago. Today a spicy pickled Chinese cabbage product known as *kimchee* is a major part of the diet of Koreans.

You and your students can make kimchee and study lactic acid fermentation in a 2-liter bottle by using the following recipe and procedure.

### Teaching Objectives
**Beginning concepts:**

- Bacteria are involved in the making of some of our foods.
- Acid-forming bacteria can live in an acidic environment in which other organisms cannot live.
- The release of a gas is a sign that a chemical reaction is taking place.

**Advanced concepts:**

- Acid-forming bacteria (lactobacilli) thrive in oxygen-lacking environments.
- Fermentation is the breakdown of sugars in the absence of oxygen to release energy, carbon dioxide and alcohol or lactic acid.

- The pH scale is a convenient method of expressing the acidity of a solution. A pH of less than 7 is acidic. The lower the number, the higher the acidity.

**Time required for exercise:** Construct the bottle: 1 hour; set up the fermentation chamber: 1 hour; making kimchee: 7 to 14 days.

**Exploratory questions:** Ask your students questions and discuss ideas they might have, such as:

- Where does the liquid come from?
- When you push down on the sliding seal, what gas is released?
- Why do you need the sliding seal?
- If cabbage doesn't taste sour, why does the kimchee that's produced taste sour?
- What other foods are made by this process?
- Why does pickling preserve foods?

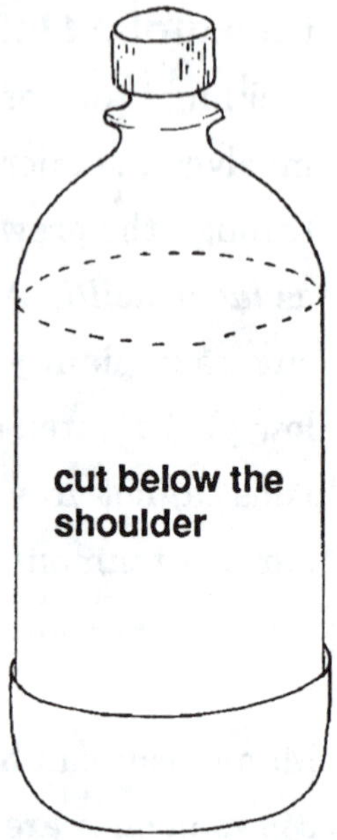

cut below the shoulder

**Figure 1**

## Exploration

1. Cut a 2-liter bottle as indicated in Figure 1. Be sure to cut the top of the bottle just below the shoulder so that it may be used to form the sliding seal (see Step 4).

2. Alternate layers of cabbage, garlic, red pepper and pickling salt in the soda bottle, pressing each layer down firmly until the bottle is packed full. The final layer should be a sprinkling of pickling salt (use up all of the salt). Notice the aroma of the garlic and pepper. These ingredients flavor the

---

**Materials needed:**

- one 2-liter soda bottle with cap
- large lid (92 mm diameter) of a plastic petri dish or pint Hagen Daz® lid
- pH indicator paper (Hydrion brand, available from lab suppliers)
- small plastic pipet
- 1-1 $\frac{1}{2}$ kg head of Chinese cabbage (*Brassica rapa*; also called napa or petsai), leaves cut into 5-7 cm chunks. Do not wash the cabbage!
- 1 hot red chili pepper, chopped (or a small packet of dried red pepper, e.g., from a pizza parlor)
- 2 cloves garlic, thinly sliced
- 3 tsp or 1/2 film can of non-iodized (or pickling) salt

product. *Caution: If working with fresh chili pepper, take care not to touch eyes or mouth. Wash hands thoroughly when finished.*

3. Place petri dish lid, rim side up, on top of ingredients and press down again (Figure 2). Note: Within a few minutes liquid begins to appear in bottom of bottle as salt draws liquid from the cells of the Chinese cabbage.

4. Press down occasionally for an hour or two.* After that there should be sufficient space to fit the cut-off top of the soda bottle into the cylinder, forming a sliding seal (Figure 3).

5. Upon pressing firmly with sliding seal, cabbage juice will rise above the petri plate and air will bubble out around the edge of the petri plate.

6. The Chinese cabbage will pack to two-thirds or half the volume of the bottle. Press daily on the sliding seal. Keep the cabbage covered by a layer of juice at all times.

7. Notice bubbles of carbon dioxide ($CO_2$) gas escape each day when pressed. The gas is produced as lactic acid bacteria grow on the sugary contents of the Chinese cabbage juice in the salty solution.

8. Measure and record the acidity of the fresh juice on top each day with the pH paper. Tape the indicator paper on the bottle and write the pH (acidity level) above it.

9. Each day take up a quantity of the juice with a plastic pipet and observe the degree of *turbidity* (cloudiness) representing the growth of lactic acid bacteria in the fermentation solution.

10. Note the increase in turbidity and change in acidity together with the continued production of gas as the pickling proceeds.

**Figure 2**

petri dish lid

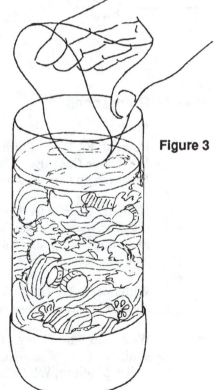

**Figure 3**

After a few days to a week or more (depending on the room temperature), the pH will have dropped from 6.5 to about 3.5, and you will have kimchee!

* petri dish lids sometimes crack while pressing. One-pint Hagen Daz® lids are perfect.

## Accompanying Activities

- A gray-line turbidity strip (Figure 4) for measuring the increasing cloudiness of the juice can be drawn on the side of the plastic pipet with a fine-tipped black marker. Hold pipet with gray line strip away from you. Look through the cabbage juice-filled pipet to the lines on the opposite side. As turbidity increases, the finer, lighter lines will disappear. After some time, the darker lines will become less visible. This provides a quantitative measure of the turbidity.

**Figure 4: Gray-Line Turbidity Strip**

- After the kimchee is mature (pH of 3.5 or less), remove the lid of the kimchee bottle. Let the kimchee bottle stand for one hour, then replace the lid. After a few days, check the chamber for evidence of bacteria or mold. Has there been any bacterial or mold growth in the chamber? Why or why not? Do the same with a can of sauerkraut or a jar of dill pickles. Compare what happens with the results obtained with the kimchee chamber.

- Research the food preservation methods of other cultures. Why and how do various cultures pickle foods?

- When the kimchee is ready, organize a multi-cultural lunch or ethnic food fair. Serve the kimchee, along with foods from other cultures.

## References

### Books

Chun, J. K. 1981. Chinese Cabbage Utilization in Korea: Kimchee Processing Technology. In *Chinese Cabbage*. N. S. Talekar and T. D. Griggs, eds. Taiwan, China: Asian Vegetable Research and Development Center.

National Council for Agricultural Education. 1994. *Using Fast Plants and Bottle Biology in the Classroom*. Reston, VA: National Association of Biology Teachers. A teacher manual including background information and 12 detailed lessons incorporating agricultural and biological science. See Lesson 5, "Silos and Sauerkraut."

Williams, P. H. 1993. *Bottle Biology*. Dubuque, IA: Kendall/Hunt Publishing Co. An idea book full of ways to use recyclable materials to teach about science and the environment.

Wisconsin Fast Plants. 1989. *Kimchee: The Korean Delight*. An information document available from Wisconsin Fast Plants, UW-Madison, Dept. of Plant Pathology, 1630 Linden Drive, Madison, WI 53706.

# Stories, Modeling and Games

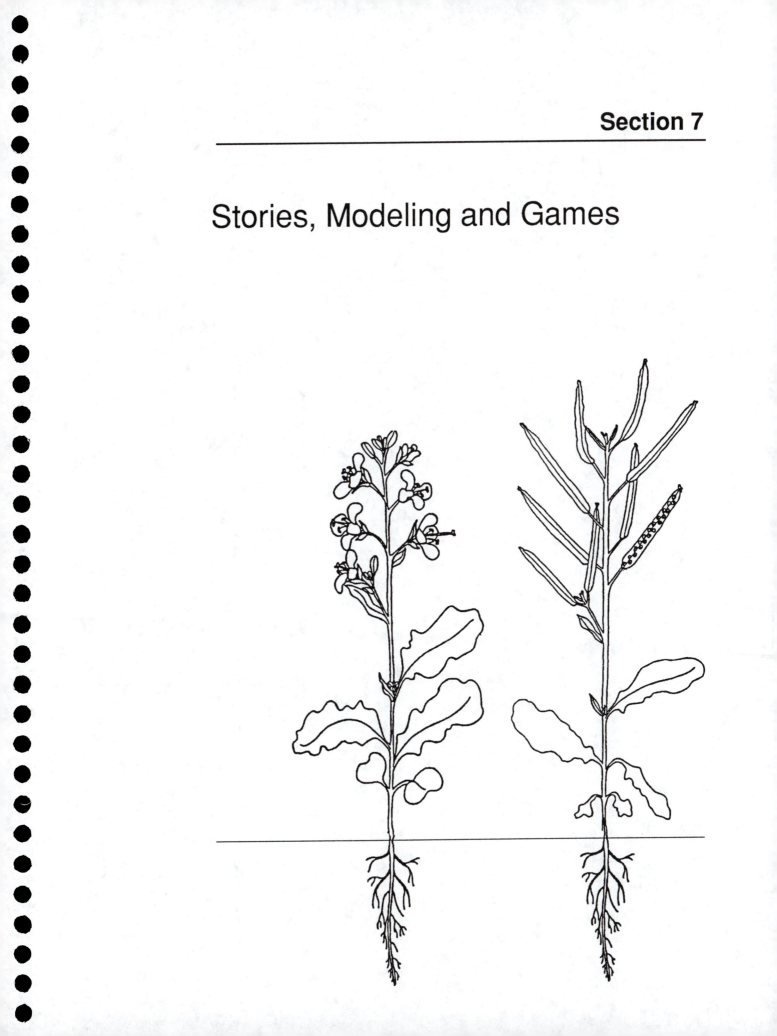

# The Story of the First Fast Plants

*Most fairy tales begin with the words, "Once upon a time in a faraway land......"*
*Sometimes, though, even real stories, begin this way.*

The story of the Fast Plants ancestors begins many, many years ago in the faraway kingdom of Nepal. High up on a rugged mountainside of the Himalayas, a farmer walked out to check his newly planted field of barley.

It was late in the spring. The snow had recently melted and the ground was becoming warm again. The barley grass he had planted a week ago would grow and provide grain for cereal and for the fried bread, called japati, that his wife made. The farmer was intending to just check the field as farmers do, but he didn't expect to see any barley plants yet.

Imagine his surprise when he spotted patches of weedy looking brassica plants, growing sturdily in the early spring sunlight. These "weeds" must have sprouted very fast. The farmer thought a bit. It had been a long winter and a long time since his family had had any fresh vegetables to eat. It would also be three months before the barley he had just planted could be harvested. So instead of pulling up the weedy plants and throwing them away, he took some home for a salad for the family's supper.

In a few days, the farmer went back to his field. By this time, the little plants were flowering. The bright yellow flowers looked like sunshine on the mountainside. Each time, the farmer took a few plants for his family to eat. The remaining plants attracted many hungry honeybees and soon produced pods with plump seeds. The farmer's wife pressed some of the seeds for oil that she could use in cooking. The farmer wisely kept the rest of the seeds to plant the following year.

The next spring he scattered his field with two kinds of seeds, the brassicas and the barley. Both of the crops grew fairly quickly, but the weedy brassica plants came up first and were already flowering while the barley was still spreading its shoots across the ground. The farmer harvested the brassicas before the barley was tall enough to shade them from the sun. He was able to produce two crops on one piece of land, providing enough food for his family and for the farm animals, the yaks.

Year after year, the farmer saved and replanted some of the brassica seeds. The little weedy brassica was a relatively "primitive" plant that required no special fertilizer and was well-adapted to survive there on the mountainside.

Time passed. Soon the farmer's grandchildren were farming the same crops on the terraced mountain field. And so it continued, generation after generation.

Then one day early in this century, a plant explorer from the other side of the world visited the mountainside farm in Nepal. Discovering the field of weedy little plants, she recognized them as a kind of brassica. She was familiar with the whole family of plants called brassicas. Many brassicas are common vegetables such as broccoli and various cabbages. Other brassicas are mustard and canola oil plants.

Since the little brassicas on the Nepalese farm had been grown for hundreds of years in the same location, they represented a unique plant stock. They could be called a "land race" and would be genetically different from other brassica plants anywhere. The plant explorer knew the importance of preserving land races of plants. She collected some of the seed of this brassica land race to take home to America. The seed was stored and saved in the United States Department of Agriculture's brassica seed collection at Iowa State University in Ames.

The seed brought by the plant explorer to the seed storage collection in Iowa stayed there for a long time. No one seemed particularly interested in it. And then, a few years ago, a plant scientist at the University of Wisconsin was seeking new genetic material for his research. This research involved trying to breed vegetable brassicas like cabbage, broccoli and turnips so that they wouldn't get particular diseases. These diseases had names like "black leg," "soft rot," and "yellows." Scientists call plants that don't become diseased with fungi, bacteria or viruses "disease resistant."

The scientist wrote to the curator of the brassica seed collection in Iowa and asked for samples of different kinds of seed of brassica land races. When they arrived, he planted them outside in a field called a research plot. There, in the middle of the research plot, appeared the little, weedy brassica from the mountainside of Nepal. This plant was about to connect the efforts of the observant farmer of long ago and the modern day research scientist.

The scientist noticed the little brassica right away because it flowered much more quickly than any of the other brassicas. What value could a weedy little brassica be to his research? Standing there in the field, ideas began to race through his mind. The plant didn't look like much, but it was very fast to flower. Normally, crossbreeding one cabbage with another takes about a year, so the results of his research were slow in coming. What if he could use this plant to develop a really fast flowering plant that could be used to test for disease resistance?

Like the farmer, the scientist decided to save the seed. He would grow the weedy brassica and its progeny (children) under constant light and with only a small amount of soil, encouraging them to reproduce faster and faster. He would choose those plants that were shortest and sturdiest, that flowered the fastest, and that produced the most seed. Then he would have a "model plant" that he could use to crossbreed with disease-resistant brassicas. Eventually he would transfer the disease resistance into his cabbages.

This is exactly what has been happening. The scientist called his model plants "Fast Plants." And thus, the little weedy brassica from Nepal was the great, great . . . . grandmother of the Fast Plants. Today scientists, students and teachers are all working with Fast Plants. They are studying how plants grow and how they produce new generations of plants.

Some students will go on to become plant geneticists, molecular biologists and plant breeders, and they will write the next chapter in the story of the Fast Plants.

How do you think it will end?

Story by Coe Williams

# Speedy Bee and the Brassica Morning

Speedy Bee woke up one Monday morning, shook her
wings and poked her nose out of the hive. What a beautiful,
sunny morning it was! Speedy was very hungry. She considered
where to go for breakfast. Should she go to the big flower garden
down the street? No, not today. What she really wanted was the delicious
nectar from the bright yellow flowers in the field behind Farmer Montero's barn.
Yesterday, on her way home from collecting nectar and pollen, she had noticed that
the whole field had turned yellow with tiny brassica flowers and smelled delicious.

Speedy set off in a hurry. Not only did she have to get the sweet nectar for herself so
that she'd have lots of energy for the day, but she also had to collect pollen from the
flowers to bring back to the hive to feed the new baby bees, called larvae. She
wanted some pollen, too, to keep her muscles in good shape.

She was flying merrily down the road when she decided to take a short cut across
the school grounds. All of a sudden she stopped and hovered in the air, her wings
beating very fast. She saw something bright yellow through the window of Mrs.
Lee's classroom. Speedy loved yellow and she zipped over to investigate.

"My goodness," she thought, "where did those brassica flowers come from? And why
are they growing in little boxes?" Just then she noticed Mrs. Lee opening the window to let in some of the fresh breeze before the stu-
dents arrived. Speedy waited until Mrs. Lee
turned and walked out into the hall. How
wonderful! This was closer to the hive than
Farmer Montero's field. She wouldn't have to
fly so far this morning. Besides, for the
moment she had all these flowers to herself.

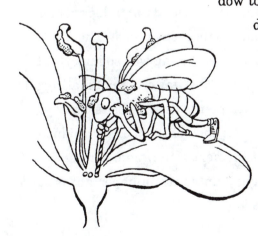

Into the room she flew, making a beeline
for the closest plant. She perched on a petal

and pushed her head deep into the flower to reach the nectaries at the bottom. As she sipped the liquid nectar with her long proboscis, her body brushed against the other parts of the flower. The sticky pollen from the stamens on the flower stuck to the feather-like hairs on her head and body.

Speedy worked very fast. She always worked hard. Each time she finished collecting nectar and pollen from the flowers in one little box, she hovered in the air for a minute and cleaned herself off. Using the brush-like part of her two front legs, she combed the pollen off her head and thorax and transferred it to the platform on her back leg.

When the platform was full of the bright yellow pollen, she snapped up the bottom of the leg against the top part and packed the pollen into some special long, curved hairs. Pretty soon there was so much pollen there that it looked as if she had baskets of pollen on both hind legs.

Speedy was having a wonderful time. She wasn't sure why there was a garden of brassica flowers in the school. She didn't think there was a farmer going to school with the children. On the wall near the plants was a sign that said "Fast Plants," but Speedy Bee couldn't read. So she just kept on with her job.

The plants were happy too. Every time pollen from one plant brushed off Speedy's body onto the flower of another plant, the second plant smiled. The pollen from its friends that collected on the stigmas of its flowers seemed so good, whereas its own

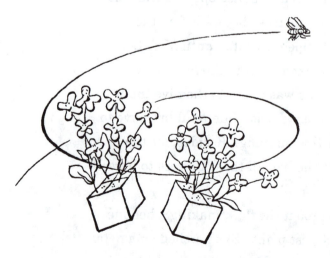

pollen was yucky. The flowers knew that pollen from their friends would grow and help them produce new seeds. That's why what Speedy was doing was so important to the plants. She was cross-pollinating all the brassica plants in Mrs. Lee's classroom, so that each of them could produce seeds for the next generation. Cross-pollinating plants was an important part of Speedy's job.

She had just moved to the last box of four plants, when she heard a bell ring and suddenly there was lots of noise in the school. It was the students laughing and talking as they walked down the hall towards Mrs. Lee's room. Speedy thought perhaps she'd better finish quickly. Besides, she had collected so much pollen that she almost couldn't carry any more. She buzzed louder as she hurried over the flowers in the last box and then flew toward the open window just as the children burst into the room.

They seemed very excited about something. She heard Mrs. Lee say that today they could pollinate their Fast Plants. Did Mrs. Lee mean Speedy's brassica flowers? She watched for a minute and sure enough, each of the children went over to pick up a little box of the brassicas.

"Well," thought Speedy, "I guess this time I won't tell all of my friends at the beehive about the special garden of brassica plants. It looks as though the children will be taking care of them. Tomorrow, I'll have to fly to Farmer Montero's field after all." She headed back home, with her stomach full of nectar and laden with pollen for the new baby bees.

As she flew away, the children in Mrs. Lee's class carefully moved around the room, cross-pollinating each other's Fast Plants. By the end of the week, as they examined their flowers, the pistils on every single flower were getting longer. Every flower that they had pollinated would be producing seed. They were very proud of themselves and Mrs. Lee was pleased with the plant skills they were developing. Nobody realized that part of that success was due to the visit from Speedy Bee.

And the Fast Plants never told.

Story by Coe Williams

# Modeling

The use of models can be extremely helpful to both teachers and students. For the teacher, the use of a model can sometimes be the best way to explain a procedure, interpret an observation or describe a process occurring over time.

For the student, the building of a model allows the student to develop a concrete visualization of a structure that may not be easily studied. Each functional part of the structure must be created by the student and placed in the proper orientation. When the model-building is complete, the student has a better understanding of both structure and function.

**Seed Sponge Model: A teaching model**

To help students visualize the effect of water intake (imbibition) on a germinating seed a model can be constructed from a grocery store sponge.

- Cut the pattern out of a household sponge, as shown in Figure 1.

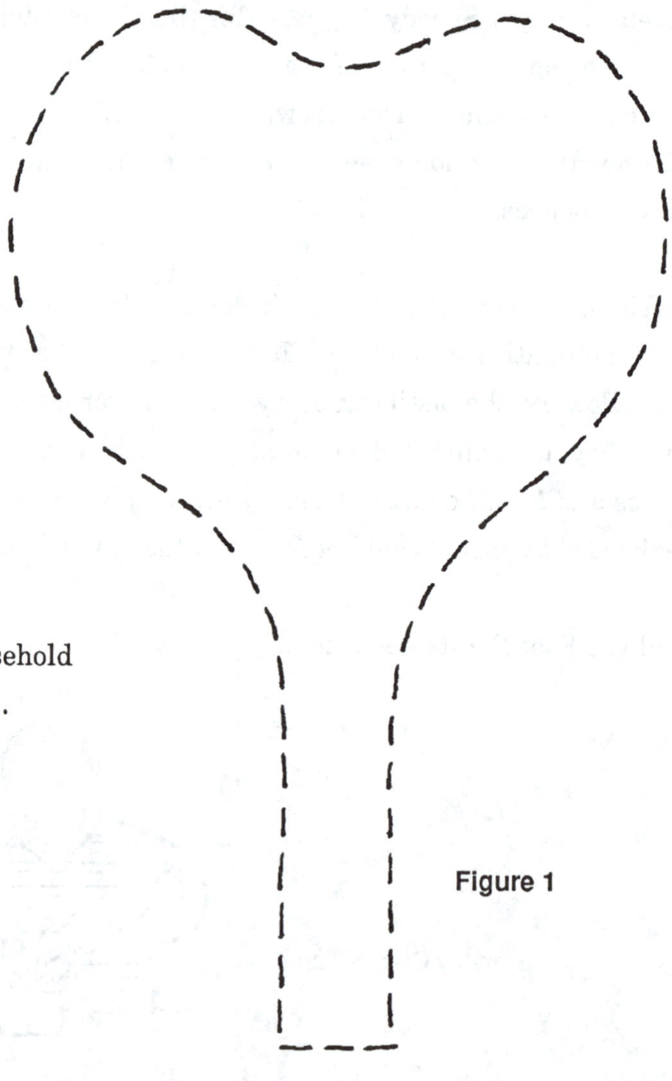

Figure 1

- Cut the cotyledon part lengthwise to form two cotyledons (Figure 2).

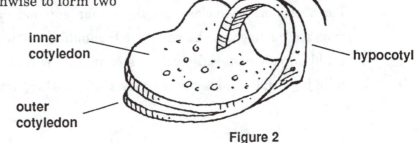

inner cotyledon

hypocotyl

outer cotyledon

**Figure 2**

- Thoroughly wet the sponge and roll it into a tiny ball (Figure 3), folding the radicle inside and wrapping the cotyledons around it.

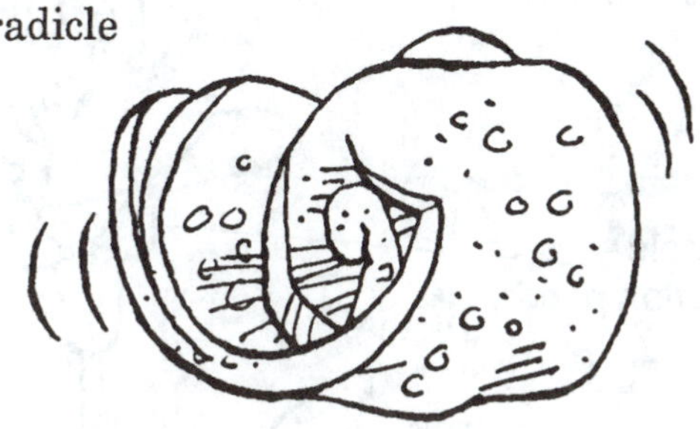

**Figure 3**

- Wrap tightly with string and let dry completely, approximately 2 days (Figure 4).

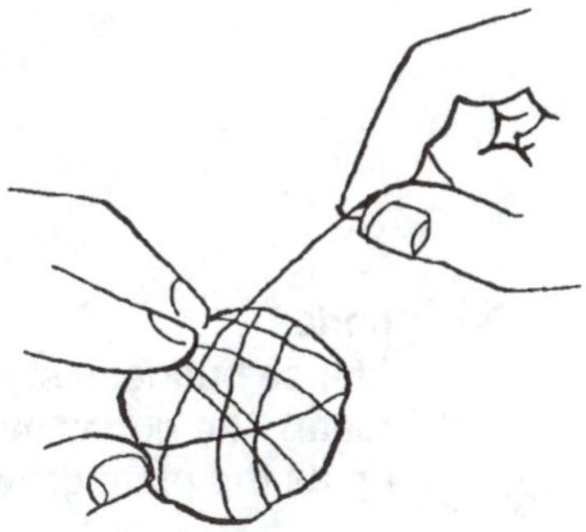

**Figure 4**

- Remove string and wrap the "seed" with one layer of tissue (kleenex) to simulate a seed coat. Secure with a tiny piece of tape.

- Pop into water and watch it germinate (Figure 5).*

**Figure 5**

* Lynnette Eddington, 3rd grade teacher at Mapleton Elementary School in Mapleton, Utah, refers to the germinating seed sponge as "a 10-second lifetime learning experience."

## Brassica Plant Model:  A student model

For homework or in class, ask the students to make a model of a brassica flower such as the diagram shown.  Models should be as accurate as possible.  The teachers could provide materials such as straws, thin wire, construction paper, empty plastic milk jugs and various scrap materials for making flower models in class.

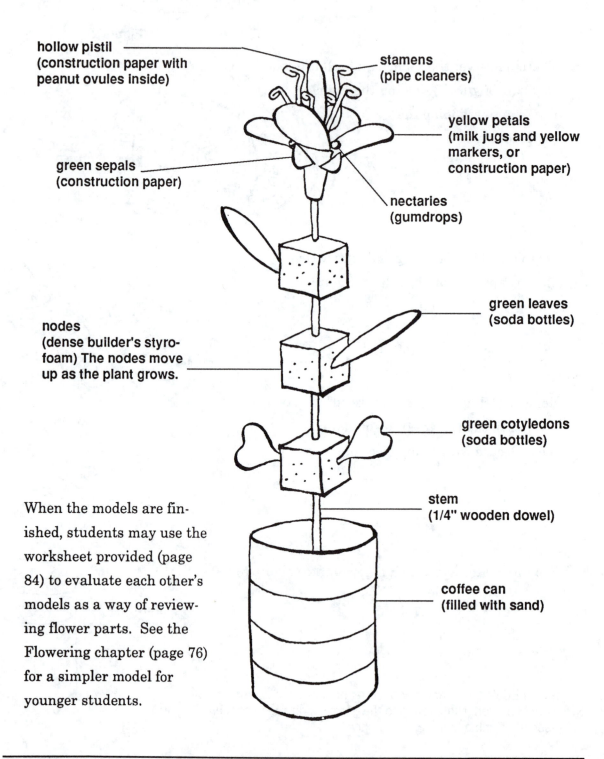

hollow pistil
(construction paper with
peanut ovules inside)

stamens
(pipe cleaners)

yellow petals
(milk jugs and yellow
markers, or
construction paper)

green sepals
(construction paper)

nectaries
(gumdrops)

nodes
(dense builder's styro-
foam) The nodes move
up as the plant grows.

green leaves
(soda bottles)

green cotyledons
(soda bottles)

stem
(1/4" wooden dowel)

coffee can
(filled with sand)

When the models are finished, students may use the worksheet provided (page 84) to evaluate each other's models as a way of reviewing flower parts.  See the Flowering chapter (page 76) for a simpler model for younger students.

## Honeybee Model: A student model

In the life cycle adventure, the honeybee is an integral part of the pollination process, ensuring the continuity of the species. Students and/or the teacher can reinforce what is being learned by constructing a model bee.

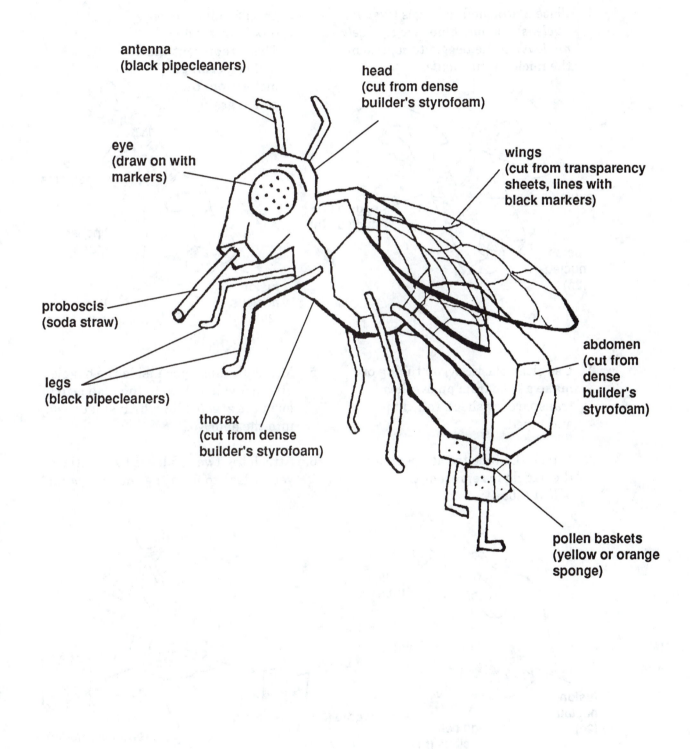

antenna
(black pipecleaners)

head
(cut from dense
builder's styrofoam)

eye
(draw on with
markers)

wings
(cut from transparency
sheets, lines with
black markers)

proboscis
(soda straw)

abdomen
(cut from
dense
builder's
styrofoam)

legs
(black pipecleaners)

thorax
(cut from dense
builder's styrofoam)

pollen baskets
(yellow or orange
sponge)

## Fertilization Model: A teaching model

Demonstrate the process of double fertilization with a clear polyethelene tube (e.g., roll up an overhead transparency), some small 1 cm legos and a clear plastic bag.

1. Place 2 attached red legos (*fusion nucleus*) and one blue lego (*egg cell nucleus*) in the baggie to represent the nuclei in the *ovule*.

4. Drop 2 yellow legos down the tube. These represent the male (sperm) gametes from the pollen grain.

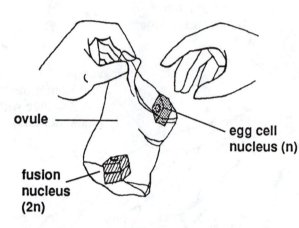

ovule

egg cell nucleus (n)

fusion nucleus (2n)

male gametes

pollen tube

fusion nucleus (2n)

egg cell nucleus (n)

2. Use clear plastic tygon tubing or make a tube from an overhead transparency sheet, rolled up and taped.

3. Attach the tube to the opening of the baggie to represent the *pollen tube*.

5. Manipulating legos inside the baggie, attach a yellow lego to the blue lego to form the *zygote* (2n) which will develop into the embryo.

6. Attach the two red legos to the other yellow lego to form the *endosperm* (3n).

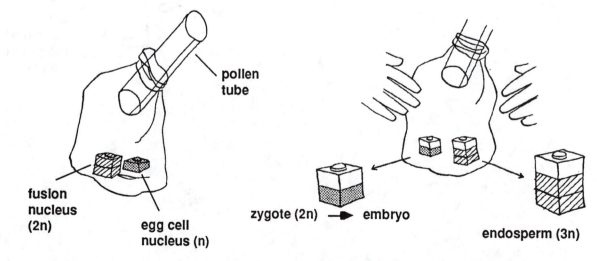

pollen tube

fusion nucleus (2n)

egg cell nucleus (n)

zygote (2n) ➔ embryo

endosperm (3n)

# Brassica Flower Role Playing Game

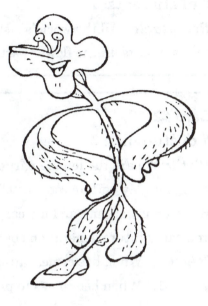

**Objectives:**

- To show students the structure of a brassica flower.
- To teach (or reinforce) students the function of the brassica flower parts.
- To present the concepts of plant fertilization.
- To reinforce vocabulary.

**How to play:**

1. **Preparation:** Before the day of the activity, the teacher and/or students should prepare the flower parts from colored construction paper. Props for the bee could be made by the teacher.

2. **Materials:**
   - yellow construction paper (for petals, receptacle and stamens)
   - green construction paper (for sepals)
   - construction paper (wings of bee)
   - four small, green balloons (for nectaries)
   - plastic bag (for pollen bag of bee)
   - heavy string (for pollen tube — wind around one pollen grain to simulate germinating pollen tube)
   - two balls of newspaper (for pollen grains)
   - masking tape (to hold pollen grains to top of pistil)

3. **The activity:**
   Select students to come up and read the description of the plant parts. Call on another student to name the part. Then that person, or persons take the props and assume the position to form the flower.

## Cue Cards

---

**Card #1**

**# of students: 1**

*Receptacle:* All the world's a stage and so am I because I am on top of the flower stalk that supports all the flower parts. My name is?

---

**Card #2**

**# of students: 2**

*Pistil:* We are the female part of this plant made up of three basic parts. My top is called a stigma. My bottom consists of two fused carpels (or ovaries) containing many ovules. Between my stigma and my carpels is my style. Once fertilized, I will become a seed pod and carry future generations of brassica. My name is?

**\*\*Action:** When bee comes, after all flower parts assembled and identified.

1. When bee comes to pistil to deposit first pollen grain, shout, "Yuk! This pollen is incompatible!"
2. When second pollen grain is deposited, shout, "Yum, yum, we're compatible!" Pull down rope from pollen grain (= germinating pollen) through the hole in stigma to ovule.

---

**Card #3**

**# of students: 1**

*Ovule:* I rest inside the carpels with lots of my friends. We each contain a female egg cell. Here we wait until fertilization takes place. Then we each grow into a seed. My name is?

**\*\*Action:** Curl up at the base of the pistil.

---

**Card #4**

**# of students: 4**

*Nectary:* My buddies and I surround the base of the pistil. Two of us are very busy producing a sweet liquid which attracts many insect friends. However, two of my buddies are freeloaders. They are simply non-functional. My name is?

---

**Card #5**

**# of students: 6**

*Stamen:* I am one of six in this plant. four of us are tall and two of us are short. We are the male parts of this plant. The most important part of us is our anther. This is where my pollen is produced. My pollen will fertilize the ovules in a brassica plant. My anther is supported by a little stem called a filament. My name is?

**Card #6**

**# of students: 4**

*Petal:* I am often the reason people and insects notice this plant. My color attracts bees which help in pollination. On a brassica there are four of us. My name is?

**Card #7**

**# of students: 4**

*Sepal:* I am on the outer limits of the flower with three other cohorts. We enclose the other flower parts in the bud until blooming time. My name is?

**Card #8**

**# of students: 1**

*Honeybee:*

**Action: The honeybee arrives wearing pollen bag on hip.

1. Tastes nectar.
2. Flies to pistil to fertilize.
3. Puts incompatible pollen on pistil.
4. Puts compatible pollen onto masking tape of pistil. At this point the Carpels (Pistil) help to pull the rope down to the ovule.

Credits: Debbie Bevan and Wesley Licht, Glendale Elementary School, Madison, WI.

# Build a Brassica

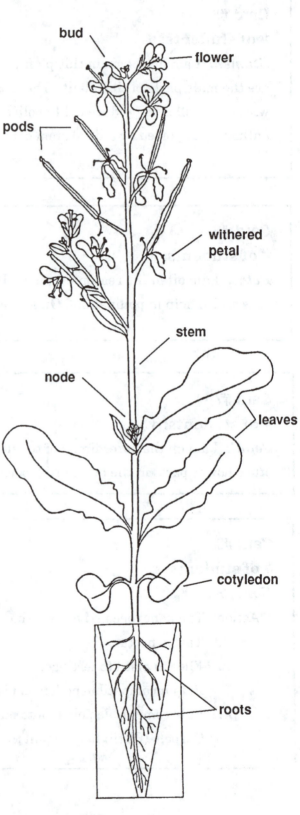

1. Divide the class into three teams. Assign each team a section of chalkboard

2. Directions to teams:
   Draw and label as many parts of a brassica plant as you can. Suggestions: Draw a ground line and suggest they begin with the roots.

3. Rules:
   Each team member may draw and label only one part when it is their turn. They may correct a mistake that a teammate made before they add their new part.

4. Scoring:
   The drawing with the most correctly drawn and labeled parts wins. If there is a tie, use spelling or neatness of the drawing as criteria.

5. Suggestions:
   Deduct a point if teammates shout out. Allow team members to pass turns if they can't think of anything towards the end of the game.

Credits: Jeanette MacMurdo, Lloyd Street School, Milwaukee, WI.

# Brassica Word Match

Give students envelopes with vocabulary words on small cards and the definitions on strips. Photocopy and cut the sample provided. Ask students to work in pairs to match words and definitions. The same words and definitions are in the "Plant Crossword Puzzle" (page 239).

| | |
|---|---|
| **ovary (carpel)** | The bottom part of the pistil that holds the ovules. |
| **cotyledons** | The seed leaves. |
| **stigma** | The top flat part of the pistil that pollen sticks to when the flower has been pollinated. |
| **pollen** | The powder on the anther. |
| **stamen** | The part of the flower producing pollen. |
| **flower** | The colorful part of the plant that attracts bees. |
| **Brassica** | Belongs to the crucifers — a family that includes mustards, radishes and cabbage. |
| **sepal** | The outer part of the flower bud that protects the flower before it opens. |

Credits: Phyllis Pickarts, Allis Elementary School, Madison, WI.

| | |
|---|---|
| **pedicel** | The stem of the flower. |
| **seed** | It has a baby plant inside that grows into a big plant. |
| **thorax** | The middle part of a bee's body. |
| **pollination** | The bee carries the pollen from one flower to another flower. |
| **ovule** | The part of the plant that holds the egg. |
| **petal** | The part of the flower that is usually colored. |
| **root hairs** | Part of the root that draws in water and minerals from the soil. |
| **root** | The part of the plant below ground that anchors and feeds the plant. |
| **anther** | The top part of the stamen that holds the pollen. |
| **pistil** | The middle flower part the which has the stigma, style and ovary (carpel). |

# Plant Crossword

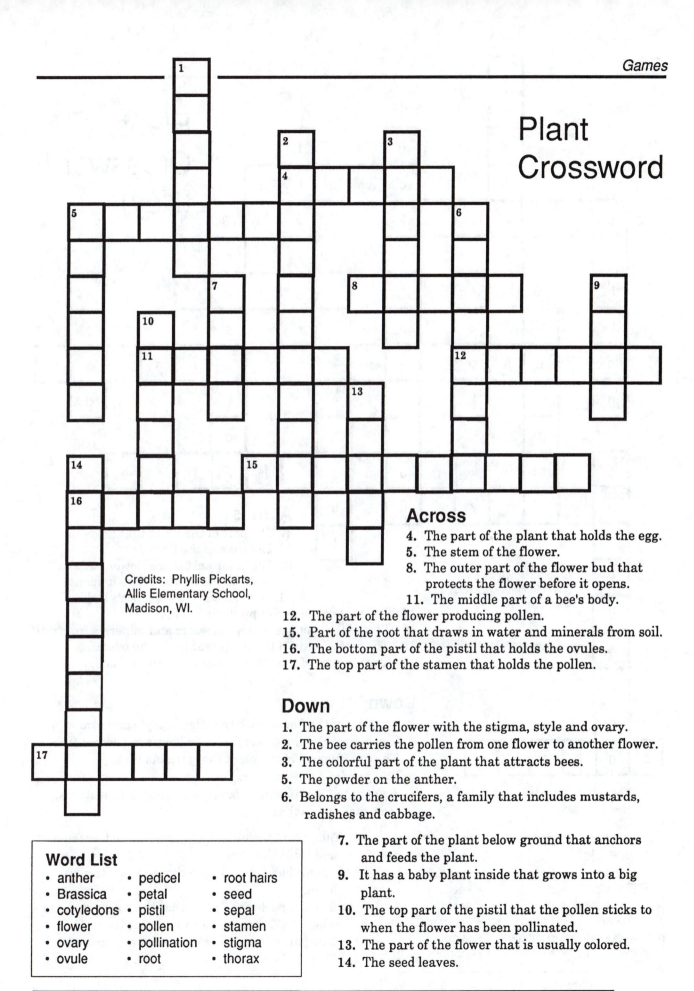

Credits: Phyllis Pickarts, Allis Elementary School, Madison, WI.

## Across

4. The part of the plant that holds the egg.
5. The stem of the flower.
8. The outer part of the flower bud that protects the flower before it opens.
11. The middle part of a bee's body.
12. The part of the flower producing pollen.
15. Part of the root that draws in water and minerals from soil.
16. The bottom part of the pistil that holds the ovules.
17. The top part of the stamen that holds the pollen.

## Down

1. The part of the flower with the stigma, style and ovary.
2. The bee carries the pollen from one flower to another flower.
3. The colorful part of the plant that attracts bees.
5. The powder on the anther.
6. Belongs to the crucifers, a family that includes mustards, radishes and cabbage.
7. The part of the plant below ground that anchors and feeds the plant.
9. It has a baby plant inside that grows into a big plant.
10. The top part of the pistil that the pollen sticks to when the flower has been pollinated.
13. The part of the flower that is usually colored.
14. The seed leaves.

## Word List

- anther
- Brassica
- cotyledons
- flower
- ovary
- ovule
- pedicel
- petal
- pistil
- pollen
- pollination
- root
- root hairs
- seed
- sepal
- stamen
- stigma
- thorax

# Plant Crossword (Key)

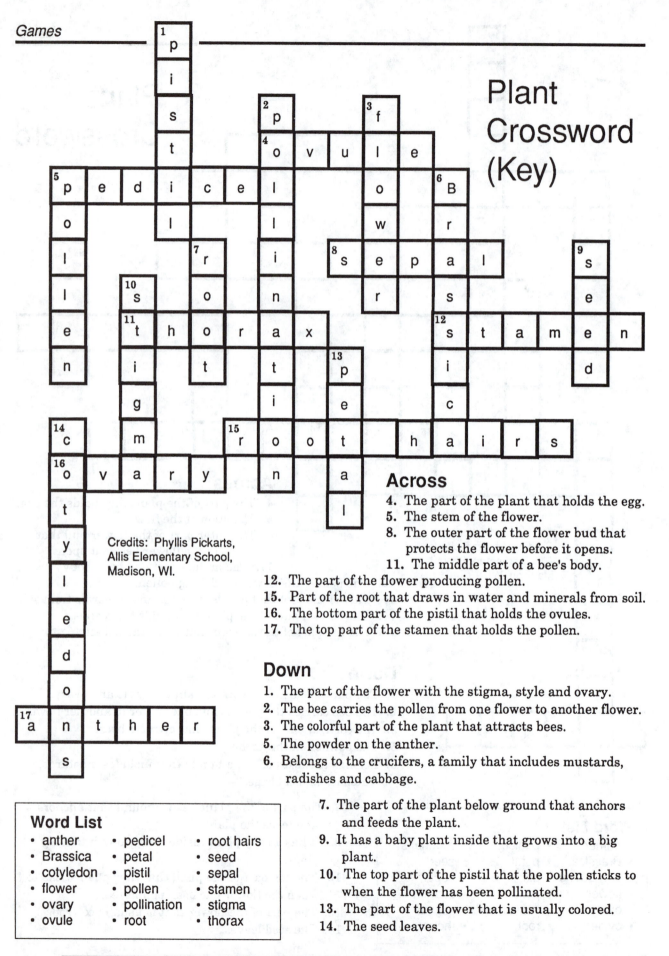

Credits: Phyllis Pickarts, Allis Elementary School, Madison, WI.

## Across

4. The part of the plant that holds the egg.
5. The stem of the flower.
8. The outer part of the flower bud that protects the flower before it opens.
11. The middle part of a bee's body.
12. The part of the flower producing pollen.
15. Part of the root that draws in water and minerals from soil.
16. The bottom part of the pistil that holds the ovules.
17. The top part of the stamen that holds the pollen.

## Down

1. The part of the flower with the stigma, style and ovary.
2. The bee carries the pollen from one flower to another flower.
3. The colorful part of the plant that attracts bees.
5. The powder on the anther.
6. Belongs to the crucifers, a family that includes mustards, radishes and cabbage.
7. The part of the plant below ground that anchors and feeds the plant.
9. It has a baby plant inside that grows into a big plant.
10. The top part of the pistil that the pollen sticks to when the flower has been pollinated.
13. The part of the flower that is usually colored.
14. The seed leaves.

### Word List

- anther
- Brassica
- cotyledon
- flower
- ovary
- ovule
- pedicel
- petal
- pistil
- pollen
- pollination
- root
- root hairs
- seed
- sepal
- stamen
- stigma
- thorax

# Brassica Bingo

1. Make several copies of the Fast Plants words from the Brassica Word Match.

2. Make multiple copies of your blank plant bingo form.

3. Cut Fast Plants words apart and glue in spaces on card. See the sample card below. Remember a word can be in more than one column but not more than once in a column.

4. Make teacher recording card. Cover all game parts with clear contact paper to prolong their use.

5. Copy definitions, color code by column and cut apart.

6. Play game like bingo -- identify letter for column, read definition, players cover the word if they have it in the correct column, and caller covers it on the recording card.

7. Shouting "Brassica" signals a win. The winner must clear his or her card.

| P | L | A | N | T |
|---|---|---|---|---|
| ovule | flower | root hairs | pedicel | seed |
| petal | anther | cotyledons | root | pollen |
| root hairs | stigma | | stamen | ovary (carpel) |
| anther | pollen | ovule | Brassica | root |
| Brassica | ovule | pedicel | stigma | flower |

Original idea and text by Nan Alexander, Readstown Elementary, Readstown, WI.

# Design a Plant
## A cooperative learning activity/game for intermediate students

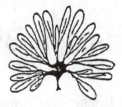

As a group you are to design a plant which will be able to live for generation after generation. This plant must be a nonwoody dicot that lives for only one season. It is an annual.

This plant must be able to survive the following conditions:

| Season | Frost | Ground Temp (°F) | Precipitation | Wind |
|--------|-------|------------------|---------------|------|
| Fall | first,10/15 | 40 | mostly rain | windy |
| Winter | one meter | 30 | snow | moderate |
| Spring | gone, 4/15 | 45 | rain | windy |
| Summer | none | 55 | very little rain | moderate |

There are no flying insects in this place, but there are all the other usual creatures which live in a place such as this.

In each of the sketches be sure to *label all parts.*

1. Sketch a leaf from your plant.

2. Sketch the stem of your plant.

3. Sketch the roots of your plant.

4. Sketch the flower of your plant and indicate how many of each part it has.

5. Sketch whatever the ovary (carpel) becomes after the egg has been fertilized, e.g., a fruit, a pod?

6. Sketch the seed of your plant.

7. How will your plant be pollinated?

8. How will your plant's seeds be dispersed?

9. Under what conditions will the seeds germinate?

10. Describe the life cycle of your plant (indicate the seasons.)

11. Name four adaptations your plant has which helps it to live and compete successfully generation after generation.

Credits: Peter Howell, Pollard Middle School, Needham, MA.

# Environment, Lighting and Alternative Growing Systems

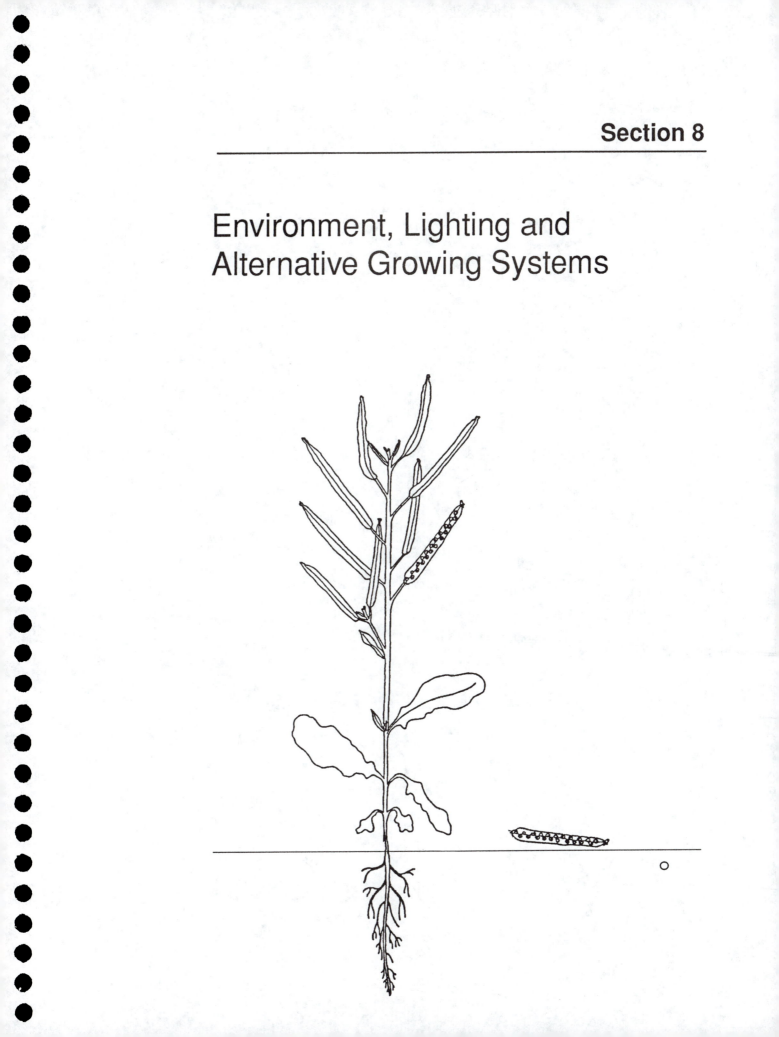

# Environment, Lighting and Alternative Growing Systems

Adequate lighting is perhaps the most important factor in the success of your Fast Plants projects. **Please read this page and "Seeing the Light" (pages 245-248) before you begin your Fast Plants project.**

## Lighting tips and suggestions

*   Fast Plants require 24 hour/day fluorescent lighting. They will not grow well in windowsills or under less than 24 hour/day lighting.
*   Use a minimum of 6 bulbs in your light bank; 8 bulbs are ideal.
*   Always remember the following equation:

---

## Formula for growing successful Fast Plants:

| | | | | | | |
|---|---|---|---|---|---|---|
| Six 40 W bulbs or the new 32 W high efficiency bulbs* should be used for growing Fast Plants | + | Rotate your plants. Irradiance (light intensity) grades off from the center of the light bank. | + | Keep tops of plants between 5 and 10 cm from the lights. | = | **Healthy Fast Plants** |

---

**Figure 1**

The light rack available from Carolina Biological Supply Company (Figure 1) is made with 1-inch PVC tubing. You can construct your own PVC tubing rack by using the same specifications for the wooden light stand (page 249).

\* new federal specifications require the use of 32 watt high efficiency bulbs (instead of the 40 watt bulbs). These 32 watt bulbs are satisfactory for Fast Plants but will require different fixtures than the 40 watt bulbs.

# Environmental Parameters

Various physical, chemical and biotic components of the environment impact on the growth of Fast Plants. Below are some major parameters that should be considered when growing Fast Plants.

**Temperature:** Monitored under each light bank using hi-low thermometers or bimetal (copper-constantan) thermocouples and recorded continuously in degrees Celsius. Note fluctuations in ambient temperature and variation in temperature among light banks.

**Irradiance:** Sources of irradiance are 40W cool white fluorescent bulbs spaced at 5-6 centimeters. Measurements were taken at 10, 20, and 30 centimeters from the light bulbs on a 10 centimeter by 10 centimeter grid, using a Licor LI-188 integrating quantum radiometer/photometer. Irradiance units in the photosynthetically active range (PAR) are $\mu Em^2 sec^{-1}$. See "Seeing the Light" (pages 245-248).

**Soil:** Growing substrate is peatlite, JiffyMix® brand, a mixture of ground sphagnum peat moss and fine vermiculite in a mixture of 1:1.

**Nutrients:** Nutrients are added to the substrate as a solution of Peters® brand general purpose fertilizer containing available NPK at 20% by weight (20-20-20). Primary nutrient sources are urea, ammonium phosphate, and potassium nitrate. A soluble green dye is added for mixing.

> Total nitrogen (N)...........................................20%
>     5.61% nitrate nitrogen
>     3.96% ammoniacal nitrogen
>     10.43% urea nitrogen
> Available phosphoric acid ($P_2O_5$)......................20%
> Soluble potash ($K_2O$)....................................20%
> Potential acidity is 597 lb calcium carbonate equivalent per ton.

- Nutrient solution contains 7 grams of Peters 20-20-20 fertilizer per liter of deionized water.
- Nutrient solution is applied to the growing substrate at the rate of 2 ml of solution on Days 3, 7, 14, 21 and 28 for each plant that will be grown to maturity.

**Soil Moisture:** Growing substrate (soil) is maintained at 'field capacity' through capillary wicking from a water reservoir through a felt wick to a water pad then to the wick pot via a second felt wick.

**Atmosphere:** Ambient air, N (78%), $O_2$ (21%), $CO_2$, $H_2$, He (<1%). $CO_2$ in air is approximately 350 ppm.

**Gravity vector:** 1g; normal vertical.

**Biota:**
- unknown, variable soil microflora and microfauna in rhizosphere
- unknown, variable microflora in phyllosphere.
- watch for phytophagus arthropods, mites, thrips, lepidopteran larvae on plant surfaces.
- watch for mycophagus insects, usually dipterans emerging from soil around plant.
- note variable algal populations on moist soil substrate surface, frequently blue-green, cyanobacteria (*Ocillatoria*) and green algae.

# Seeing the Light
## When growing Fast Plants, the more light the better

Among the various environmental factors that influence the growth and development of Wisconsin Fast Plants, light is one that can have the greatest long term impact on the success of your classroom activities.

Continuous high light is essential to the growth of vigorous, robust plants that are capable of producing lots of flowers and seeds. Fast Plants were purposely developed to grow under inexpensive, white fluorescent lamps and have been bred for many generations to perform well when illuminated continuously (24 hours/day) with the relatively high light intensity provided by six or eight four foot 40 W fluorescent bulbs spaced at 5-6 cm apart (center to center).

High light provides energy for photosynthesis to support the accelerated growth of the Fast Plants and also is the source of energy that regulates the form and color of the plants. Basic rapid-cycling *Brassica rapa* plants growing with normal nutrition and temperature under the **ideal lighting** provided by eight 4-foot 40 W fluorescent bulbs will be stocky and dark green with purple anthocyanin pigment strongly expressed in the stem, leaves and buds. The plants will bear many flowers which, when pollinated, will produce abundant seed in the normal life cycle of 40 days.

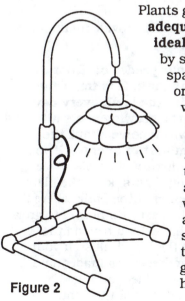

Plants growing under the **adequate, but less than ideal**, lighting provided by six 40 W bulbs spaced at 10 cm apart, or a 30 W circle light, will be somewhat less stocky and may require staking as the plants grow taller. Purple anthocyanin color will be less intense and seed set will be somewhat less than that from plants growing under higher light.

**Figure 2**

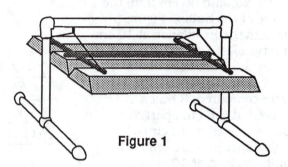

**Figure 1**

Plants growing under **less than adequate light** provided by four or fewer 40 W bulbs will be spindly and tend to fall over easily. The leaves will be thinner and plants will have weak expression of the purple color in their stems and leaves. Such plants may be delayed in flowering and will produce fewer flowers and seeds.

Our experience with Fast Plants is that the more fluorescent light they receive, the better they grow. Light intensity, or *irradiance*, is quantified as the flow of photons in the light spectrum and is measured in micromoles (μmoles) of photons impacting on a meter square surface ($m^2$) each second ($s^{-1}$). Irradiance can be measured by various kinds of photometers that provide an indication of the μMol $m^2$ $s^{-1}$ of photons.

### Measurement of Irradiance

In order to determine the relationship between light intensity and Fast Plant growth, we have measured the irradiance in the space under various combinations of 40 watt white fluorescent lamps, Figure 1, as well as under 22 W and 30 W fluorescent circle lights, Figure 2, and observed the growth of Fast Plants under various levels of irradiance.

Irradiance measurements in μMol $m^2$ $s^{-1}$ of photons were made with a Licor L1-188 integrating quantum radiometer/photometer with a filter that transmitted photons in the photosynthetically active range (PAR) of 400-700 nanometers. Because it is known that irradiance from fluorescent lamps decreases with use, we measured irradiance with both new and used (<1000 hour) bulbs.

## Measurements under 40 W bulbs

Measurements under 40 W bulbs were made on a 60 x 120 cm grid at 10 cm intervals, and at 10, 20, and 30 cm from the plane of the bulbs. Figure 3 depicts the irradiance at 10 cm intervals 10, 20 and 30 cm below a 6-bulb light bank. Four configurations of bulbs were compared, 8 bulbs spaced at 5-6 cm apart, 6 bulbs spaced at 10 cm, 4 bulbs spaced at 10 cm and 2 bulbs spaced at 10 cm apart centered on the measuring grid. As expected, light intensities were greatest under eight lamps, Figures 4 and 5. Irradiance decreased rapidly at the edges of the light banks with lowest intensities in the corners. Intensities decreased 20-30% with each 10 cm increase in distance from the plane of the bulbs. Plants growing at irradiances of greater than 200 µMol m$^2$ s$^{-1}$ exhibit ideal growth and development, plants growing between 199 and 100 µMol m$^2$ s$^{-1}$ grow adequately, whereas plants grown at less than 100 µMol m$^2$ s$^{-1}$ perform less than adequately.

**Figure 3:** Irradiance on a 120 x 60 cm grid measured at 10 cm intervals, 10, 20, and 30 cm below six 40 W fluorescent bulbs.

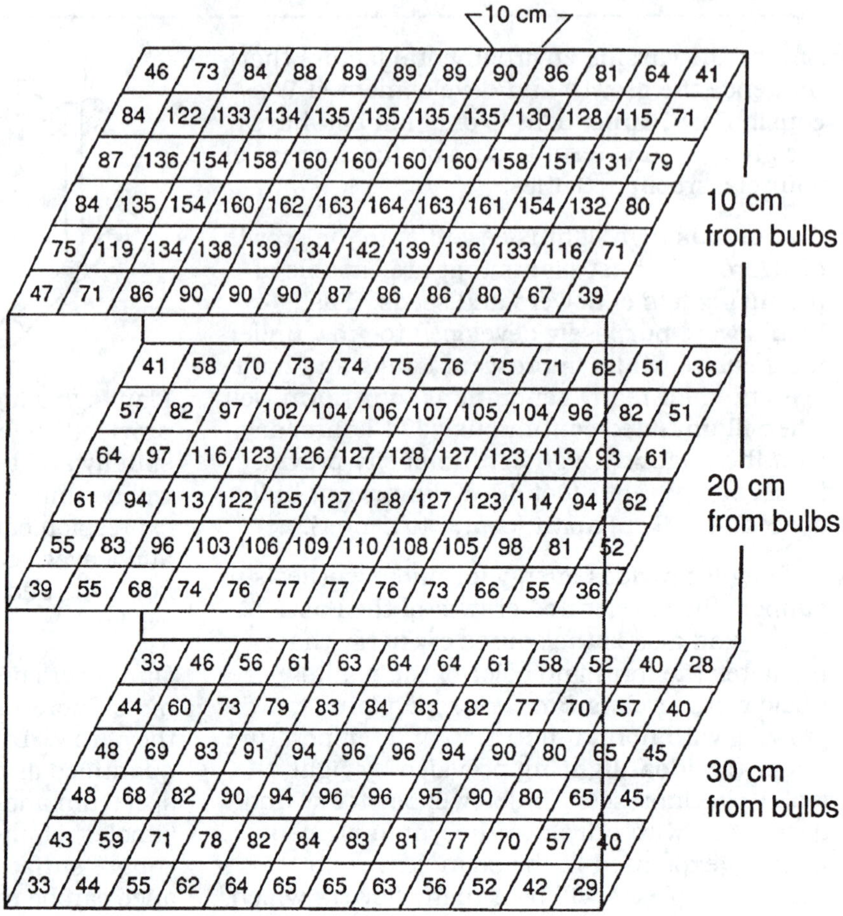

**Our research indicates that light banks with a minimum of six 40 W bulbs should be used for Fast Plants. Eight or more bulbs spaced over a 60 x 120 cm area is preferred.** More light is better and reflective sides placed along the edges of light banks can increase the irradiance received by plants by a few percent. Four and two bulb units generally provide **inadequate** lighting for Fast Plants.

**Since the irradiance grades off from the center of the light bank, it is important to rotate plants under the bank every day or two so that over the growing cycle all plants will receive about the same amount of energy.** If you have the luxury of ample space under your lights, keep the plants in the center of the bank where the light is highest. Do not try to grow plants that extend beyond the edges of the light bulbs. If your plants are receiving inadequate light they will let you know by "reaching" toward the light.

---

### How many 4-foot fluorescent light bulbs do you need to grow Fast Plants?

**8 tubes** = ideal growth
**6 tubes** = adequate growth
**4 tubes or less** = less than adequate growth

---

**Figure 4:** Irradiance on a 120 x 60 cm grid measured at 10 cm intervals, 10 cm below eight 40 W fluorescent bulbs. Numbers are µMol of photons (PAR) m$^2$ s$^{-1}$. These numbers conform to grid A in Figure 5.

| 88 | 124 | 148 | 150 | 150 | 156 | 160 | 155 | 149 | 133 | 111 | 80 |
| 161 | 231 | 257 | 259 | 257 | 256 | 255 | 260 | 248 | 249 | 219 | 136 |
| 196 | 280 | 314 | 320 | 324 | 324 | 325 | 323 | 318 | 304 | 261 | 166 |
| 189 | 275 | 308 | 316 | 318 | 319 | 320 | 320 | 315 | 304 | 260 | 169 |
| 147 | 217 | 243 | 251 | 252 | 252 | 252 | 249 | 249 | 242 | 212 | 140 |
| 78 | 124 | 142 | 147 | 150 | 153 | 156 | 153 | 144 | 132 | 112 | 75 |

An interesting experiment is to place plants at various fixed distances and positions from the lights and observe and record their responses. It is best to keep young plants as close to the bulbs as possible without overheating them. Plants grow best if they can be kept within 10 cm of the bulbs. **Young seedlings kept between 4 and 6 cm from the plane of the bulbs will produce stocky stems that are less likely to fall over when the plants elongate.**

**Measurements with 22 W and 30 W circle lights**

Thirty-watt fluorescent circle lights ("energy saver" type) are also suitable for growing Fast Plants. Measurements were made at 5 cm distances on four 20 cm radii from the center of the circle light. One radius transected the attachment point of the circle light. Measurements were made at 5 cm distances from the plane of the bulb up to 30 cm distance from the light. Measurements were made with both new and used bulbs and with and without a white reflective shade.

Figure 6 (page 248) shows irradiance patterns for a new 30 W circle light with a plastic reflector. **The 30 W light provides adequate irradiance as long as plants are grown within a 30 cm diameter circle 10 cm from the plane of the bulb.** Irradiance is lower under the attachment point and plants should be rotated to equalize light distribution.

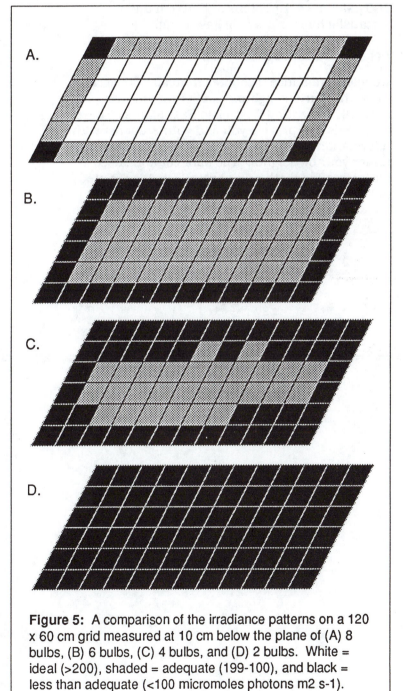

**Figure 5:** A comparison of the irradiance patterns on a 120 x 60 cm grid measured at 10 cm below the plane of (A) 8 bulbs, (B) 6 bulbs, (C) 4 bulbs, and (D) 2 bulbs. White = ideal (>200), shaded = adequate (199-100), and black = less than adequate (<100 micromoles photons m2 s-1).

Since the circle light provides energy only from a single bulb, it is particularly important to grow the plants within the cylinder of space defined by adequate irradiance. A convenient way of defining the adequate area under the 30 W lamp and of rotating the plants is to use a dinner plate or to place the Fast Plant growing systems on a 27 cm (10.5 inch) diameter circular Rubbermaid™ 'lazy susan'. The 22 W circle light produces less than 100 µMol m2 s-1 photons at 5-10 cm and is unsatisfactory for growing Fast Plants.

### Detailed irradiance data available

Detailed irradiance measures from all of the grids under the various lighting configurations are available by writing Wisconsin Fast Plants. These data grids can provide you and your students with information for understanding the irradiance under your own lights. The data could be used for interesting math and physics activities related to Fast Plants.

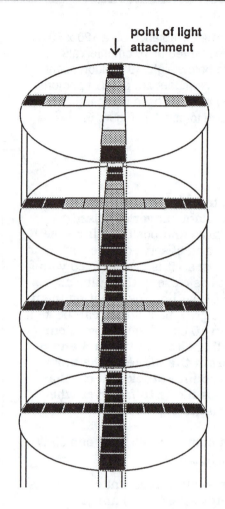

point of light attachment

**Figure 6:** Irradiance patterns for a 30 W circle light with a white plastic reflector (see Figure 2, page 245) measured at 5 cm intervals on four radii at 5 cm distances from the bulb. White and shaded areas depict zones of ideal and adequate irradiance for growing Fast Plants.

# Constructing a Wooden Light Rack

### Tools
- flathead screwdriver, Phillips screwdriver, pliers, $\frac{1}{2}$" wrench

### Hardware
- four $\frac{1}{4}$" x 3" wood screws
- four $\frac{1}{4}$" x $3\frac{1}{2}$" lag bolts with four flat washers
- four $\frac{1}{8}$" x $1\frac{1}{2}$" bolts with eight flat washers and four nuts
- two $\frac{1}{8}$" x $2\frac{1}{2}$" bolts with four flat washers and two nuts
- four (18") lengths of chain
- eight S-hooks
- one power cord
- one sash handle with screws

### Parts
- two $1\frac{1}{2}$" x $1\frac{1}{2}$" x 24" wood pieces (A)

- two 2" x 4" x 26" wood pieces (B)

- two $\frac{3}{4}$" x $3\frac{1}{2}$" x 16" wood pieces with metal eye screws on each end (C)

- one 1" x 2" x $46\frac{1}{2}$" wood piece (D)

- one 2" x 4" x 52" wood piece with four metal eye screws attached (E)

### Instructions
Attach one 2" x 4" x 52" wood piece (E) to two 2" x 4" x 26" wood pieces (B) using four $\frac{1}{4}$" x $3\frac{1}{2}$" lag bolts with washers. Then attach $1\frac{1}{2}$" x $1\frac{1}{2}$" x 24" horizontal pieces (A) to parallel pieces using four $\frac{1}{4}$" x 3" wood screws (Figure 1).

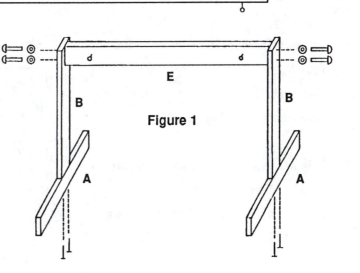

Figure 1

# Assembling a Light Bank

## Instructions

Remove all light fixtures from boxes. Using screwdriver, remove center panel from underside of fixtures (Figure 1), exposing holes in light fixtures that will be used for attaching fixtures to $3/4$" x $31/2$" x 16" wood pieces (C).

remove screw ———————————————————— remove screw

**Figure 1**

Place 1" x 2" x $461/2$" wood piece (D) on a table. Center the two $3/4$" x $31/2$" x 16" wood pieces on each end of D (Figure 2). Place the 1st light fixture on the two $3/4$" x $31/2$" x 16" (C) wood pieces so that its holes line up with the center of wood pieces C and the ends of wood piece D; then bolt the three pieces together using two $1/8$" x $21/2$" bolts, nuts and washers (Figure 3). Attach 2nd and 3rd fixtures to each end of $3/4$" x $31/2$" x 16" wood pieces (C) in same manner using four $1/8$" x $11/2$" bolts, nuts and washers. Replace center panels on underside of fixtures.

Use screws to attach sash handle to center of wood piece D. Attach light bank to support frame using four chains and S-hooks (Figure 4).

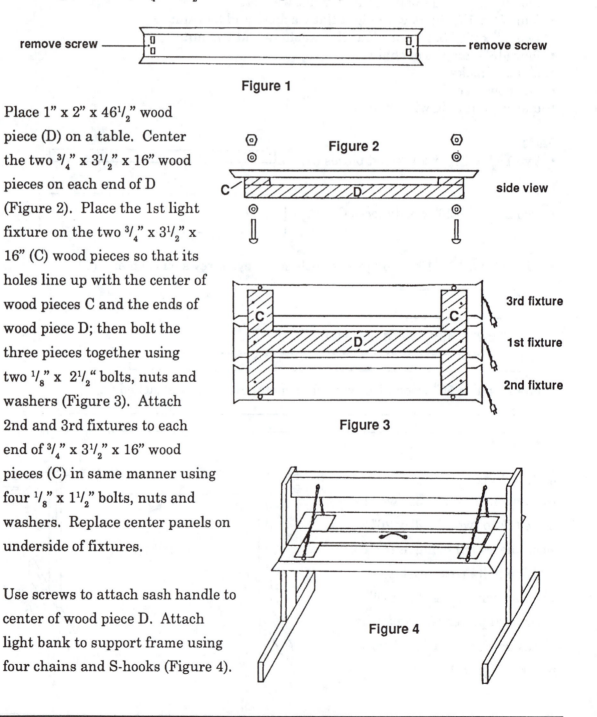

**Figure 2**

side view

**Figure 3**

3rd fixture

1st fixture

2nd fixture

**Figure 4**

# Portable Stacking Light Bank Design

Plans and original text by Irving Granderson, Elmwood Junior High School, Rogers, AR.

Storage space is often in short supply or almost nonexistent for most teachers. This light bank is very sturdy, easy to set up and collapses for storage when not in use.

Although it stands 28 inches tall, it occupies only 8.5 inches of height on the shelf, including the light fixture, when it is fully collapsed. The support rack folds up. Four of its eight bolts remain intact so it sets up in a couple of minutes when you put in the other four bolts. Two or more racks can be stacked.

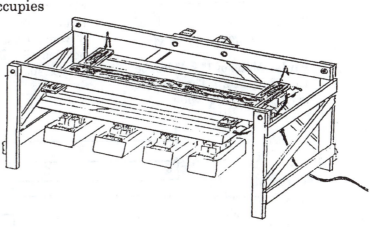

## Hardware
- four 1/4" x 2" bolts
- two 1/4" x 3 1/2" bolts
- two 1/4" x 4 1/2" bolts
- 26 washers

- lightweight chain, about 5 feet in length
- four hooks and eyes, medium weight
- "three to one" plug

## Parts
Ends:
- four 1" x 2 1/2" x 28" wood pieces
- four 1" x 2 1/2" x 18 1/2" wood pieces
- two 1" x 1 5/8" x 25" wood pieces

Tops:
- two 1" x 2 1/2" x 56 1/2" wood pieces
- one 1" x 2 1/2" x 12" wood piece

Braces:
- two 1" x 1 5/8" x 37" wood pieces, cut at 45° angle at both ends
- four 2" x 2" x 5 1/2" wood pieces, cut at 45° angle at both ends

Light Rack:
- one 1" x 4" x 46 1/2" wood piece
- two 1" x 4" x 18" wood pieces

Note: All 1" lumber is actually 3/4" thick. The width and length dimensions are exact.

## Lights
- three "Shop Lights of America"
- 12 wood or metal screws, 5/8" long, about #10

## Instructions

Construct your light support rack as shown in Figures 2-6.

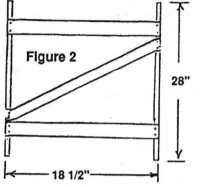

**Figure 2**

28"

18 1/2"

**Ends:** Made of 1" x 4" lumber ripped to 2 1/2". The crosspiece is ripped to 1 5/8" wide.

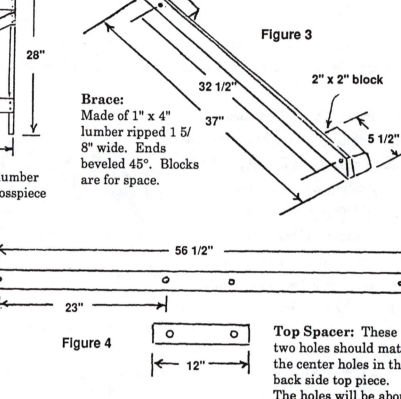

**Figure 3**

32 1/2"

37"

**Brace:** Made of 1" x 4" lumber ripped 1 5/8" wide. Ends beveled 45°. Blocks are for space.

**2" x 2" block**

5 1/2"

**Tops:** Made of 1" lumber ripped to 2 1/2". Only one (the back side top) needs the center holes.

56 1/2"

23"

**Figure 4**

12"

**Top Spacer:** These two holes should match the center holes in the back side top piece. The holes will be about 7 3/4" apart. Make them about 1/2" wide for an easy fit.

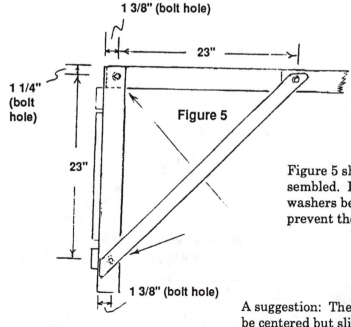

1 3/8" (bolt hole)

23"

1 1/4" (bolt hole)

23"

**Figure 5**

1 3/8" (bolt hole)

Figure 5 shows how the back is assembled. It is strongly suggested that washers be put between all boards to prevent the paint from sticking.

A suggestion: The holes on the end piece should not be centered but slightly (about 1/8") closer to the inside. This will allow it to fold without binding.

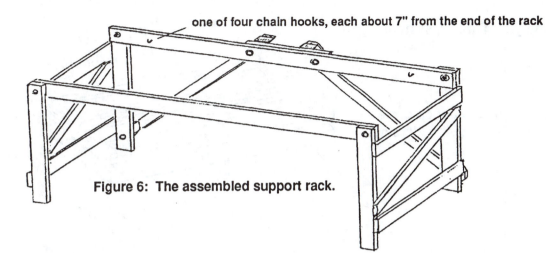

one of four chain hooks, each about 7" from the end of the rack

Figure 6: The assembled support rack.

## Instructions

Construct your light bank as shown in Figures 7-9.

**Note:** This light bank is almost identical to the Wisconsin Fast Plants model offered by Carolina Biological Supply Company.

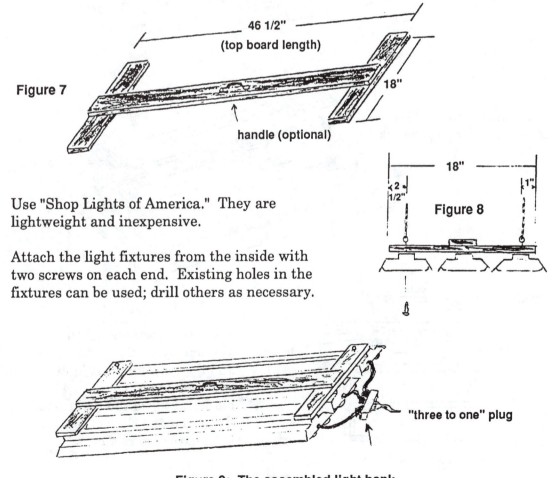

46 1/2"
(top board length)

Figure 7

18"

handle (optional)

Use "Shop Lights of America." They are lightweight and inexpensive.

Attach the light fixtures from the inside with two screws on each end. Existing holes in the fixtures can be used; drill others as necessary.

18"

2 1/2"

1"

Figure 8

"three to one" plug

Figure 9: The assembled light bank.

**Storing your lighting system**

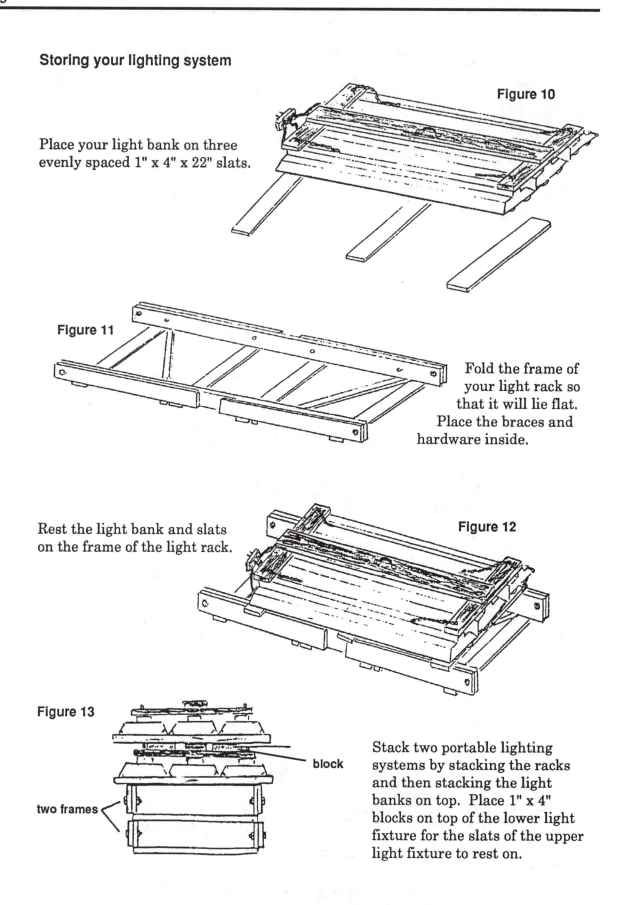

**Figure 10**

Place your light bank on three evenly spaced 1" x 4" x 22" slats.

**Figure 11**

Fold the frame of your light rack so that it will lie flat. Place the braces and hardware inside.

Rest the light bank and slats on the frame of the light rack.

**Figure 12**

**Figure 13**

block

two frames

Stack two portable lighting systems by stacking the racks and then stacking the light banks on top. Place 1" x 4" blocks on top of the lower light fixture for the slats of the upper light fixture to rest on.

# Alternative Growing Systems

There are a variety of options for creating Fast Plants growing systems. Depending on space available and the number of plants you plan to grow, you can design your own growing system; almost anything will work if you have the proper wicking.

## Reservoirs

### Bottle reservoirs

Fill a 2-liter bottle with hot (50-60°C) water and, after several seconds, peel off the label. Cut off the top of the bottle, leaving a total height of about 10-11 cm. Twist the opaque base off a second 2-liter bottle using hot water again to soften the glue.

Place the base into the opening of the first bottle (Figure 1). Put a petri dish, Hagen Daz® lid, plastic disc or other lid open end down into the base to act as a platform for your pots.

**Wicks:** Wicking material provides a continuous supply of water to the plants via capillary action. Use any material that works. WaterMat™ (Florist Products at 1-800-828-2242) is ideal. Teachers also report using pre-washed Pellon™, felt, old bath towels and HandiWipes®.

Run a 20 cm x 1 cm wick strip with tapered ends from the bottom of the reservoir up through a hole in the upper bottle base and well over the platform. Cut an 8 cm square mat of wicking material to cover the platform and place it on top of the wick strip. Presaturate your wicks and mats before use.

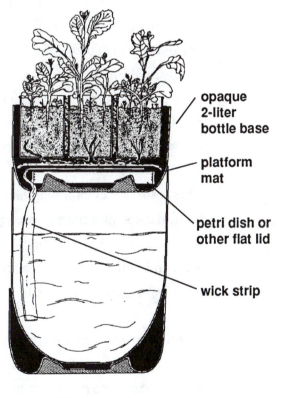

opaque
2-liter
bottle base

platform
mat

petri dish or
other flat lid

wick strip

**Figure 1**

This reservoir accommodates 7 film can pots, 7 tube cap wick pots, 7 bottle cap wick pots, or one quad or square pot with room for a couple of film cans. It holds enough water so that you can leave your plants unattended for 3-4 days. Cylindrical wick pots can be clustered in groups of 7, 4 or 3 with two strong rubber bands (size 64).

## Rubbermaid™ reservoirs

Square 2.4-liter or round 5-liter Rubbermaid™ containers also work as reservoirs. The lid serves as the platform for the pots. Prepare the platform by heating the open end of a 17-20 mm diameter Pyrex® test tube and melting a hole midway along each of the four sides at the inside edge of the "trough" (Figure 2). *Caution: melting plastic gives off fumes, perform this step under a hood or in a well-ventilated area.*

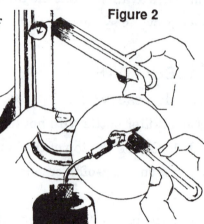

**Figure 2**

**Wicks:** Use the same kind of wicking material as previously described for the bottle reservoir. For a 2.4-liter reservoir, cut two 20 cm x 1 cm wicks with tapered ends. Cut a platform mat to fit inside the trough, with the mat corners trimmed off. Run one wick through each of two opposite holes in the platform (Figure 3) and well over the platform lid. Snap the lid in place and place the mat on top of the wicks. Presaturate the wicks and mat before use. You can fill and replenish the reservoir by carefully pouring water through one of the open holes in the lid.

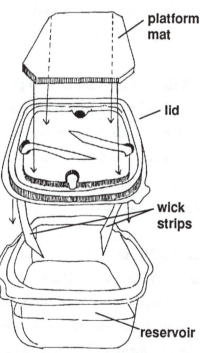

platform mat

lid

wick strips

reservoir

**Figure 3**

This reservoir accommodates 9 square pots, 9 quads, 25 film cans, 36 tube cap wick pots, 36 bottle cap wick pots or four 7-pot clusters of tube caps or film cans and will hold enough water so that you can leave your plants unattended for 3-5 days.

**Algal control (optional):** Copper sulfate solution at a concentration of 100 ppm (parts per million) will reduce algae growth in your water reservoir. To achieve 100 ppm copper sulfate solution, add 10 ml of concentrated stock solution to each liter of water in your reservoirs. Add the copper sulfate to your reservoir only once in the growing cycle, preferably when you first fill it. Concentrated stock solution can be made by dissolving 10 grams of copper sulfate crystals in one liter of distilled or deionized water (10,000 ppm). The stock solution can be stored indefinitely at room temperature.

# Potting Systems

## Film cans

Construct a minipot (Figure 4) using an opaque 35 mm film can. You can get film cans from local film processing centers. Film can wick pots can support up to 4 mature plants. Drill or use a heated large nail or soldering iron to melt a 5 mm hole in the center of the bottom of the can.

film can

string wick

**Figure 4**

**String wicks:** Presaturate a 5 cm length of thick, unpolished cotton string. To effectively saturate the string, wet your hand, run it around a bar of soap and then squish the string(s) in your hand. The soap acts as a wetting agent for the string.

Fold the piece of string in half to make a loop, or hold the center of the wick with forceps. Push the loop through the hole in the can, leaving the two ends sticking out about 1 cm each. The string will make solid contact with the reservoir mat.

**Diamond wicks:** You can also use a small diamond of WaterMat™ or other wicking material to wick your film can pot (see Figure 6 as an example). Insert the presaturated diamond about halfway into the wick pot. The emerging end of the wick will make contact with the presaturated reservoir mat.

## Tube cap wick pots

Plastic size 25 mm diameter test tube caps can also be used as wick pots. Use two large rubber bands to group 7 tube cap wick pots together for stability and ease of transport. Each tube cap wick pot can support one plant to maturity. Drill a 5 mm hole in the center of the bottom of the cap and use small diamond wicks as described above.

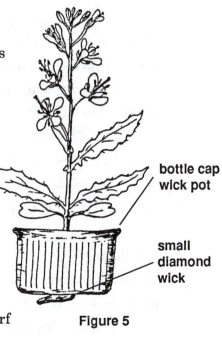

bottle cap wick pot

small diamond wick

**Figure 5**

## Bottle cap wick pots

Construct a minipot (Figure 5) using caps from plastic beverage bottles. Each bottle cap wick pot can support one plant to maturity. Again, drill a 5 mm hole in the center of the bottom of the cap and use small diamond wicks. The dwarf stock (*dwf1*) is particularly suited to bottle cap wick pots.

### Square pots

Square 2 1/4-inch pots are available from gardening stores or can be ordered from Hummert International at 1-800-325-3055. The pots have four holes in the bottom through which diamond-shaped wicks can be inserted (Figure 6). A 2 1/4-inch square pot supports up to 4 mature plants.

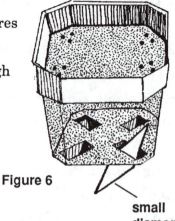

**Figure 6**

small
diamond
wick

# Planting and maintaining your Fast Plants

### Soil

Use a commercially available peat/vermiculite mixture such as Jiffy Mix® or Terralite Redi-earth®, or mix peat moss and vermiculite yourself in a 1:1 ratio. Carolina Biological Supply Company also provides a suitable soil, available in bulk. You will need to supplement the soil with fertilizer (see below).

### Planting

The soil should be very lightly moistened; it should not be wet enough for water to be squeezed out of it. Fill the potting container loosely, tapping several times to settle the soil. Scrape the excess soil off the top, but do not push down or pack the soil mixture. Water carefully until the wick drips (the soil will recede about 1/2 cm).

Drop seeds on top of soil using twice or 3 times the number of seeds as plants you intend to grow to maturity. Check the maximum number of plants recommended for the container you are using in "Potting Systems" (page 257). Cover the seeds with vermiculite and water lightly to wet the vermiculite.

Fold the pot wick under the pot and place it on the saturated platform lid. The wick will make solid contact with the platform mat. Label the pot. On Day 3, thin to the desired number of plants.

### Fertilizer

There are two major options for fertilizing your Fast Plants: solid pellets and liquid fertilizer solution. Both contain supplemental nitrogen (N), phosphorus (P) and potassium (K). The NPK pellets available from the Carolina Biological Supply

Company have been screened for size. If you buy NPK pellets (14-14-14) from a garden store, pellet size will vary.

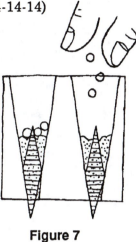

NPK pellets must be introduced as you fill your planting container with soil. They should be positioned at approximately half of the depth of your potting system (Figure 7). The number of pellets used depends on the volume of soil, and thus on the potting system used. Use the table below as a guide.

**Figure 7**

| Potting system | Number of NPK pellets |
|----------------|-----------------------|
| film can | 6 |
| tube cap | 4 |
| bottle cap | 2 |
| square pot | 4 |
| quad | 3/cell |

You can also use a liquid fertilizer solution to provide nitrogen, phosphorus and potassium to your plants. Make a solution of one soda bottle cap full of Peters™ brand fertilizer crystals per liter of distilled or deionized water. See "Environmental Parameters" (page 244). You can also use other commercial brands; follow the manufacturer's instructions to mix the appropriate concentration. Apply 2 ml of the NPK solution to the soil surface at Days 3, 7, 14, 21 and 28 for each plant that will be grown to maturity.

# Supplementary Materials
# for the Teacher

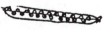

# In case you've forgotten your plant biology...

Is a plant a "green animal?" One might immediately say, "No," but think again. There are some fundamental similarities between the plant and animal kingdoms. Both plants and animals face similar problems of survival. These include the need for space, acquisition and utilization of food, the maintenance of water balance, and a need for the integration of body functions. Plants and animals develop from a fertilized egg or zygote and undergo progressive differentiation as each individual organism grows and develops. This developmental process involves orderly and predictable changes that lead to the adult organism. Plants and animals face a common challenge of maintaining and integrating all their various functions in response to changes in their environment.

Though plants and animals have many fundamental similarities they are really quite different. Land plants cannot simply be thought of as "green animals." The most obvious difference lies in the basic body plan. Land plants are anchored and cannot move from place to place and therefore must meet their nutritional needs internally. Green plants are *autotrophs*; they have the unique ability to manufacture their own food from carbon dioxide, water, inorganic salts and solar energy. Green plants are producers as opposed to members of the animal kingdom which are consumers.

Through the use of specialized parts and the process of *photosynthesis*, plants manufacture food to sustain themselves throughout their growth cycle. An underground root system allows plants to take in water and minerals including nitrogen, phosphorus, and potassium from the soil. One part of the vascular system (*xylem* tissue) carries these minerals and water from the roots to the leaves, the major sites of photosynthesis. The leaves maximize the absorption of carbon dioxide

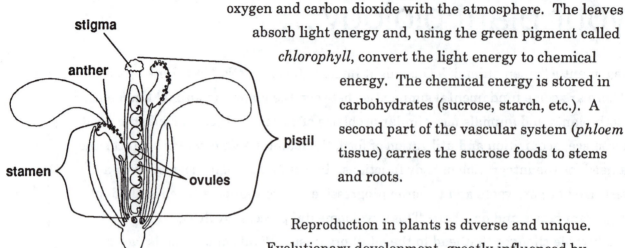

and light with a large surface area. Special openings on the outer layer of the leaves called *stomata*, located between *guard cells*, allow for the exchange of water vapor, oxygen and carbon dioxide with the atmosphere. The leaves absorb light energy and, using the green pigment called *chlorophyll*, convert the light energy to chemical energy. The chemical energy is stored in carbohydrates (sucrose, starch, etc.). A second part of the vascular system (*phloem* tissue) carries the sucrose foods to stems and roots.

Reproduction in plants is diverse and unique. Evolutionary development, greatly influenced by environmental factors, has brought special adaptations to different plant species to ensure survival. In the majority of plants sexual reproduction starts in the flower where male and female sex cells (*gametes*) are located. The *ovules* (housed in the carpels [ovaries] within the *pistil*) and the *pollen* (produced in the *anthers* of the *stamen*) combine their genetic information beginning with a process called *pollination*. Pollination is the transfer of pollen from the anthers to the tissue on the pistil known as the *stigma*. Transfer of pollen from the anther to the stigma of the same flower or between the flowers of the same plant is called *self-pollination*. Many plant species need the pollen from another plant of the same species in order to produce seeds. The transfer of pollen from one plant to the stigma of a different plant is called *cross-pollination* and is also accomplished with help from insects, water, and wind.

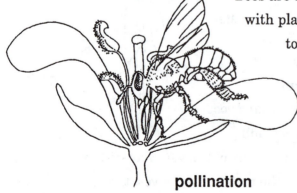

**pollination**

Bees are the primary insect pollinators and have coevolved with plants. Brightly-colored flower petals attract the bees to plants where they move from flower to flower to gather nectar from nectaries at the base of the pistil. During nectar-gathering, pollen from the anthers is picked up by the bee's hairy body parts and is deposited on the sticky surface of the stigma. Some plant species (*Brassica rapa* is one) contain special recognition compounds (*glycoproteins*) in the stigma. These compounds are unique to each plant and are recognized as "self," causing the stigma to abort the pollen from its own anther but to accept the pollen from another plant of the same species as compatible. This *self-incompatibility* mechanism ensures that genetic information (genes) within the species will be well mixed, ensuring genetic variation within the species.

Within a day or two after pollination, *fertilization* takes place. In flowering plants a unique process known as *double fertilization* occurs. From the germinating pollen grain on the stigma, a pollen tube grows through the style tissue of the pistil to an ovule housed in the carpels. Two male gametes (from the pollen grain) travel down the pollen tube. One will join with the female gamete (egg) within the ovule. The union of one male gamete and the female gamete produces a one-celled fertilized egg called a *zygote*. The zygote develops into an embryo through a process called *embryogenesis*. The second male gamete from the tube joins with a fusion nucleus and develops into the *endosperm*. The endosperm is the food for the developing embryo. When the embryo is mature, the ovule tissue dries around it and the remaining endosperm to form the seed.

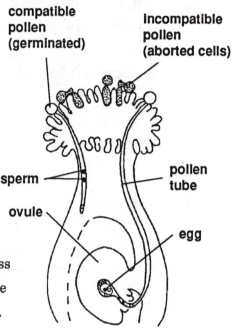

**fertilization**

Seeds are dispersed by wind, water, animals and through a wide variety of self-propulsion mechanisms. When environmental conditions are favorable, *germination* of the seeds will take place. The ability of a seed to grow into a new plant, *viability*, is the true measure of the plant's reproductive success. Adequate moisture and appropriate temperature are needed for the seed to swell, the coat to crack and growth to begin. A *radicle* (embryonic root) extends downward and *cotyledons* (seed leaves) emerge along with the *hypocotyl*. In some plants, including brassicas, the hypocotyl will extend to raise the two cotyledons above ground. As growth continues, the *meristem* (growing point) produces a

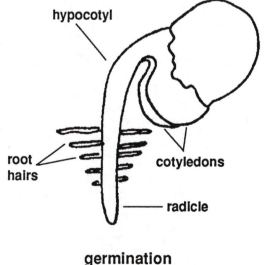

**germination**

a stem and leaves, a young plant, with various combinations of characteristics of the parent plants, which continues the cycle of life. No one can argue the importance of plants in the web of life. They are the foundation of our food chains and without these primary producers there would be no animal kingdom. Their structure, function, pattern of development and reproduction are distinctively different from that of animals and should be understood and appreciated on their own terms.

See Section 3 for explorations of these basic plant processes.

## References

### Books

Schuman, D. N. 1980. *Living with Plants, A Guide to Practical Botany*. Eureka, CA: Mad River Press, Inc. Excellent introductory chapter for background information entitled, "Introduction to a Plant," as well as other topics such as nutrients, soils, and plant hormones.

Stockley, C. 1986. *Dictionary of Biology (Usborne Illustrated)*. London: Usborne Publishing, Ltd. A densely illustrated, clear guide to key terms and subject areas of plants and animals.

# Interdisciplinary Activities with Fast Plants

During the growth of one life cycle of Fast Plants, activities can include most of the disciplines in the elementary curriculum. Journal keeping (language arts) and life cycle illustrations (art) are easily incorporated. Measuring and graphing (math), as well as observing and experimenting (science), are fundamental to the growing of the plants. Story writing can be introduced. Plan to use a multi-disciplinary approach with Fast Plants.

## Suggestions

### Language Arts

- journal writing
- whole language development approach coordinated with Fast Plants unit for primary students
- poetry
  — haiku
  — limericks
  — cinquain
  — first person poems from a plant's perspective
- story-writing
  — news article
  — first person from a seed's perspective
  — conversations with a honeybee
  — science fiction, for example "What Would Happen If A Fast Plant Just Kept Growing?"
- outline the planting or pollination procedures
- list
  — relatives of the Fast Plants and illustrate them
  — characteristics of Fast Plants
  — variations within a population
- spelling
  — brassica-related words
  — brassica crosswords and wordsearch puzzles, computer program may be useful
  — oxymorons

### Math

- graphing
  — plant height during growth

— seed harvest (number of seeds per pod, number of seeds per plant, etc.)
— using computer program

- averaging
  — seeds per pod, flowers per plant, aphids per quad, etc.

- estimating
  — seeds per pod

- counting
  — flowers, leaves, seeds, flower parts, pods, etc.

- comparing
  — germination times of Fast Plants and other plants
  — harvest times of Fast Plants and other plants
  — seed prices in garden catalogs

## Social Studies

- mapping
  — where brassicas are grown around the world

- culture
  — importance and preparation of brassicas as food
  — various uses of brassicas: oils, fodder, etc.

## Social Skills

- working with partners

- cooperative decision-making

- responsibility in caring for plants

## Science (see Sections 3 and 4)

- investigate plant processes (tropisms, for example) by doing an investigation with Fast Plants

- investigate why brassicas are recommended as part of a cancer-preventing diet

## Art

- construct a model brassica flower or honeybee (see page 228)

- detailed illustrations of life cycle of Fast Plants integrated with journal keeping or charts

- create a collage of the life cycle of Fast Plants, the *Brassica* family, etc.

## Creativity

- ask students to develop their own Fast Plants game (like Trivia, Hollywood Squares, etc.)

## Gardening

- try growing relatives of Fast Plants (turnip, Chinese cabbage, mustard, cabbage, etc.) in your home or school garden (see Plant Breeding, page 205)

# Fast Plants Learning Objectives

It is often difficult to focus on what truly is being learned by your students because of the many tasks of the teacher. To reflect on the potential learning outcomes attained through the use of Wisconsin Fast Plants, the following learning objectives are presented.

### General learning objectives
- The student shall use living plants, honeybees (dried), journals, and a variety of models as resources for learning about the life of a plant.
- The student shall make accurate observations using his/her own senses and instruments such as a ruler, hand lens and microscope.
- The student shall quantitatively describe the properties of a living plant with such quantities as number of leaves, height of plant, number of flowers, number of seed pods, number of seeds per plant, etc.
- The student shall observe that living plants grow, age, change and complete their life cycle.
- The student shall observe that living plants reproduce their own kind.
- The student shall use journal-writing as a means of keeping accurate records.
- The student shall use mathematics as a means of analyzing data.

### Specific learning objectives for each exploration
**Germination:**
- The student shall understand that a plant begins to grow only under certain environmental conditions.
- The student shall understand that food stored in the seed is the initial source of energy for plant growth.

**Plant Growth:**
- The student shall observe that plants grow and change.
- The student shall observe the development of leaves, stem and flowers.
- The student shall observe variations in growth within a population.
- The student shall understand that normal growth requires a favorable environment.
- The student shall understand that variation in growth depends on both the environment and the genetic makeup of the organism.

### Flowering and Pollination:

- The student shall understand that flowering is an adaptation in reproduction that leads to diversity.
- The student shall understand that flowering plants and the honeybee have a beneficial relationship.

### Double Fertilization and Seed Pod Development:

- The student shall understand the process of sexual reproduction.
- The student shall observe the development of a plant embryo.

### Seed Maturation and Dispersal:

- The student shall observe variation in nature by noting variation among seeds, pod production and seed production.

# Glossary

**adaptation:** in an evolutionary context, a heritable feature of an individual's phenotype the improves the organism's chances of survival and reproduction in its existing environment.

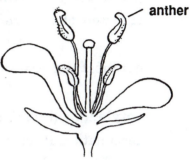

**annual:** a plant which completes its life cycle in one growing season.

**anther:** the portion of the stamen which produces the pollen.

**artificial selection:** in an evolutionary context, the human-influenced process by which individuals possessing desirable characteristics increase in proportion to others through successful reproduction in a specific environment normally created by humans (agroecosystems). Contrast with "natural selection."

**biennial:** a plant which requires two growing seasons to complete its life cycle.

**bioassay:** a test of a substance, found in the environment, in which a living organism is exposed to various concentrations of that substance to determine what concentrations are harmful.

**blade:** the broad part of a leaf.

**capillary action:** the process by which water and nutrients are carried from the root up through the stem of the plant to the leaves and flowers.

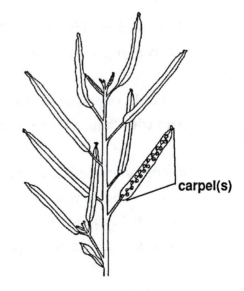

**carpel:** the structure in fruit-producing plants which encloses one or more ovules. Also called the "ovary."

**cell wall:** the rigid outer layer of a plant cell.

**chlorophyll:** (klor-o-fill) a green pigment in plant cells necessary for photosynthesis.

**chloroplast:** (klor-o-plast) the body in green plants which contains chlorophyll.

**compatible:** refers to the condition of the pollen and stigma which permits pollen to germinate. In *Brassica rapa*, pollen from one plant will only germinate on the stigmas of flowers of a different plant: they are compatible. Compare with "incompatible."

**composting:** controlled biodegradation of organic matter.

**cotyledon:** (kot'l-ee-d'n) the seed leaf, first to be seen after germination. It serves as a food source (energy) until true leaves form.

cotyledons

**cross-pollination:** the transfer of pollen from the anther of one plant to the stigma of a flower on another plant.

**cuticle:** (kyoo-te-kl) the waxy protective outer covering of a leaf.

**decomposition:** the breakdown of organic matter by decay organisms (bacteria, fungi and animals).

cross-pollination

**dicotyledon:** (dy-kot'l-ee-d'n) a plant whose embryo has two cotyledons (dicot).

**diploid:** refers to cells which contain two sets of chromosomes (2n = diploid). Compare with "haploid" and "triploid."

**dormancy:** seeds are dormant if they require some special event or "trigger" before they resume growth, e.g., fire, scarification or cold treatment. Contrast with "quiescence" (when seeds will resume growth at any time upon exposure to favorable conditions: water, oxygen, warmth).

**embryo:** a young plant before the start of germination.

**endosperm:** a fine granular liquid that forms in the ovule after fertilization as food for the developing embryo.

**epidermis:** the outermost layer of cells of the plant.

**F$_1$ generation:** the offspring of a cross between two parent plants; first filial generation.

**F$_2$ generation:** the second generation of offspring from the original two parents, resulting from a cross of members of the F$_1$ generation; second filial generation.

**fertilization:** the union of two reproductive cells to produce a new embryo.

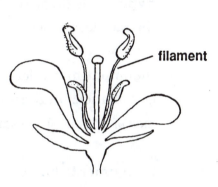

filament

**filament:** the stalk of the stamen which supports the anther.

**flower:** the reproductive structure of fruit-producing plants.

**fruit:** the mature, ripened ovary containing the seeds.

**gamete:** (ga-meet) a mature reproductive cell carrying the genetic code of the parent in a single set of chromosomes (n). The ovule contains the female gamete; pollen carries male gametes.

flower

**gene:** the unit that carries hereditary traits.

**genotype:** the genetic composition of an organism. Compare with "phenotype."

**germination:** the beginning of growth by a seed.

**gravitropism:** the direction of growth influenced by the force of gravity.

germination

**guard cells:** specialized pairs of cells in the epidermis which surround the stomata.

**haploid:** refers to cells which contain one set of chromosomes (n = haploid). The sex cells of some plants and animals (including humans) are haploid. Compare with "diploid" and "triploid."

**heredity:** the genetic transmission of characteristics from parents to offspring.

**humus:** (hyoo-mus) decayed organic matter which provides nutrients to plants.

**hybrid:** a variety of plant resulting from the cross of two pure breeding lines.

**hypocotyl:** (hi-po-cot'l) the part of an embryo or seedling between the cotyledons and the radicle or roots.

**incompatible:** refers to the condition of the pollen and stigma which inhibits pollen germination. In *Brassica rapa*, pollen from one plant will not germinate on the stigmas of flowers of the same plant: they are incompatible. Compare with "compatible."

**integument:** (in-teg-yoo-ment) the outer layer of tissue around the ovule which becomes the seed coat.

**internode:** the region of the stem between two nodes.

**monocotyledon:** (mon-o-kot'l-ee-d'n) a plant whose embryo has one cotyledon (monocot).

**natural selection:** in an evolutionary context, the process in nature by which individuals of a species possessing characteristics advantageous for survival in a specific environment survive and increase in proportion to others through successful reproduction. Contrast with "artificial selection."

**nectary:** a gland in the flower of fruit-producing plants located at the base of the pistil. A nectary produces sugary fluid (nectar) which attracts insects and birds.

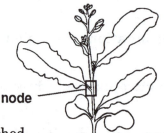

**node:** the part of a stem where one or more leaves are attached.

**osmosis:** (oss-mo-sis) the movement of a substance across a semipermeable membrane, from high concentration to low concentration.

**ovary:** the enlarged part of the pistil containing the ovules. Also called the carpel.

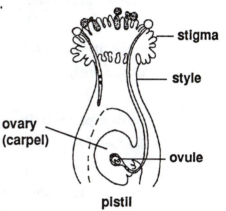

**ovule:** the female reproductive cell in seed plants.

**pedicel:** (ped-e-s'l) the stalk of an individual flower.

**perennial:** a plant that lives for more than one growing season, usually producing reproductive structures in two or more years.

**petal:** a flower part that is usually colored.

**petiole:** (pet-ee-ol) the stalk of a leaf.

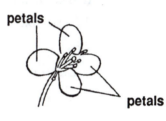

**phenotype:** (feen-o-type) the environmentally and genetically determined observable appearance of an organism. Compare with "genotype."

**phloem:** (flo-em) the tissue which carries food (sugars) made in the leaves to the rest of the plant.

**photosynthesis:** (fo-toe-sin-thi-sis) food-making by green plants; the manufacturing of carbohydrates (sugar) in the presence of light and chlorophyll.

**phototropism:** growth, turning or bending in response to the direction of light.

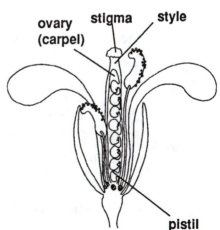

**pigment:** a substance that absorbs light.

**pistil:** the central structure of flowers, consisting of the ovary (carpel), style and stigma.

**plant wilt:** limpness of a plant due to greater moisture loss by transpiration than gain by absorption by root hairs.

**pollen:** the powder (usually yellow, cream or reddish in color) found on the anthers of stamens; spores bearing male gametes; sperm.

**pollen parent:** the plant selected to provide pollen for fertilization.

**pollen tube:** the tube formed after pollination which carries the male reproductive cell (sperm or gamete) into the ovule.

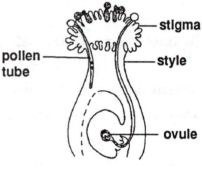

**pollination:** the transfer of pollen from the anther to the stigma.

**progeny:** next generation or offspring.

**protoplasm:** the name for all substances and bodies in a cell.

pollination

**quiescence:** (kwi-es-sense) state of suspended growth of the embryo; the resting condition of the seed. Compare with "dormancy."

**radicle:** the embryonic root which first appears after germination.

**receptacle:** the region of the flower stalk that bears the floral parts.

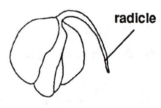

**root:** the part of the plant that normally grows into the ground; anchors the plant, and absorbs and conducts water and minerals.

**root hairs:** tiny outgrowths of the root which absorb water and minerals.

**rosette:** a plant that grows very compactly at soil level with its leaves fanning out in a circular cluster.

**sap:** the juice of plants carrying water and nutrients to all its parts.

**seed:** the part of a flowering plant that will grow into a new plant under the right conditions; formed by the maturation of the ovule after fertilization.

**seed parent:** the plant which provides the ovule and produces and supports the development of the seed following fertilization.

**seedling:** a young plant grown from a seed; not a cutting.

**self-pollination:** the transfer of pollen from the anther of one flower to the stigma of the same flower or another flower on the same plant. Fast Plants do not self-pollinate; they are self-incompatible.

**sepal:** (see-pel) the outermost flower structure; usually encloses the other flower parts in the bud.

**sexual reproduction:** the union of a male and a female reproductive cell to form a zygote.

**shoot:** the new growth above ground, consisting of stem and leaves.

**species:** (spee-cees) a population of organisms having many characteristics in common and which produce fertile offspring when crossed.

**spongy layer:** the tissue of the leaf where food manufacturing occurs in the chloroplasts.

**stamen:** the flower structure which produces pollen; consists of anther and filament.

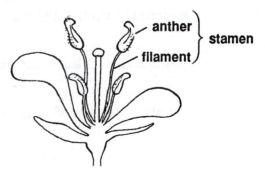

**stem:** the part of a plant that grows above ground bearing the leaves and flowers.

**stigma:** the receptive surface of the pistil on which pollen adheres and germinates.

**stoma:** a small pore in the epidermis which allows for gas exchange and water vapor release (pl. stomata).

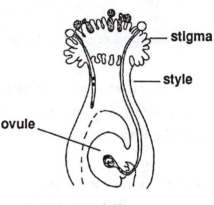

**style:** the slender top portion of the pistil through which the pollen tubes grow to reach the ovary.

**succulent:** a plant with fleshy leaves or stems for storing water.

**transpiration:** the loss of water vapor through the stomata.

**triploid:** refers to cells which contain three sets of chromosomes (3n = triploid). The endosperm in Fast Plants ovules is triploid. Compare with "diploid" and "haploid."

**tropism:** a response to an external stimulus; changes the direction of movement or growth.

**variation:** the genotypic and phenotypic differences that occur within the offspring of a particular species.

**variegated:** the appearance of green leaves being regularly or irregularly patterned with white, cream or yellow sectors.

**vascular bundle:** the tissue in plants containing the xylem and phloem.

**vein:** a rib of a leaf containing conducting and supporting tissues.

**viable seed:** a seed capable of producing a new plant.

**weed:** a plant growing wild and not wanted for use or beauty; especially one hindering the growth of desirable vegetation.

**xylem:** (zy-l'm) the tissue in plants which transports water and minerals from the roots throughout the plant.

**zygote:** the fertilized cell resulting from the union of the male and female gametes; the first cell of the new generation, which develops into an embryo.

# Index *by Jennifer Sharkey*